Solving in Style

John Nunn

This edition, first published by Gambit Publications Ltd in 2002, is an unaltered reproduction of the work originally published by George Allen and Unwin in 1985

ISBN 1 901983 66 8

DISTRIBUTION:
Worldwide (except USA): Central Books Ltd, 99 Wallis Rd, London E9 5LN.
Tel +44 (0)20 8986 4854 Fax +44 (0)20 8533 5821.
E-mail: orders@Centralbooks.com
USA: BHB International, Inc., 41 Monroe Turnpike, Trumbull, CT 06611, USA.

For all other enquiries (including a full list of all Gambit Chess titles) please contact the publishers, Gambit Publications Ltd, P.O. Box 32640, London W14 0JN. E-mail Murray@gambitchess.freeserve.co.uk
Or visit the GAMBIT web site at http://www.gambitbooks.com

Printed in Great Britain by The Cromwell Press, Wiltshire.

10 9 8 7 6 5 4 3 2

Gambit Publications Ltd
Managing Director: GM Murray Chandler
Chess Director: GM John Nunn
Editorial Director: FM Graham Burgess
German Editor: WFM Petra Nunn

Contents

Introduction

Chess is full of artificial divisions. Over-the-board players have little contact with postal players and neither of these groups talks to problemists. Even in the little world of chess composition there is a division between problem composers and study enthusiasts. This book aims to help break down some of these barriers by introducing over-the-board players to chess problems and studies.

Basically, a chess problem is a composed position together with a target which must be achieved in a specified number of moves (e.g. mate in two, selfmate in three, etc.). There should be a (unique) solution achieving the target and it is the solver's task to uncover this solution, which is usually well hidden. A study is again a composed position, but in this case the objective is either to win or to draw, without limit on the number of moves. This is precisely one's ambition when playing a game over the board, so studies are much closer to practical play than problems and, indeed, they are frequently of value in endgame play.

On one level problems and studies may be looked on as puzzles, more refined than the daily crossword perhaps, but still puzzles. This is the point of view taken by most over-the-board players who take an interest in solving, and it is the one adopted in this book. The composer will probably have a different opinion. He may be more concerned with the fact that he has conceived a novel theme, never shown before in precisely the same way, than with whether or not his creation makes a good puzzle.

One of the most frequently debated questions about chess is whether it is a sport, a science or an art. If the hurly-burly of tournament play emphasises the sporting aspect, and the cool calculation of postal play the scientific, then the artistic element finds its best expression in the world of chess composition. Chess problems are an unusual art form in that the audience (solvers) have to participate actively, by solving the problem, in order to appreciate the artist's message. Those who peek at the solutions are missing out on the pleasure and satisfaction gained when the crystal-clear point of the problem is suddenly revealed after an hour's careful study.

Chess problems are frequently published in magazines and newspaper columns, but all too often over-the-board players just turn to the next page. They are put off by the unnatural appearance of the positions, the jargon used by problemists and the fact that they don't know how to go about solving problems. There isn't much to be done about the positions, although I have tried to introduce each type of problem with a few natural examples. In order to discuss any technical subject a certain amount of jargon is necessary, but I have kept this to an absolute minimum. Finally, this book explains how to tackle all the common types of problem with the aim of finding the solution in the shortest possible time. Each chapter ends with a selection of problems for the reader to try himself. Detailed solutions are included at the back of the book. After having read the book, the reader will be fully equipped to study specialist problem magazines and books. I hope that some will be tempted to enter solving competitions such as the annual Lloyds Bank Chess Problem Solving Competition, which attracts nearly 2,000 entries each year.

No one will pretend that solving problems is going to help over-the-board play, but there is more to chess than going up (or down) a few rating points each year. Endgame studies are of help in improving tactical vision, while the more didactic examples offer a painless way to learn some endgame theory. Those who prefer to enter the problem environment gradually are directed to Chapters 2 and 5, but otherwise it is sensible to read the chapters in numerical order. The pace gathers momentum as the book proceeds and towards the end some of the elementary details are taken for granted.

The remaining comments are directed at readers who are already problemists. They may find that I have missed out their favourite type of problem; for example, there are no stalemate problems, no retractors and no fairy pieces. On the other hand, many of the problems have been analysed in greater depth than usual, so they should find something of interest. I have kept to normal problem conventions, with the single exception of using 'N' for knight, as opposed to 'S'. The arguments for using the German S seem very weak and a mixture of two different notations appears very strange to the player's eye. I hope that problemists who have not taken much interest in studies will be encouraged to pay a closer look by the examples in this book. Study supporters should note that I have not repeated any of the positions given in my earlier book *Tactical Chess Endings* by the same publisher.

Finally, here is a brief round-up of conventions and abbreviations used throughout the book.

Composing competitions are held regularly all over the world, often in conjunction with newspapers or chess magazines. These are called tourneys and I have abbreviated this by T. or Tny. Awards are given for the best problems in each tourney; in descending order, these awards are Prizes (Pr.), honourable mentions (h.m.) and commendations (comm.).

The condition under the problem is abbreviated as follows:

$\neq$n	mate in n
h$\neq$n	helpmate in n
s$\neq$n	selfmate in n
r$\neq$n	reflexmate in n
sh$\neq$n	serieshelpmate in n
ss$\neq$n	seriesselfmate in n
sr$\neq$n	seriesreflexmate in n

Black moves first in helpmates and serieshelpmates; White moves first if any of the other conditions appear under the diagram. In Chapter 10 on retro-analysis, unusual conditions occur; in this case the solver normally has to deduce from the diagram which player is to move.

The diagram position of a problem must be legal, i.e. it must be possible to start at the initial array for a game and reach the diagram by a sequence of legal moves, however unlikely. Promoted men are permitted by this convention, but they are nevertheless frowned upon and are used by composers only in exceptional circumstances. Two problems in this book contain promoted pieces.

Many players believe that problems aren't allowed to start with a check. This isn't so, but because a check severely restricts Black's options it is unlikely that there will be many interesting variations, so very few short problems start with one. Longer problems and studies quite often start with a check.

1 Two-movers

It is logical to start with two-move problems, not only because they are easier to solve than longer problems, but also because many of the techniques used for solving them are applicable throughout the book. The solver's aim is to find the unique White first move, called the key, which leads to mate in one against any Black reply. Since the time-scale of a two-mover is so short, it may seem surprising that very much of interest can occur. However, the past century has seen a great increase in the complexity of problems of all types, so that the modern two-mover can take considerable unravelling.

As part of the composer's aim is to puzzle the solver, the key will probably not be an obvious move. The capture of a pawn is a permissible key, but the capture of a piece or a check is considered too brutal to make an effective key. Once in a while an iconoclastic composer produces a problem with a checking key, but there is little point in considering a check as a possible key unless all else fails. Similarly composers favour paradoxical keys which appear either to limit White's possibilities or to extend Black's. A key which pins a White piece or unpins a Black piece is more highly regarded than a neutral key which has no special effect on the position. The key may even expose White's king to an immediate check, provided, of course, that the check may be met by an immediate mate. Often composers aren't able to incorporate one of these favoured types of key into their creations, but we shall see many examples of problems in which a surprising key enhances the impression created by the composition. At one time a spectacular key was considered essential in a first-rate two-mover, but now less emphasis is placed on the key and more on the strategy embodied in the problem. Consequently the solver has to be rather more sophisticated to appreciate fully the composer's idea.

There are no such difficulties with Diagram 1, by one of the great nineteenth-century composers.

#2

What should the first step be when the solver is confronted by a board full of pieces and no obvious mating idea in sight? The most sensible approach is to decide whether the key might put Black in zugzwang. If this is impossible then the key will have to carry a threat of mate in one. In most cases it is quite clear whether or not zugzwang is likely. Black may have several irrelevant moves which obviously cannot allow mate in one, in which case zugzwang is out of the question. This is not the case in Diagram 1, however, and if we look at Black's available moves we soon find the variations 1...Ke5 2 Nd3, 1...N moves 2 Bg3, 1...B moves 2 Qxb8, 1...Qe5 2 Ne2, 1...Q elsewhere 2 Qd6 (or Q takes Q). Thus Black is already in zugzwang and White only needs a waiting move to solve the problem.

Some of the White pieces are fully employed in the above variations and moving one of these might disrupt the mates which are already arranged, so we have to look around for pieces irrelevant to the pre-arranged mates. This narrows the choice down to the K on a3, B on g6 and R on a4. However, moving the B on g6 allows Black's g-pawn to move, while king moves run into trouble from pins and checks, for example, 1 Ka2/b3? Be6+, 1 Kb4? Nd5+ or 1 Kb2? Qe5!. Can the rook at a4 move without affecting the status quo? Certainly it cannot move along the fourth rank, for then Black has a check with his queen. Similarly a7 and a8 may be eliminated. a5 gives Black the move ...bxa5 so we are left with a6. This has no harmful effects so must be the key. **1 Ra6!** is an even more mysterious rook move than Nimzowitsch's famous ...Re8! Looking back at Diagram 1, a more experienced solver would suspect zugzwang even before he had begun to explore Black's possible moves. Every piece has a purpose in a problem and the function of White's b5 pawn looks likely to be simply the prevention of the pass move ...b5. The immobilisation of the g7, h5 and e4 pawns by blockading pieces provides further evidence that the problem's construction is motivated by the necessity to prevent nondescript moves by Black.

2

Problems in which the key is simply a waiting move preserving a zugzwang position are easy to solve, but one must be careful not to fall into a trap, as in Diagram 16.

In many cases, although zugzwang may appear probable, the situation before the key is not yet zugzwang. Some of Black's moves do not allow White to deliver immediate mate and the key must either prevent these moves or prepare mates for them.

2 M. Lipton, 1st Pr. De Waarheid, 1965

a) Diagram b) b5→e5 ≠2

This is a two-in-one problem, called a **twin**. When the diagram position has been solved the pawn is moved from b5 to e5 to provide a second mate in two problem. Much of the interest in twin problems centres on the way an apparently insignificant change in the position can completely alter the solution. Usually, as here, the twin is formed by moving one piece in the diagram. Sometimes the removal or addition of a piece is preferred, while in a few cases more exotic twinning mechanisms may be used, such as rotating the board or moving the entire position to the left or right. Dealing with the first part of the problem, Black has just four legal moves and only one of these, 1...axb5, is already provided with a mate. Nevertheless, it looks likely that zugzwang will be used to dislodge Black's king from its relatively secure refuge at a4. The second prominent point is the line-up on the fourth rank. At present there is a good deal of wood between the h4 rook and Black's king, but the rook has to come into play quickly if it is to serve a purpose in the problem, so the key will probably be made by one of White's minor pieces. Operating on the assumption that zugzwang will be used, Black's f6 pawn presents an obvious difficulty. The move ...f5 will foil White's plans if he doesn't prevent it, so the two most likely keys are 1 Nxf6 and 1 Bf5. 1 Nxf6? destroys the mate prepared for 1...axb5 without replacing it by another, so the key is **1 Bf5!**, with the lines 1...Kxb3 2 Nxc5 and 1...Kxb5 2 Nc3 verifying our hypothesis. Now move the pawn from b5 to e5 in the diagram. The same type of logic

3

applies, but this time 1 Bf5? fails to 1...fxe5!. Now **1 Nxf6!** succeeds, with two new mates arising after Black's king moves, namely 1...Kxb3 2 Bd1 and 1...Kb5 2 Bd7.

Diagram 17 is similar in that all Black's moves apart from 1...d6 have a mate prepared, so White's key is designed to set up a reply to this defence.

One of the ways in which composers attempt to mislead solvers is by arranging tempting White moves which look as if they should be the key, but which in fact fail to a subtle refutation. Such moves are called **tries**. It is a convention that the refutation of a try should be unique, so that solvers are more likely to be taken in by them. Tries form an integral part of many modern problems, although they have been around for a long time, as the following composition demonstrates.

3 B. Sommer, 1st Pr. Teplitz–Schönauer Anzeiger, 1922

‡2

Once again it is helpful to explore what would happen if it were Black to move in the diagram position. This is called the **set play** and the White mates arising in the set play are the **set mates**. Here 1...dxc6 2 Qxc6, 1...R moves 2 Rxd7 and 1...N moves 2 Qc5 form the set play so White need only arrange a mate for the remaining move 1...Ke7 to solve the problem. After ...Ke7 Black has f6 and f8 available for his king and the double pin of e6 and d7 resulting from the king move suggests a mate along the a3–f8 diagonal. It follows that the key must cover f6. 1 Qf2? abandons the attack on c6 and allows 1...dxc6, so it seems likely that the White rook on e5 should move. The pin on the knight must be maintained, or else 1...Ke7 2 Qc5 will not be mate, but at first sight any move of the rook down the e-file will do. This is where the tries come in, for only one of these moves actually works. The first point is that almost all the intended rook moves allow Black's king to move to d5, pinning the e6 knight and allowing White to mate by playing his rook to the d-file. The two exceptions are 1 Re4? Kd5, since 2 Rd4 obstructs, or **interferes** with, the b2 bishop, and 1 Re3? Kd5 when 2 Rd3 blocks the queen's guard of e4. The second

4

point is that White has to abandon the mate 2 Qc5 set for Black knight moves.

If the knight moves anywhere apart from c5 White can reply 2 Ba3, but after 1...Nc5 White can only mate by 2 Qh2. Therefore the rook must avoid e2 obstructing the queen's path. By elimination the key must be **1 Re1!**, which does indeed place Black in zugzwang. This problem contains some new features. The key gives the Black king an extra escape square, or **flight**, not present in the diagram, a desirable feature since it seems unlikely that Black's king will be given any extra freedom if mate is to be administered next move. Moreover, one of the set mates (after 1...N moves) is abandoned and new mates are introduced to cope with Black knight moves. This is an example of **changed play**. The problem does have one slightly unfortunate feature, namely that Black's king has the **unprovided flight** e7. Black king moves are prominent defences and if one of them doesn't have a set mate the solver is given a helpful clue to the key, which must either arrange a mate or prevent the king move altogether. The key will normally not take away a flight from Black's king, unless another is given in return, and there will only be a small number of moves providing a mate for the king move. In Diagram 3 this defect isn't too serious as the composer's main idea is to trap the solver into moving to the wrong square on the e-file.

If Black is in zugzwang in the initial position, one is naturally tempted to try to maintain the set mates. In many problems it proves impossible to find a waiting move so the solver is obliged to change some of the mates. In Diagram 19 the alteration to the set play is slight, but in Diagram 4 White can only mate in two by completely destroying the initial zugzwang and replacing it by a quite different one.

4 D. Bannij, =1st Pr. Moscow 22 Olympiad, 1980

#2

The set play is 1...exd3 2 Qf3, 1...f1=Q 2 Qxd2 and 1...f1=N 2 Qe2. It doesn't take long to see that there is no waiting move. The only plausible

5

try is 1 Kc4? but now the king is too far from d2 and Black can reply
1...f1=Q. White has various moves which carry a threat, but these also fail,
for example 1 Nc5? (threat 2 Qxe4) f1=N! or 1 Qf1? (threat 2 Qe2) exd3!.
Fortunately White doesn't have very many legal moves so that one
eventually arrives at **1 Nxf2!**, putting Black in zugzwang. The new variations are 1...Kf4 2 Qxe4, 1...gxf2 2 Qg5 and 1...Nxf2 2 Qxg3. This
spectacular problem features a particularly drastic form of changed play in
which Black's defences and White's mates are all changed. It is especially
hard on the solver when this type of changed play occurs, for the set play
is no guide to what happens after the key and may even be positively
misleading.

Changed play can also occur in positions which are nowhere near
zugzwang. Even if the key must threaten something, it is still good solving
practice to imagine that Black is to play in the diagram. If Black has a
prominent defence such as a king move or the capture of an important
White piece, see if mates are already set for these defences. If not, the key
will have to provide mates or prevent the defences. If so, the key will
either maintain the set mates or introduce changed play.

5 M. Persson, 5 h.m. Uppsala All. S.J.T. 1945

≠2

Here three Black pieces can capture on e4, while the king can move to
e5. We soon find the mates 1...Bxe4 2 Nf3, 1...Rxe4 2 Bg7 and 1...Qxe4 2
Nc6 set for the captures, in each case exploiting the **self-pin** arising along
the fourth rank. However, no mate is set for 1...Ke5 and if one were to be
provided by the key, White would have to cover d6, e6, f6, e5 and d4 in
the mating position. With only two moves to play with this looks extremely
unlikely, so one is led to consider moves which prevent 1...Ke5. Only two
come into consideration, namely 1 f4 and 1 Rh5. Nevertheless, 1 f4 may
be met by 1...Kxe4 when there is no mate, so we try **1 Rh5**, threatening 2
Qd3. 1...Kxe4 is met by 2 Qe3, while the three captures on e4 which led
to self-pins in the set play now lead to **self-blocks**, taking away the flight at

6

e4 from Black's king: 1...Bxe4 2 Ne2, 1...Rxe4 2 Bxc5 and 1...Qxe4 2 Nxb5. Thus the replies to all three moves are changed. The only other defence to the threat is 1...c4, met by 2 Qe3. Although the key gives a flight at e4 in compensation for the one taken at e5, the unprovided flight is a serious defect and doubtless led to the relatively lowly position attained by this problem in the 1945 composing tourney. Such constructional defects can make the solver's task much easier, if he knows what to look for.

6 A. Servais, 1st Pr. U.T.F., 1947

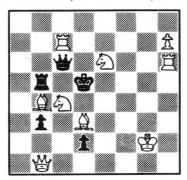

‡2

This problem can be solved without the analysis of any variations at all! Looking over the board, there is one unit which has no obvious purpose — the pawn at h7. Clearly this pawn can play no direct part in mating Black's king unless the key is the extremely unlikely 1 h8=Q, which is adequately met by 1...Qxe6. There seems no reason why the composer needed to prevent either of the White rooks moving to h7, but the bishop is another matter. The only conceivable reason for the pawn is to prevent a **cook** (an unintended second solution) by 1 Bh7. Since this is impossible, it seems reasonable to try **1 Bg6** instead, threatening 2 Qe4, and this leads to the spectacular variations 1...Kxe6+ 2 Be4, 1...Kxc4+ 2 Qe4, 1...Qxe6 2 Qd3 and 1...Qxc4 2 Qf5. The problem won first prize despite the pawn at h7 because the astonishing key not only grants two flights to Black's king, but both king moves deliver check! In one case the bishop returns to its original square (a **switchback**) to deliver mate by discovery and in the other Black self-pins his queen so that White can mate by playing onto the line of Black's check. These two variations are examples of **cross-checks**, that is checks by Black answered by interpositions which themselves give check. Cross-check problems are popular with composers and solvers alike and if a problem contains an arrangement of pieces aimed at White's king, it is worth considering the possibility that cross-checks will occur in the solution.

7

7 V. Melnichenko, 2nd Pr. 64, 1974

#2

A linear arrangement of two pieces aimed at the opposing king, in which a move of the front piece delivers discovered check from the rear piece, is called a **battery**. In the diagram White has a bishop + rook battery aimed at Black's king while Black has a queen + king battery aimed at White's king. At the moment White can't deliver mate by playing his rook along the third rank because the enemy queen attacks b1, but if the queen were deflected the battery could fire. In view of the above comments, we should consider whether Black's battery might fire after the key. The only reasonable way to give Black's king a move is for the White queen to go away, allowing 1...Kxf5+ which can be met by 2 Rd5 mate. This spectacular mate indicates that we are working along the right lines and it only remains to decide on the queen's destination. The queen's move must create a threat, so there are just two possibilities, 1 Qh3 and 1 Qh7. 1 Qh3? threatens 2 Rd4 but Black can simply take the queen, so we try **1 Qh7** (threat 2 Rxf4). This gives two cross-checks by 1...Kxf5+ 2 Rd5 and 1...Qxh7+ 2 Rh3, with two less important lines 1...Bxf5 2 Qxb7 and 1...Ne5 2 Rxe5. The last variation shows that there is a third battery in position after the key, which can only fire after the masking knight has moved away.

It is important that Black's checks should not be too obvious in cross-check problems since the theme depends on the surprise element for its effect. If Black had a check or two with no mates provided in the initial position, the composer's idea would be only too obvious. It is therefore normal for the key to expose White's king to the attack of Black's pieces and in the best examples of the genre the key looks so preposterous that one is inclined to overlook it completely.

8

8 G. Guidelli, 2nd Pr. L'Eco degli Scacchi, 1917

#2

Knowing that this is a cross-check problem renders the key obvious, but starting from scratch is another proposition entirely, for there are no Black checks in sight. The solver's attention would probably be drawn to Black's flight 1...Ke5, for which the mate 2 Nc4 is set. White's threat must cover d6 and e5, but it isn't clear how this can be achieved since White's knights can't reach f7 while c4 is defended twice. The evidence points to a mate along the h2—b8 diagonal, but Black has a choice of two interpositions after Bxf4. Finally the solver would overcome his natural inhibitions and consider **1 Kf7**, threatening 2 Qb8, even though two Black batteries can fire at White's king. However, 1...e5+ 2 N7d5 exploits the pin of the f6 bishop, while the analogous line 1...B at random + 2 N3f5 utilises the pin of the e6 pawn. Such a situation, in which two Black pieces lie between a White piece and the enemy king, is called a **half-pin**. Usually there are paired variations when Black moves one or other of the intervening pieces, the resulting White mates depending on the pin of the remaining piece. The final variation arises after 1...Be5+, which prevents the mate occasioned on other bishop moves by unpinning the rook, but allows a new mate 2 N7f5 as a result of the self-block at e5.

Four of the problems for solving at the end of this chapter involve cross-checks, but to preserve the element of surprise I will leave the reader to discover which they are.

As in Diagram 6, the next problem is most readily solved by focusing on the function of one particular piece.

9 V. Chepizhny, 1st Pr. The Problemist, 1982

#2

The a3 rook must be brought into play and this immediately suggests that the key will be by one of the minor pieces on the third rank. The bishop has a limited number of moves since control of c4 must be retained, but 1 Bd5? Kxd4+ and 1 Be6? Ke3+ allow the bishop + king battery to fire. If the knight moves there is no threat with the bishop because Bd5+ and Be6+ both interfere with White pieces to give Black's king a flight. So the threat must be from another piece. Most moves by the c3 knight are answered by simple captures (e.g. 1 Na4/d1/b1/e2/d5/b5 just allow Black to take the knight) so by a process of elimination one is led to **1 Ne4**, which blocks off the f4 rook and so threatens 2 Nxc2 mate. It does allow Black to check with his king but this leads to the surprising mate 1...Ke3+ 2 Bc4. Two of the variations are particularly interesting. 1...Rxe4 2 Be6 and 1...cxd4 2 Bd5 both feature self-blocks of Black's king by other Black pieces, but these self-blocks are exploited in an unusual way by White interferences. The mating move cuts off control of a flight, permissible since Black has already blocked it. There are some less interesting variations too: 1...Nb4/c7 2 Nxc5, 1...Bc4 2 Bxc2, 1...Nxf7 2 Bxf7, 1...Bf2 2 Nxf2 and 1...Rxf5 2 Nxf5. It goes without saying that a position like that of Diagram 9 cannot involve zugzwang, since Black has numerous non-committal moves such as 1...Ng6 or 1...Qg5.

The theme of White interference after self-blocks arises in the next problem in a more symmetrical fashion.

10 A. Ellerman, 1st Pr. Guidelli Mem. Tny. 1925

≠2

Some of Black's prominent defences already have mates arranged, for example 1...Qxb7+ 2 Bxb7 and 1...Qh8+ 2 Nd8, but there are many others which do not, such as 1...e2 and 1...Bf2, giving the Black king flights at d3 and f3 respectively. Dealing with the latter defence first, the opening of the White queen's path to h1 and the interference with Black's queen suggest that White's reply to 1...Bf2 will be 2 Qxh1. Hence the key must either defend d3 or be a move by the d3 rook. The only move to protect d3 is 1 Rad5? and this allows 1...Qxb7+, so the rook must travel along the d-file, creating the threat of 2 Qf4. d1, d6, d7 and d8 are the possible squares, but d1 can be rejected at once on account of 1...Qd2 allowing the king access to d3 and d4. 1 Rd6 fails to 1...Qd4, when 2 Nc5 gives the Black king e5. The refutation of 1 Rd8 is particularly subtle, since it isn't obvious that d8 must be left vacant for White's knight. However, 1...Qf2 shows up the defects of 1 Rd8 as the only two available checks with the knight block one of the rooks and allow the king to flee to d4 or e5. **1 Rd7!** is the key when there are two symmetrical variations 1...Qd4 2 Nd6 and 1...Qe5 2 Nc5, each showing a White interference. The other variations are quite interesting, including two more self-blocks: 1...Bf3 2 Qd3, 1...Rd4 2 Re7, 1...Qxb7+ 2 Bxb7, 1...Qf2 2 Nd8 and 1...Qh8+ 2 Nd8.

Diagram 21 shows a combination of a half-pin and self-blocks with White interference.

Many problems involve pinning and unpinning strategy, but this is usually not sufficiently interesting to make a good problem on its own. In the next position self-blocks are combined with pins.

11 A. Ellerman, 3rd Pr. American Chess Bulletin, 1921

#2

A quick examination shows that there is no set play at all, so all the defences have to be introduced by the key, which must carry a threat in view of Black's pawn promotions. One would certainly expect the White queen to play a major part in the proceedings, but at the moment she is just pinning Black's rook, a task which could just as well be performed by a bishop. So the key is probably a queen move. The bishop + rook battery aimed at White's king might indicate a cross-check problem, but it is easy to see that White cannot arrange a mate to counter 1...Rxd5+. So if the queen moves, it must be **1 Qd7** to shield the king from checks. The threat is 2 Qa4 and apart from the trivial 1...Bxd6 2 Nxd6 Black's only defence is to move his unpinned rook, at the same time pinning White's queen. Four self-blocks arise after 1...Re5 2 R5d4, 1...Rxd5 2 Re3, 1...Rf4 2 Nc3 and 1...Rf3 2 R3d4, with a bonus interference variation 1...Rg5 2 Nxf6.

Diagram 23 centres on the unpinning of Black's queen.

Most of the problems we have examined so far in this chapter have been over fifty years old and it is now time to move on to more modern compositions. We have already seen changed play in which mates set before the key are transformed to new mates after the key. Many contemporary problems contain a different type of changed play involving tries by White. The idea is that certain prominent Black defences are answered by different mates after the key and the try. There may even be several tries, with further changed mates after each one. The difficulty with this type of problem is that the solver is looking for the solution rather than the near misses and if he finds the right move first time he will overlook the tries and the point of the problem. Try-play problems therefore work best when there is a strong common link between tries and key, so that it is harder for the solver to miss some of the possibilities. The tries and key may all be moves of the same piece, for example, or they may be moves of different pieces to the same square.

12 H. Knuppert, 1st Pr. Key Stip TT, 1973

≠2

Three White pieces are poised to create the threat of 2 Qg4 by capturing on f5. Which one is correct? After 1 Rxf5 the defences based on moving the queen fail, for example 1...Qe5 2 Rf4, 1...Qxd6 2 Rf6 and 1...Qxg6 2 Bd5. The first variation shows self-block with White interference and gives a clue to the refutation of 1 Rxf5, for 1...Ne5! blocks e5, but White is unable to exploit it because his rook is still pinned. What about 1 Nexf5? Now 1...Ne5 is met by 2 Rf4 and the unpinning defences 1...Qe5 2 Ng3 and 1...Qxd6 2 Nxd6 still lead to mate, but now 1...Qxg6! defends because White has abandoned his guard of d5. The key is **1 Ngxf5!**, which leads to the same mates as 1 Nexf5?, except that with d5 defended White has Bd5 against 1...Qxg6. In this case the tries and key are all captures on the same square, creating the same threat, and it is hardly possible for the solver to miss the changed mates after 1...Qe5 and 1...Qxd6.

Diagram 26 is somewhat similar, although in this case the threat does not remain the same after the different tries.

13 V. Chepizhny & L. Loshinsky, 1st Pr. Leipzig Olympic Tny, 1960

≠2

This example is much more complex and is a typical top class modern two-move problem. In the diagram the White queen simply gets in the way, preventing mate in one by d7, so it is logical to try a queen move as the key. To decide on a destination, we have to look at Black's possible defences to the threat of d7 mate. Suppose White makes a random queen move, 1 Qh3 say. Then Black has three moves to control the bishop + pawn battery, namely 1...Nf7, 1...Rh7 and 1...Re8. Now the pieces at b8, g8 and h4 share the responsibility of preventing mates by b4, Rc4 and Nb3, but it doesn't matter if one of the pieces moves away because any two of the three Black men are capable of preventing all the White mates. But what happens if White's queen move is used to interrupt the control of one of the three Black men? White might try 1 Qg4, 1 Qb7 or 1 Qe6. After 1 Qg4, for example, 1...Nf7 and 1...Re8 leave just one Black piece trying unsuccessfully to stop three mates and allow 2 Rc4 and 2 b4 respectively. Clearly Black should use the piece which has already been obstructed to stop the threat and play 1...Rh7. However, this gives up control of the fourth rank and the queen is able to move along Black's former line of control to mate by 2 Qd4. The refutation of 1 Qg4 is subtle and easily overlooked. White has given up his double guard on c6 by moving the queen away and Black can exploit this by 1...Bd5! giving his king a flight at c6. Turning now to 1 Qb7, which maintains the guard of c6, there is an analogous set of three lines, 1...Nf7 2 Nb3, 1...Rh7 2 b4 and 1...Re8 2 Qb6, the last again showing the queen moving along one of the three thematic lines. This time the refutation is 1...Re4! allowing the king to slip away at d5. The key is **1 Qe6!**, with the variations 1...Rh7 2 Rc4, 1...Re8 2 Nb3 and 1...Nf7 2 Qd5. The refutations of the tries don't work after the key because d5 is under double control and ...Bd5 has been physically prevented.

Diagram 27 is another example of tries and key all being made with the same piece.

The last two examples in this chapter involve tries which have a common aim.

14

14 L. Loshinsky, 1st Pr. Probleemblad, 1967

#2

White's ambition is to bring the rook at d8 or the queen at c7 to the e-file, mating Black's king. This is not easily countered, since Black's attempts to arrange an interposition have mates set, for example 1...f5 2 Qe5 or 1...Nc3 2 Bxc5. First of all, let's try bringing the rook to the e-file by 1 Rd6. This has the unfortunate side-effect of interfering with the e7 bishop and allowing 1...Nc3!, since Bxc5 is not possible. So the queen must come to the e-file instead. Perhaps e6 is the destination? In view of the line 1...f5 2 Qe5 White should keep e5 under observation, so 1 Qd6 is sensible, particularly as 1...Nc3 is met by 2 Qxc5. The refutation is 1...Rf2! which prevents Qe6 by cutting off the other guard of f4. Looking at the diagram we see that 1...Rf2 is met by 2 Rxd3 and the flaw in 1 Qd6 is that it interfered with the rook at d8. Still sticking to the plan of bringing the queen to the e-file, it now seems that the e7 bishop must move to threaten 2 Qe7. 1 Bd6 is one attempt, when 1...Rf2 doesn't stop the threat and 1...Nc3 is still answered by 2 Bxc5. Unfortunately the bishop interferes with the queen's path to e5 and allows 1...f5!. Thus the three tries are all moves by different pieces to the same square and fail because of a cycle of White interferences, rook interferes with bishop, queen interferes with rook and finally bishop interferes with queen. After all that, what might the key be? Simply **1 Bf8!**, which has all the beneficial features of 1 Bd6 but avoids obstructing the queen. Many modern problems have almost irrelevant post-key play, as in this example, since the main purpose is to show interesting relationships between the tries and the key. Perhaps the most satisfactory type of problem is one which combines the older clear-cut themes with modern try-play. The following problem is a fine example.

15 V. Wilson, 1st Pr. American Chess Bull. 1956

#2

In the diagram Black has two checks from the bishop + king battery, but these lead to set mates after 1...Kd4+ 2 Neg2 or 1...Ke5+ 2 Nfd5/g2. At the moment neither of White's rook + knight batteries can fire because the squares d3 and f5 are not covered by any other piece. White's threat will have to be a battery mate since there is no other way to cover e4, d4 and e5 simultaneously, so it seems likely that the key will be either 1 Bc4, guarding d3 and threatening 2 Nf4 moves, or 1 Qh3, guarding f5 and threatening 2 Ne3 moves. After 1 Bc4 Black still has his checks, but they are of no avail, for example 1...Kd4+ 2 Nfd5 or 1...Ke5+ 2 Nfg2. White can shut off Black's attempt to interpose at g4 after 1...Bc8 2 Ne6, but the fourth rank battery can be completely nullified by 1...Rf6! and White has no mate. So the key must be **1 Qh3!**, when the replies to Black's checks are completely changed to 1...Kd4+ 2 Neg2 and 1...Ke5+ 2 Ned5. By controlling f5 instead of e5 with his queen, White arranges for the other battery to fire and the roles of the squares d5 and g2 are interchanged between try and key. There are three unimportant variations after the key: 1...d1=Q or N 2 Nxd1, 1...Ba6 2 Nc4 and 1...Rd3 2 Ng6, the last variation being a pleasant bonus in which the other battery fires to exploit the self-block at d3.

Now there is a selection of problems for the reader to solve, which provide further useful illustration for many of the points made in this chapter. The solutions may be found at the back of the book.

16

Problems for Solving

16 C. Mansfield, V. Massman & L. Loshinsky, 3rd Pr. Problem, 1959

‡2

17 W. Shinkman, 1st Pr. Huddersfield College Mag., 1877

‡2

18 A. Ellerman, 3rd Pr. Good Companions Meredith Tny, 1919

‡2

19 H. D. O'Bernard, Western Morning News, 1903

‡2

20 C. Mansfield, 1st Pr. Good Companions, 1917

‡2

21 C. Mansfield, 1st Pr. Hampshire Telegraph & Post, 1919

‡2

22 C. Mansfield, 1st Pr.
British C. F., 1974

≠2

23 H. Knuppert, 1st Pr.
Europe Echecs, 1973

≠2

24 G. Anderson, 1st Pr.
Il Secolo, 1921

≠2

25 A. Ellerman, 1st Pr.
Good Companions, 1916

≠2

26 G. Rinder, 1st Pr.
Die Schwalbe, 1975

≠2

27 C. Sammelius, 1st Pr.
Schakend Nederland, 1964

≠2

28 Y. Cheylan, 1st Pr.
The Problemist, 1976

≠2

29 Touw Hian Bwee, 1st Pr.
Het Parool, 1976

a) Diagram   b) Remove Nf8   ≠2

2 Studies I

In this chapter we enter a world halfway between problems and over-the-board play, the world of endgame studies. Like problems these are composed positions, but the aim is not to force mate in a specified number of moves but to force a win or draw. The number of moves required is left unspecified since there is no definite point at which the win becomes obvious; what is obvious to one solver may be unclear to another. Most endgame studies have positions which could plausibly arise in practical play and, indeed, solving a study is similar to analysing an adjournment in tournament play. The difference is that with a study you know that the win or draw is there is you look hard enough, while in an adjournment one can only hope.

Despite these connections to the competitive game, many of the principles applying to problems hold for studies too. The principle of economy must be observed; every piece has a purpose and the composer won't use two where one will do just as well. The composer's idea will involve some unusual behaviour on the part of the chessmen, perhaps a surprising tactical point or maybe an exception to one of the usual rules of endgame play. It is usually much harder to guess the composer's intention from the diagram with a study, because there may be several introductory moves before the hidden point comes to light and in the course of these moves the position may have been changed radically. Study solvers face another difficulty. Many compositions involve analysis of considerable complexity, taxing enough for a strong tournament player and doubly so for those whose main interest is in problems. However, those who turn their backs on studies are missing a good deal of pleasure. One of the aims of chess composition is to extract the maximum effect from the minimum material, and studies are better able to fulfil this objective than any other form of composition. Look at Diagrams 34 and 45, for example, to see how much play can be extracted from a position of king and pawn v. king and pawn. The over-the-board player also has much to gain from taking an interest in endgame composition, since many study ideas are applicable to practical play. Would you see how to win in Diagrams 35 and 42, if you had not seen the ideas before in these positions by Speelman and Mattison, strong over-the-board players of different eras?

In this chapter we will examine studies which do not involve too much difficult analysis, while Chapter 5 deals with more complex positions.

Before the mid-nineteenth century there was no clear distinction between endgames composed for artistic purposes, i.e. studies, and didactic positions intended to advance endgame theory. Consequently studies are of fairly recent origin, dating mainly from the turn of the century. Two composers of this period, Rinck and Troitsky, laid the foundations for the rapid development occurring in the twentieth century. The period 1905–35 was perhaps the Golden Age of the study and many of the lightweight positions considered classics today were composed in this period. The territory was largely unexplored and new discoveries came thick and fast. Here are three famous studies from the Golden Age.

30 V. & M. Platov, Deutsche Schachzeitung, 1907

Draw

The first consideration is to identify Black's threats. Here any move of Black's bishop will win the White rook in return for the d2 pawn, but it is particularly urgent to do something to counter ...Bf3+. Only three first moves by White come into consideration, namely 1 Rd3, 1 Rc8+ and 1 Rh3+. The first fails after 1 Rd3 Bf3+ 2 Ka7 d1=Q 3 Rxd1 Bxd1 4 Kb6 d5 5 Kc5 Bf3, while the second is pointless as Black easily evades the checks by 1 Rc8+ Kg7 2 Rc7+ Kf6.

1 Rh3+

Even though we may have no idea yet why this move is correct, a process of elimination is often the best way to arrive at the solution!

1 ...   Kg7

The situation has not substantially changed, so the same logic as above implies that White must check again.

2 Rg3+

Now it is possible to see some point in White's checks, in that if Black moves to the f-file White can reply Rd3 winning the d2 pawn, for ...Bf3+ can be taken with check.

21

2 ...	Kh6

At some point White will have to stop checking, for otherwise Black brings the king up to the rook and White will be finished, so at each move White should look at Rd3 to see if the position of Black's king can be exploited.

3 Rd3!

In fact the crucial point is that Black's king is on the third rank, so 2...Kh7 3 Rh3+ Kg6 would also have been met by Rd3.

3 ...	Bf3+
4 Ka7!	d1=Q

If Black plays 4...d1=R 5 Rxf3 d5 White draws by 6 Kb6 d4 7 Kc5 since Black's king is cut off by the rook and cannot support the d-pawn.

5 Rxd6+

This only works because it is check. **5...Qxd6** is stalemate thanks to White's fourth move, while after a king move White just takes the queen.

Although the introductory moves of a study can often be found by straightforward analysis, there usually comes a moment when none of the available moves seem to offer a chance of success and the solver has to wait for a flash of inspiration to strike. The next study provides a good example.

31 V. & M. Platov, 1st Pr. Rigaer Tageblatt, 1909

Win

Black's pawn is about to promote so White's choice is limited. 1 Bg5+ just forces Black to take a useful White pawn, so the first move is easy.

1 Bf6	d4

Now it seems that the only way to counter Black's promotion is by 2 Nf3 to win the new queen by Bxd4+. Unfortunately 2 Nf3 a1=Q 3 Bxd4+ Qxd4 4 Nxd4 Kxd4 5 Kf4 Kxd3 6 Kg5 Ke4 7 Kh6 Kf5 8 Kxh7 Kf6 is

22

manifestly a draw after 9 h6 Kf7 or 9 Kg8 Kg5. Another problem is that if this were the right line then 2 Ne2 would work just as well, for 2...Kxe2 3 Bxd4 Kxd3 4 Ba1 wins for White (if Black goes to win the bishop White is much too quick taking the h-pawn, while otherwise White's bishop is the right colour for the rook's pawn). The solution can only be discovered when one has the idea that Black's queen does not have to be won immediately, provided White can generate a mate threat.

2	Ne2!	a1=Q
3	Nc1!!	

A superb move threatening Bg5 mate and preventing Black's queen delivering check at e1 or g1. Of course, 3 Bxd4+ repeats the above draw.

| 3 | ... | Qa5 |

3...Qxc1 4 Bg5+, 3...Kd2 4 Nb3+ and 3...h6 4 Be5! are also lost for Black.

| 4 | Bxd4+! |

The final point. Black cannot avoid a knight fork by Nb3+ winning the queen and keeping an extra piece.

32 M. Liburkin, 2nd Pr. Shakhmaty v SSSR, 1931

Win

White's passed pawns are dangerous but Black threatens both ....Rxb5 and ....Kxa2. Since 1 Nb4 Rxb5 leads to nothing White's first move is forced.

| 1 | Nc1 | Rxb5 |

Black has other moves to meet the threat of Nb3+:
1) 1...Kb1 2 Nb3 Rc3 (2...Rxb5 3 c7 Rd5+ 4 Nd2+ or 2...Rc4 3 Nd2+) 3 Na5 followed by b6 wins.
2) 1...Rc3 (or c4) 2 Nb3+! followed by 3 Na5, or 2...Rxb3 3 c7 Rc3 4 b6 promoting a pawn.

23

3) 1...Rd5+ 2 Kc2 (2 Ke1/e2? Rxb5 3 c7 Re5+ and ....Re8 draws, or 2 Nd3? Rxd3+ 3 Kc2 Rd5 and White loses a pawn) Rc5+ (2...Rxb5 3 Nb3+ and 4 c7) and now White must be careful. 3 Kd2? Rxb5 4 c7 (4 Nb3+ Rxb3 5 c7 Rb2+ draws — White must even take care not to lose by 6 Kc3? Kb1) Rb2+ 5 Kd1 Rc2! draws since 6 Kxc2 is stalemate and 6 Nb3+ Kb2 wins the pawn. The correct line is 3 Kd3! Rxb5 (3...Rxc1 5 Kd4 and the pawns win easily after Kd5 followed by b6) 4 c7 Rb8! 5 cxb8=B!, the only move to win as Q and R give stalemate, while N reaches the K+2N v K draw.

2	c7	Rd5+
3	Nd3!	

3 Ke1/e2 Re5+ and ....Re8 draws.

3	...	Rxd3+
4	Kc2	Rd4!

Black can't stop the pawn promoting so he sets the trap 5 c8=Q? Rc4+! 6 Qxc4 stalemate. 5 Kc3 Rd1 6 Kc2 Rd4 just repeats the position, so how does White win?

5	c8=R!	

Threatening 6 Ra8 mate. Black has only one defence.

5	...	Ra4
6	Kb3!	

and wins, as Black must lose his rook in order to prevent mate by Rc1. Some readers may recognise the position after White's fourth move as being the Saavedra position, so called because the winning underpromotion was found by the Revd. F. Saavedra in May 1895. Liburkin's contribution was to add the bishop underpromotion after 1...Rd5+.

After the Second World War composers found more and more difficulty composing such elegant lightweight studies, since most had already been discovered. Consequently there has been a trend towards greater analytical complexity even in positions with few pieces. Often the uniqueness of White's moves can only be proved by deep and lengthy variations so some composers have followed a different path. They have turned towards heavier positions with a marked middle-game character. In this way they have been able to compose studies with clear-cut variations not requiring much supporting analysis, but at the cost of less natural positions. Happily some composers have persevered with light positions and have made new discoveries overlooked by earlier generations.

33 D. Gurgenidze, 3rd Pr. Mhkedruli, 1976

Win

This forms a companion to Liburkin's composition. White can't promote immediately and after 1 Kc4? Rd2 2 Kc3 (2 Ne2? Rxe2) Rd5! White has nothing better than 3 Kc4 repeating the position since 3 c8=Q Rc5+! 4 Qxc5 is stalemate rather as in Liburkin's piece. In practice, White might very well try 3 c8=R but in a study one always assumes that Black will play perfectly.

1 Ne2   Ka5!

1...Rd2 2 Nc3+ and 3 c8=Q wins, but now White must once again avoid promotion because 2 c8=Q Rc3+ 4 Nxc3 is another stalemate while 2 c8=R Ka6 (but not 2...Ka4? 3 Kc4 and wins) is drawn.

2 Kc4!   Rd6!

Black's tricks still aren't exhausted! Now he is aiming for 3 c8=Q Rc6+ 4 Qxc6 stalemate.

3 Nd4!   Rc6+

Black cannot prevent the pawn advancing any longer, so he sets one last trap.

4 Nxc6+   Kb6
5 c8=R!

The only move to win as 5 c8=Q is once again stalemate. A short but sharp promotion battle in which White must sidestep four different stalemate traps.

The complexity of apparently simple endgame positions is familiar to over-the-board players and study composers have thoroughly explored such endings as K+P v K+P, often uncovering surprising finesses. The Soviet composer Grigoriev (1895–1938) was the undisputed master of the pawn ending, producing over 150 king and pawn studies.

34 N. Grigoriev, Shakhmaty v SSSR, 1932

Win

Black's king is within the square of White's pawn so 1 a4? Ke4 is no good, while after 1 Kf6? Ke4 2 Ke6 c5 both sides promote.

1 Kf5!		**Ke3**

1...c5 2 Ke5 Ke3 3 Kd5 and 1...c6 2 a4 are easy wins for White.

2 Ke5		**c6!**

2...Kd3 3 Kd5 Kc3 (or 3...c6+ 4 Kc5) 4 Kc5 followed by a4 wins.

3 a4	

There is nothing better as 4 Kd6 Kd4 5 a4 (5 Kxc6 Kc4 wins the a-pawn) c5 is a sure draw.

3 ...		**Kd3**

Black has to waste a vital tempo before he can push his own pawn.

4 a5	**c5**
5 a6	**c4**
6 a7	**c3**
7 a8=Q	**c2**

The introduction is over and the main content of the study lies in the next two moves. Normally Q v c-pawn on the seventh is a draw because Black has a stalemate defence; when his king is on b1 and White plays Qb3+ Black can avoid obstructing his pawn by playing ...Ka1. The pawn is invulnerable and Black threatens to promote, so White has nothing better than to repeat the position. If White's king is near he may still be able to win, but only if he is within the zone bordered by a4, b4, c4, c3, d3, e3, e2 and e1 — thus d4 is too far away. At the moment Black's king is on the wrong side of the pawn for the stalemate defence so White must prevent Black's king crossing to the b-file unless White can bring his own king within the winning zone. How can White make progress? 8 Qa1 Kd2 9 Qa2 is an obvious try since 9...Kd1 10 Kd4! c1=Q 11 Kd3 wins, but Black has the subtle defence 9...Kc3! which keeps White's king out and forces a repetition. Other moves are similar, for example 8 Qe4+ Kd2 (not 8...Kc3? 9 Qd4+ and Qa1) 9 Qd4+ Ke2 and now:

1) 10 Qc3 Kd1 11 Qd3+ Kc1 (White has a free move while Black crosses to the right side of the pawn but he still can't win because he cannot bring his king into the winning zone in one move) 12 Kd4 Kb2 13 Qe2 (or 13 Qd2 Kb1) Ka1! (not 13...Kb1? 14 Kc3 c1=Q+ 15 Kb3 and wins) 14 Kc3 c1=Q+ 15 Kb3 Qb1+ draw.

2) 10 Qb2 Kd1 11 Qb3 Kd2 12 Qa2 Kc3! as before.

3) 10 Qe4+ Kd2 11 Qd5+ Ke1! draw.

It seems that once Black's king is on d2 White cannot win, so if White is to triumph he must exploit the position of the king at d3 immediately and in such a way as to prevent the drawing ...Kd2. 8 Qd8+ Ke2! leads to nothing after 9 Qg5 Kd1 so there is only one plausible move.

8 Qd5+!!

The only move to win.

8 ...   Ke2

8...Ke3 (8...Kc3 9 Qd4+ and Qa1) 9 Qg2! (the only move, e.g. 9 Qd4+ Ke2 or 9 Qd6 Ke2 with a draw as White's queen cannot reach a2) Kd3 10 Qg5 wins.

9 Qa2!

With the king on e2 rather than d2 Black lacks the defence ...Kc3 which saved the day against 8 Qa1.

9 ...   Kd2

Setting a last trap. 9...Kd1 10 Kd4 c1=Q (10...Kd2 11 Qb2) 11 Kd3 and 9...Kd3 10 Qb2 Kd2 11 Kd4 are no better.

10 Kd4   Kd1
11 Kc3 (or e3)

But not 11 Kd3?? c1=N+!

11 ...   c1=Q+
12 Kd3

and finally Black must give up.

The next position is also far more subtle than the diagram suggests.

35 J. Speelman, EG, 1979

Win

Rather than attempt to solve this by trial and error it is far better to try to uncover the basic principles governing the play. First, if both kings are on the queenside then the position is a draw. For example, with White Kb6,Ph6 v Black Kb8,Ph7 Black draws by 1...Ka8 2 Kc7 Ka7. Alternatively with White Kc5 v Black Kc7 and White's pawn on h6, 1...Kd7 2 Kd5 Kc7 3 Ke6 Kc6 4 Kf7 only draws even though White wins the race because Black can continue 4...Kd7! 5 Kg7 Ke7 6 Kxh7 Kf7 and White's king cannot escape. If White keeps his pawn on h5 to preserve the tempo h6 needed to free his king in the above line then Black draws by taking the opposition with a timely ...h6. It follows that White must prevent Black's king reaching the queenside. The second important point is that if White threatens to march to b7 with his king Black has to oppose kings, for in any race White's a-pawn will win by a mile.

1 Kg5

Not 1 Ke5? Kd7 and White has the choice between 2 Kd5 Kc7 drawing as above and indulging in a race by 2 Kf6, not a great success as Black promotes first.

1 ...   Kf7

Black loses the race: 1...Kd6 2 h4 Kc5 3 Kh6 Kb5 4 Kxh7 Kxa5 5 h5 b5 6 h6 b4 7 Kg7! (not g6, when Black promotes with check, nor g8 blocking White's queen) b3 8 h7 b2 9 h8=Q b1=Q 10 Qa8+ and 11 Qb8+ winning the queen.

2 Kh6

Not 2 h4? Kg7.

2 ...   Kg8
3 h4

28

White aims to return to the diagram position with the pawn on h4 rather than h3 so that the line 1 Ke5 Kd7 2 Kf6 becomes a White win thanks to the extra tempo.

	3 ...	Kh8

Now 4 h5 Kg8 5 Kg5 Kf7 6 Kf5 h6 is completely drawn. White has to gain the opposition to make progress.

	4 Kh5!	Kg8

4...Kg7 5 Kg5 Kf7 (or 4...h6+ 5 Kf5 Kf7 6 h5 winning the pawn at h6, when White's spare tempo h6 decides the game) 6 Kf5 transposing to the main line.

	5 Kg4	Kf8
	6 Kf4	Ke8

Black can't go to the g-file as White heads for b7. 6...h6 7 Kf5 Kf7 (must prevent Ke6) 8 h5 wins more easily. After 6...Ke8 White must arrange a bypass to regain the opposition with the kings two squares closer, but he must be careful. The opposition breaks down when Black's king is near enough to the queenside to win races, for then the White king is dragged inexorably further left which, as we already know, leads to a draw. So White must bypass here. After 7 Ke4? Kd7 it is too late.

	7 Kg5!	Kf7

Black loses the race so he has to come back.

	8 Kf5	

White's objective is achieved and Black will soon be in a fatal zugzwang.

	8 ...	Ke7
	9 Ke5	Kd7

9...h6 10 h5 is no better.

	10 Kf6	Kc6

11 h5 (or Kg7) Kb5 12 h6 (or Kg7) Kxa5 13 Kg7 b5 14 Kxh7 b4 15 Kg7! b3 16 h7 b2 17 h8=Q b1=Q 18 Qa8+ and 19 Qb8+ wins.

Diagram 45 is another king and pawn ending containing a trap for the unwary solver!

An idea which occurs frequently in studies and in the longer problems of Chapter 4 is that of a foreplan. White may have a forcing continuation which almost, but not quite, succeeds in its objective. It may be possible, though the immediate execution fails, to devise a preliminary manoeuvre which may deflect a vital Black unit or introduce some other element unfavourable to Black, so that the delayed execution succeeds. In studies this foreplan may be just one move and often amounts to a sacrifice deflecting a Black piece. The following example should make the idea clear.

29

36 S. Kaminer, 2nd Pr. Shakhmaty, 1925

Win

| 1 | b7 | Rf8 |

Black threatens ....Rb8, so White's knight manoeuvre is forced.

| 2 | Nb4+ | Ke4 (or e3) |
| 3 | Nc6 | |

White's plan involves running Black's rook out of squares on the eighth rank, so 3 Na6 is less promising as it leaves d8 unguarded. After 3 Nc6 White intends to play g4—g5 safeguarding the g-pawn and then to win Black's rook by b8=Q.

| 3 | ... | Kf4 |

3...Kf5 4 Ne7+ and 5 Nc8 wins. After 3...Kf4 White cannot promote immediately as Black can win the g-pawn by ...Kg3. At first sight 4 Kg7 Re8 5 Kf7 Rh8 is tempting since Black's rook is completely bottled up and hasn't a single move along the eighth rank, but how can White proceed? 6 g4 h6! (intending ...Rh7+), 6 Ke7 (threat Nd8) Rg8! 7 Nd8 Rg7+ 8 Nf7 Rg8 (threat ...Rb8) 9 Nd8 Rg7+ and 6 N moves Rb8 all lead to a draw.

| 4 | g4! | |

White threatens 5 g5 so Black is forced to accept the sacrifice, which deflects his king onto a bad square. 4 g3+? Kxg3 doesn't work as the king is safe from knight forks at g3.

| 4 | ... | Kxg4 |

Now the manoeuvre which failed last move comes into effect.

5	Kg7	Re8
6	Kf7	Rh8
7	Ke7	Rg8

7...h5 8 Nd8 Rh7+ 9 Nf7 is no better.

| 8 | Nd8 | Rg7+ |
| 9 | Nf7 | Rg8 |

Now White reveals the point of 4 g4!.

10 Nh6+ and wins.

The foreplans in Chapter 4 are generally more subtle than the simple deflections of this chapter, but the study settings are more elegant. Diagrams 46 and 47 also feature preliminary sacrifices.

In the remainder of this chapter and Chapter 5 we will look more closely at a few of the typical themes in endgame studies. Perhaps the most basic of all is mate. Of course, mate is the object of the game so if it constitutes the main idea of a study there must be some special element of surprise involved. If White's force is very limited, for example, or if the mate arises suddenly after a long period of interchanges in which there is no hint of mating threats, then the solver is likely to be astonished by its unexpected appearance.

37 T. Gorgiev, L'Echiquier de France, 1957

Win

1 Ra5!

White's e-pawn is in serious danger, so drastic action is necessary. 1 Nxf2+? Kxe2 2 Ra5 can be refuted by careful play: 2...e3 3 Ra2+ (3 Rxa6 exf2 4 Ra2+ Ke1 5 Rxf2 Nb5 6 Kf3 Nc3 and Black's knight reaches d1 to give a draw, or if 6 Rf3 in this line, then 6...Kd2) Ke1 4 Ne4 (so that ...Bb7 isn't check) Bb7 5 Kf3 Kd1 6 Rxa7 (6 Kxe3 Nb5 draw) Bxe4+ 7 Kxe4 e2 8 Kd3 e1=N+ with a theoretical draw.

| 1 | ... | f1=Q+ |

1...Kxe2 2 Nf4+ Ke1 (2...Ke3 3 Rxa6) 3 Ra1+ Kd2 4 Rxa6 e3 5 Rxa7 wins.

2	Kxf1	Bxe2+
3	Kf2	Nb5!

Black sacrifices his bishop to bring the knight into the game. 3...Bg4 4 Nf4 Nc8 (4...Nc6 5 Rd5+ Kc2 6 Rc5+ Kd2 7 Rxc6 e3+ 8 Kg3 e2 9 Rd6+ Kc2 10 Kf2 or 9...Ke3 10 Kxg4 and White wins) 5 Rg5 Bf3 (5...Bd7 6 Rd5+) 6 Rd5+ and 7 Rc5+ wins.

4	Ra1+	

White has nothing better than to accept since 4 Ke3? Nc3 5 Nf2+ Kc2 6 Rc5 Kb3 7 Kd2 e3+ draws easily.

4	...	Kd2
5	Ra2+	Kc1!

Black aims to trap White's rook, so he must cover b2.

6	Rxe2	

Of course not 6 Kxe2 Nc3+.

6	...	Nc3
7	Re1+	Kd2
8	Kf1!	

This restricts the rook's freedom, but it is necessary because 8 Rh1? e3+ 9 Kg2 (9 Kg3 e2 10 Kf2 allows 10...Ne4+ or 10...Nd1+ and if 10 Rh2 then simply 10...Ke3) e2 10 Ng5 (or g1) allows 10...e1=N+!. 8 Ra1? is similar while Black's threat to draw by ...Nd1—e3+ doesn't give White time for moves like 8 Ng5?.

8	...	e3
9	Ng5!	

At first sight this just loses the rook. 9 Nf4 and 9 Ng1 are the obvious moves, but these allow a surprising draw by 9...e2+! 10 Nxe2 Nd1 and White must either submit to perpetual check by ...Ne3—d1+ or lose his rook. After 9 Ng5 White threatens Nf3+ so Black must take.

9	...	e2+
10	Kf2	Nd1+
11	Kg1	

Not 11 Kg2? Ne3+ 12 Kf2 Ng4+ and White doesn't get a second chance.

11	...	Kxe1

11...Ke3 12 Kg2 Kd2 13 Nf3+, 11...Kd3 12 Nf3 and 11...N moves 12 Nf3+ all win for White.

12	Nf3 mate.	

Diagram 49 is another example with an entirely different mating position.

Queen and pawn endings often give rise to unexpected mates, but in the next diagram it doesn't look as though Black's king is in trouble.

38 H. Rinck, =1st Pr. Bohemia, 1906

Win

Black has an extra passed pawn so White must act quickly or he might very well lose! The only possible chance is to generate threats against Black's king, but the first priority is to prevent the target from slipping away via b3, b4 or d3.

1 Qb1

The threat is 2 Qb5+ Kd4 3 Qd5 mate. 1...Qf7/g8 allows 2 Qa2+, so Black's king must move.

1 ...   Kd4

Black threatens ...Qxe4+ and if 2 Kd6 Black has a chance to activate his queen by 2...Qh8 since White doesn't have a serious threat.

2 Qb3!

Checking is useless as Black's king escapes via d3. Now White's threat of 3 Qd5 mate forces Black to take the pawn.

2 ...   Qxe4+

2...Kxe4 3 Qc2+.

3 Kd6

Black must move the queen or White plays Qc3 mate, but he must retain the guard of d5. 3...Qg2/h1 allows 4 Qc3+ Ke4 5 Qc6+, so the only move is to the opposite corner.

3	...	Qa8
4	Qe3+	Kc4
5	Qc3+	Kb5

33

6	**Qb3+**	**Ka6**

Black's moves are forced thanks to the exposed position of the queen at a8.

7	**Qa4+**	**Kb7**
8	**Qb5+**	**Ka7**

8...Kc8 allows mate in two.

9 Kc7

A familiar motif in queen and pawn endings. Black must give up his queen to avoid mate in one. Here the surprise lies in White's second move, allowing Black's queen to occupy a central position with gain of time, and the subsequent impotence of her majesty to deal with the threats.

The knight has long held a fascination for chess-players and some of the most attractive mating positions involve knights. The next study needs no further introduction.

39 A. Gurevich, Revista Romana de Sah, 1948

Win

White has sufficient material advantage to win, but his pieces are badly co-ordinated and he needs to defend against the threats of ...Kxh6 and ...hxg3.

1	**Nf5!**	**Ng3!**

1...Nf3 (or 1...Kxf5 2 Rxh4 and Black loses a knight in return) 2 Nde7 Ng3 3 Rg6+ Kf4 4 Nxg3 hxg3 5 Nd5+ Ke5 6 Rxg3 wins, but Black can play 1...Ng4 2 Rxh4 Ng3! transposing to the main line.

2	**Rxh4**	**Ng4**

2...Nf3 3 Rh3 and 2...Nhf1 3 Rf4 wins without difficulty.

3 Nd4!

34

Otherwise White loses a piece without compensation.

| 3 ... | Kxh4 |
| 4 Nf3+ | Kh5 |

4...Kh3 5 Nf4 is the first of the mates delivered by the knight pair.

5 Kg7

Threat 6 Nf4 mate. If the knight on g4 moves White can mate by Nf6.

| 5 ... | Ne2 |
| 6 Kh7! | |

with a dreadful zugzwang leading to mate next move by Nf4 or Nf6.

Mate and stalemate differ only by the control of a single square, so it is not surprising that a number of studies are based on avoiding false paths leading only to stalemate and finding the one correct route through the maze.

40 J. Nunn, EG, 1978

Win

1 Be3+

The only reasonable move as 1 Nf4? b2 2 Bc5 g1=Q stops the mate by Bf8 and wins for Black, while the timid 1 Bd4? hxg6 is an immediate draw.

1 ...   f4!

1...Kg7 (1...Kxh5 2 Nf4+ followed by 3 Nxg2+ and 4 Bd4 wins) 2 Kxg2 (2 Bd4+ is tempting, to cover b2 with gain of tempo, but in fact after 2...Kh6 White has nothing better than to repeat the position by 3 Be3+) hxg6 3 h6+ (3 Bc1 also wins) Kh7 4 Bc1 f4 5 Kf3 Kxh6 6 Kg4! (not 6 Kxf4? Kh5 7 Kg3 g5 8 hxg5 b2 draw) and White wins.

2 Nxf4

Not 2 Bxf4+ Kxh5 and the bishop blocks the square needed by White's knight.

	2 ...	g1=Q!

2...b2 3 Nd3+ and 4 Nxb2.

	3 Bxg1	b2

White cannot prevent promotion so he must threaten mate in one.

	4 Bc5	Kg7

Forced, but can't White win the pawn now?

	5 Bd4+	Kh6

No! 6 Bxb2 is stalemate. It seems that White has shot his bolt, but there is a mate hidden in the position.

	6 Ne6!	b1=Q
	7 Bg7+	Kxh5
	8 Nf4+	Kxh4
	9 Bf6 mate.	

Diagrams 50 and 51 contain a similar combination of mate and stalemate avoidance.

To finish the chapter, here is one of the most famous studies ever composed.

41 L. Kubbel, 1st Pr. Bakinski Rabochi, 1927/8

Win

Black's connected passed pawns on the seventh are so formidable that White must make immediate threats.

	1 Rf7+	Kb8
	2 Kb6	Kc8

36

There is a complicated side-variation which runs 2...f1=Q 3 Bxf1 exf1=Q 4 Rxf1 Kc8 5 Kc6 Kd8 (5...Kb8 6 Rf3 d5 7 Kxd5 Kc7 8 Ke6 Kc6 9 Kf7 and the only defence to 10 Kg6 is 9...Kd5, when the knight drops to 10 Rf5+) 6 Kxd6 Ke8 (6...Kc8 7 Rf3 Kb7 8 Ke6 etc.) 7 Ke6 Ng7+ (7...Ng3 8 Rg1) 8 Kf6 Kf8 (8...Nh5+ 9 Kg6 Ng3 10 Rg1) reaching a R v N ending. This material usually results in a draw, but there are certain positions in which White can force the separation of king and knight. The win is then a matter of restricting the movements of Black's pieces, always being careful that they are not allowed to reunite. Although this process is not especially difficult, the analysis is quite lengthy because of the large number of variations. For the curious here it is, but one could skip it without missing much: 9 Rf3 Ne8+ (9...Kg8 10 Rg3 Kh8 11 Kf7) 10 Ke6+ Kg8 11 Ke7 Ng7 (11...Nc7 12 Rf5 threatens Ra5, and if 12...Na6 then 13 Rg5+ Kh7 14 Kf7 Kh6 15 Rg6+) 12 Rh3 Nf5+ 13 Kf6 and now:
1) 13...Nd4 14 Rg3+ Kh7 15 Rg7+ Kh8 (15...Kh6 16 Rg4 Nf3 17 Rf4) 16 Rg4 Nc6 (16...Nf3 17 Rf4 and 18 Kf7) 17 Rc4 Na5 18 Rc5 Nb3 19 Rc3 and 20 Kg6 wins.
2) 13...Nd6 14 Rd3! and now:
2a) 14...Ne8+ 15 Ke7 Ng7 (15...Nc7 16 Rg3+ followed by Rg5 and Ra5) 16 Rd5 Kh7 (16...Kh8 17 Kf7 Kh7 18 Rg5 Kh8 19 Rg1) 17 Kf8! Kg6/h6 (17...Ne6+ 18 Kf7 and now 18...Ng7 19 Rg5 Kh8 20 Rg1 or 18...Nf4 19 Rf5) 18 Rd6+ Kh7 19 Rd7 Kh8 20 Kf7 Kh7 (20...Nf5/h5 21 Rd5) 21 Kf6 Kh8 22 Re7 Nh5+ 23 Kg5 Ng3 (23...Ng7 24 Kg6) 24 Re1 and 25 Kg4 wins.
2b) 14...Ne4+ 15 Kg6 Kf8 16 Rf3+ Kg8 17 Re3 Nd6 18 Re6 wins.
2c) 14...Nc4 15 Rd4 and now there are five lines, but all lead to a rapid conclusion — 15...Nb2 16 Ke5 Kf7 17 Kd5 Kf6 18 Kc6! Ke5 (or else 19 Kb5) 19 Kc5 K moves 20 Kb4 and 21 Kc3, 15...Na3 16 Rg4+ Kh7 17 Rg7+ Kh8 18 Kg6 Nc4 19 Re7, 15...Na5 16 Rd8+ Kh7 17 Rc8 Nb3 18 Rc7+ Kg8 19 Rg7+ Kh8 20 Kg6, 15...Nb6 16 Ke7 Kg7 17 Kd8 and finally 15...Ne3 16 Kg6 Kf8 17 Rf4+ Kg8 18 Re4.
2d) 14...Nb5 15 Ke7 etc.
2e) 14...Nb7 15 Rd5 Kh8 (15...Kf8 16 Rd7) 16 Kf7 wins.
Now we can return to the main line of the study.

3 Rxf2!

White should not pursue Black's king along the eighth rank any further since 3 Kc6 Kd8 4 Kxd6 e1=Q allows an interposition at e8.

3 ... Nf4!

3...e1=Q 4 Rf8+ Kd7 5 Bc6+ Ke6/7 6 Re8+ and 7 Rxe1 wins. Black's knight sacrifice seems to have little effect on this line, but he is aiming to set up a stalemate.

4 Rxf4 d5!

Black stops the rook coming behind the e-pawn and prepares the trap

5 Bxd5? e1=Q 6 Rf8+ Kd7 7 Bc6+ Ke7 8 Re8+ Kd6 9 Rxe1 stalemate.
5 Rf8+? Kd7 and 5 Bh3+? Kd8 6 Rf8+ Ke7 also fail, but White has a surprising finesse which leads to a line similar to that after 5 Bxd5?, but without the stalemate.

5	**Bf1!!**	e1=Q
6	**Rf8+**	Kd7
7	**Bb5+**	Kd6
8	**Rd8+**	

and **9 Re8+** winning the queen. This study makes an interesting comparison with Diagram 50. Having given so much analysis on the R v N position in the above study, it seems a shame to put it to no further use, so I have included Diagram 52 in the positions for solving. The main line leads to a R v N position which can be speedily wrapped up using the above analysis.

Problems for Solving

42 H. Mattison,
Rigaer Rundschau, 1914

Win

43 E. Pogosjants, 1st Pr.
Shakhmatnia Moskva, 1961

Win

44 P. Benko,
EG, 1982

Draw

45 H. Adamson,
Chess Amateur, 1915

Win

46 S. Kaminer,
2nd Pr. Trud, 1935

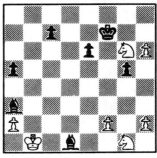

Win

47 G. Nadareishvili, 2nd Pr.
Lelo, 1950 (version)

Win

48 A. Troitsky,
Shakhmatnoe Obosrenie, 1910

Win

49 V. Pachman, 1st Pr.
Šachové Umĕni, 1979

Win

50 R. Réti, corrected by H. Rinck,
Bohemia, 1935

Win

51 E. Pogosjants, 1st Pr.
Shakhmatnia Moskva, 1964

Win

52 J. Moravec, 10th Pr. La Stratégie, 1913

Win

3 Three-move problems

Compared with the problems in Chapter 1, the extra move introduces a new order of complexity into the solver's task. Even if all else fails, a two-mover can always be solved by trial and error in fairly short order. Applying the same method to a three-mover could take hours, so it is essential to use all available short cuts.

The various bits of advice given in Chapter 1 apply here too, and we shall take it for granted that clues such as out of play White pieces, unprovided Black king flights and so on will already be familiar from the two-mover chapter. There are, however, a number of solving hints which apply especially to three-move problems and we shall concentrate on these here.

The distinction between zugzwang and threat problems, which played such an important role in Chapter 1, is of less significance. Very few three-movers are based solely on the idea of maintaining a pre-key zugzwang, or of introducing changed play in a zugzwang setting. There are a few examples, such as Diagram 69, but these are definitely the exception rather than the rule. A sense of humour is evident in the following composition.

53 E. Zepler, 3rd h.m., Thematurnier des Dresdhner Anzeigers, 1930

‡3

Black can only move his king, but there are four flights available. As with two-movers it is often helpful to see if Black's most prominent defences already have mates provided. 1...Kxg3 leads to a brutal mate after

41

2 Qe2 Kh3 3 Qg2, but the other three lead to more attractive continuations: 1...Kg1 2 Ng4 Kxh1 3 Qf1, 1...Ke1 2 Ne4 Kd1 3 Qf1 with the a1 knight revealing its function, and finally 1...Kxe3 2 Ne4 Kd4 3 Nc2, the best of the four mates. Notice that White's second move wasn't a check in any variation. There is no general rule governing this; many problems have checking second move continuations, while others do not, or both types may occur in the same problem. It is considered praiseworthy when the composer is able to incorporate quiet continuations, but often this proves impossible. As with two-movers, the key is almost never a check or the capture of a piece. Returning to Diagram 53, we have proved that a waiting move is sufficient to solve the problem and it is surprising that with the vast force at White's disposal it isn't easy to find one. 1 Kxg6 destroys the mating net after 1...Kxg3, while other king moves release the pawn. 1 Ba8, for example, fails to 1...Kg1 when 2 Ng4 stalemates, so the solver's eye is drawn to the h7 pawn. It took no part in the set play, so why should it not promote? This argument seems suspicious, for it suggests that there are four possible keys, one for each pawn promotion. Searching more carefully reveals the trap 1 h8=Q/B? Kxe3! when 2 Ne4 delivers another stalemate. 1 h8=R? Kxg3! 2 Qe2 is similar, exploiting White's newly acquired control of h3. Thus the key must be 1 h8=N!, waiting.

Three-move problems may be divided into two categories, which I shall call **Bohemian and strategic**. I will not attempt to define these terms, which is not only undesirable but also impossible. Some problems clearly belong to one group or the other, but there is a wide area in between. A Bohemian problem is characterised by a good key, often flight-giving or sacrificial, with at least two variations ending in spectacular mating positions. Since the point of the problem lies in the mates, it is only after one has found the solution that the idea is appreciated. How, then, can the solver tell from the diagram whether the problem belongs to the Bohemian school? An open position with limited Black force is a promising sign, and the name of the composer is a useful guide for more experienced solvers. The following position illustrates the solver's difficulties when faced with a Bohemian problem.

54 J. Dobrusky, Humoristické Listy, 1882

#3

The limited Black material provides no clue at all, but the a2 pawn and the position of White's king at b7 suggests that Black's king will move to the c-file during the play. At the moment no mates in two are provided for 1...Kxd4 and 1...Ke4. It seems that 1...Kxd4 is a particularly strong defence since Black's king has access to no less than six squares from d4, so our first task is to provide a mate for this defence. Bohemian problems contain elegant mating positions, so the variation 1...Kxd4 2 Nxd5+ Kxd5 3 Rh5 should attract one's eye, even though Black can escape by 2...Kc5 or 2...Kd3. The mate after 2...Ke5 3 Rh5 strongly indicates that the rook will stay on the h-file. We may reject 1 Rh5 as it deprives us of the mate after 2...Kxd5 and the only other reasonable square is **1 Rh4**. This gives flights at d2 and f2, but this is not too alarming as Bohemian keys often give flights. Checking the variations reveals an astonishing variety of mating positions for such limited material: **1...Kxd4 2 Nxd5+ Kd3** (2...Kc5 2 Qc4; 2...Kxd5 3 Rh5; 2...Ke5 3 Rh5) **3 Qd1, 1...Ke4 2 Qg3!** (necessary to cover e5) **Kxd4** (2...Kf5 3 Qg6) **3 Ne6, 1...Kd2 2 Qe2+ Kc3** (2...Kc1 3 Rh1) **3 Nxd5, 1...Kf2 2 Qe2+ Kg3** (2...Kg1 3 Qg2/e1) **3 Rg4.** The most common source of error when solving Bohemian problems is to reject the correct key through overlooking a mate in two after one of Black's defences. In the above example, it would be only too easy to consider 1 Rh4! and miss the move 2 Qg3! after 1...Ke4, for instance.

Many contemporary composers feel that the possibilities for creative innovation in Bohemian three-movers have now been exhausted, and it is certainly true that the heyday for this type of problem was the period 1880–1920. However, there are occasional happy discoveries, such as the next position.

55 L. Knotek, 1st Pr. White Memorial Tny, 1953

#3

Once again, the solver isn't helped very much by the diagram position. 1...Kc8 allows mate in one, but no mate is set for 1...Kc6 or for a random knight move such as 1...Ne5. 1...Kc6 is no problem, for example 1 Bh2 Kc6 2 Qa6+ Nb6 3 c8=Q, but the knight moves are awkward as they don't seem to create any obvious weakness. Perhaps 1 Qh8, so as to mate after 1...Ne5 by 2 c8=Q+ or 2 Qb8+? Unfortunately Black can reply 1...Nf8 or 1...Ka6, but we are on the right lines now. By playing **1 Qg7!** White prevents the knight from moving on pain of 2 c8=Q+ and 3 Qc7 mate, so we only have to check Black king moves. **1...Kxa8 2 c8=Q+ Ka7 3 Bxc5** also exploits the lateral effect of the queen, while **1...Ka6 2 Qxd7 Ka5** (or else c8=Q mates) **3 Qb5** and **1...Kc6 2 c8=Q+ Kxd6 3 Qcxd7** are rather mundane. The star variation is **1...Ka7** which leads to a beautiful switch-back after **2 c8=B!** (avoiding stalemate) **Kxa8 3 Qa1.**

Even if few Bohemian problems are produced today, many of the classics are in this style and the novice solver has a treat in store if he looks at the problems of Heathcote, Havel and Würzburg.

#3

White has no good reply to the obvious move 1...Ka1 and since the rook and bishop afford Black's king protection from checks along the a-file and the long diagonal, it is natural to try to use the queen along the first rank. The first move must therefore be by the c1 bishop or the king. A bishop move threatens 2 Kd2+ Kb2 3 Qc1, but Black can defend by 1...Bc3, not only preventing Kd2 but also preparing an interposition by ...Be1. Since Black has several other moves, such as ...Bd4 and ...Rg6, which disturb White's queen it is preferable to retain the bishop move until Black has revealed his defence. White can then move to e3 or g5 as appropriate to shut off the irritating enemy piece. 1 Kd2? looks bad since it blocks in the bishop and in fact 1...Bc3+ is fine for Black. Thus **1 Ke2!** must be the key, even though the king is exposed to two rook checks and Black is given a further flight at c2. The threat is 2 B checks (except b2!) followed by 3 Qc1. There are ten variations: **1...Rc6 2 Ba3+, 1...Re6+ 2 Be3+, 1...Rf6 2 Bf4+, 1...Rg6 2 Bg5+, 1...Ra2+ 2 Bd2+, 1...Bd4 2 Be3+** and **1...Bc3 2 Bd2+** are all followed by **3 Qc1** mate while the remaining three lines are **1...Kc2 2 Qd1+ Kc3 3 Qd2, 1...Bb2 2 Bd2+ Kc2 3 Qd1** and **1...Ra1 2 Be4+ Ka2 3 Qg8**. There are self-blocks in the last two variations. You will find two Bohemian problems in the section for solving at the end of the chapter, namely Diagrams 70 and 71.

When two variations end in similar mating positions, the lines are said to be **echoes** of each other. For echoes to be interesting the two positions should have Black's king on different squares, or else the effect is merely one of repetition. Many Bohemian problems contain echoes, as in the next position.

57 W. Shinkman, Dubuque Chess Journal, 1890

‡3

It isn't hard to see which piece makes the key, for the bishop on h5 is out of play in the diagram and even more so after 1...Kb6 or 1...Kb7. It is tempting to put the bishop behind the queen by 1 Bg4, which threatens 2 Bg1 followed by Qd7 or Qc8 mate according to Black's response. However, Black replies 1...Kb6, when the g4 bishop serves no useful purpose. Therefore **1 Be2** is the most likely candidate. Looking around for a threat one finds mate in two by 2 Qe6+, 2 Qd7+, 2 Qc8+ and even 2 Qa5. Multiple threats are frowned upon, but since the main point of the problem lies in the replies to Black's king flights it isn't too serious a flaw here. After **1...Kb7** White plays **2 Qc8+! Kxc8** (2...Ka7 3 Qa6/Qb8/Bg1 or 2...Kb6 3 Qc7) **3 Ba6**, while **1...Kb6** leads to the echo **2 Qa5+! Kxa5** (2...Kc6 3 Bf3 or 2...Kb7 3 Qa6) **3 Bc7**.

Some three-movers rely on a surprising or paradoxical key for their main effect. The extra move gives much more scope for unexpected keys here than in two-move problems, for apparently functionless pieces can come into play with a move to spare. The next position has a humorous element.

58 H. Baumann, Neue Zürcher Zeitung, 1980

‡3

It is a convention of chess problems that castling is always assumed to be legal unless it can be proved illegal from the diagram. For example, if, in the above diagram, there were an added White rook at h8 and Black bishop at f8, Black would not be able to castle. The reason is that the h8 rook could only have reached that position by two means; either by passing over e8, or by a promotion e7xf8=R followed by Rf8–h8. In either case Black's king must have moved, rendering castling illegal. We shall see in Chapter 10 that such arguments can be very involved, but Diagram 58 presents no such difficulties, for there is no reason why castling should be illegal. Thus if White attacks bluntly by 1 Qxg7?, Black can slip away with 1...0–0–0 when a threat to mate down the c-file is met by a rook move, granting a flight at d8. 1 Rxh7? 0–0–0 is a similar flop. Sometimes problem keys are so brilliant that to an experienced solver they spring to the eye in a flash. This is the case with Baumann's problem, for who could resist trying **1 Qg6?** The variation **1...fxg6 2 0–0! 0–0–0 3 Rc1** suggests that this is correct. The threat is 2 Qxh7 0–0–0 3 Qc2 and the remaining defences are **1...b3 2 Qxg7 0–0–0 3 Qc3** and **1...Rc8 2 Qe4+ Kd8 3 Qe7**. In essence White is trying to reach the c-file with gain of tempo; this happens three times in different variations.

59 S. Loyd, 1st Sp. Pr. Chess Monthly, 1857

#3

Obviously a Bohemian problem, but one with a difference! Sam Loyd was never inhibited by conventional values and this problem can cause complete bafflement. It is very deceptive, for it seems that a normal solution might be found if only one looks a little longer. The idea of a checking key only follows the exhaustion of all other possibilities. Once this is accepted, **1 Ng4+** can be found quite easily. **1...Kf1/g1 2 Ra8 any 3 Ra1** is nothing special, but the other lines are attractive: **1...Kf3 2 Qc2 g2 3 Qd3, 1...Kh1 2 Qh2+ gxh2 3 Nf2** and best of all, **1...Kh3 2 Nh2 (threat 3 Rh8) gxh2/g2/Kh4 3 Qh8**. Other composers have tried checking keys, but often their attempts are unconvincing because Black has a strong threat which practically forces White to act vigorously. Loyd's effort is free from this defect.

Diagrams 73 and 74 also have unusual keys, so take care!

In Chapter 1 a number of problems were based on the possibility of Black checks and not surprisingly the same theme can be developed in three-movers. With the introduction of a definite theme, we are moving away from Bohemian problems into the field of strategy. Most modern compositions belong to this school, which aims to explore not only the half-pins, self-blocks, White interferences and so on of Chapter 1, but also the more complex ideas which are only possible with three moves. Often this makes the solver's task easier, for he can sometimes spot the idea straight from the diagram, as in the next position.

60 E. Visserman, 4th Pr. Die Schwalbe, 1971

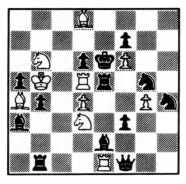

‡3

The board is congested with pieces, but our experience from Chapter 1 pinpoints the half-pin up the e-file as a likely central point for the problem. Black has two prominent checking defences by the half-pinned pieces, 1...Rxd5+ and 1...Bxd3+, so a natural first step is to see if White has replies set up for these two moves. 1...Rxd5+ 2 Ka6! threatens 3 Bd7, when Black's only defence is 2...Rb5, unpinning the d3 knight to mate by 3 Nf4. One might expect the other check to lead to an echo after 1...Bxd3+ 2 Kxa5 Bb5 (forced), but although this unpins the d5 rook there is no mate. The cure for this ailment is to attack d6, so that White can mate by Rxd6. Returning to the initial position, there is only one way to do this without upsetting the other line, namely **1 Be7** (not 1 Kc6? Rc1+). This threatens 2 Rxe5+ and 3 d5, which Black can only prevent by checking, introducing the two lines given above. Although this problem is very clear-cut, many of Black's pieces take no part at all in the play. Their only function is to prevent cooks.

In the last problem Black's checks existed in the diagram position and White's main task was to cope with them. The surprise effect is heightened if the key actually exposes White's king to enemy attack.

61 A. Kraemer, 1st Pr. Römmig Jub. T., 1955

‡3

Black has few legal moves; he may play 1...Kg2 or promote the pawn. There is a set mate 1...Kg2 2 Rxf2+ Kxh3 3 Rb3 so White must find a reply to 1...f1=Q, threatening a check on the second move. It seems White's second move must pin the queen to prevent these checks, but at the moment 1...f1=Q 2 Ba4 (or b3/c2) fails because 2...Qxb1 enables the queen to interpose at e4. 1 d3? disrupts the mate set for 1...Kg2, but 1 Rc1 is tempting, since the mate set for 1...Kg2 is preserved while 1...f1=Q 2 Bc2/b3 also leads to mate. However, Black has the ingenious defence 1 Rc1? f1=B! (1...f1=N? 2 Rf2 and 3 Bf3) and a bishop moves stalemates Black, while 2 Rf2 doesn't work because ...Bb5 is a check. A similar comment applies to 1 Ra1? f1=B!. White's king appears badly placed on a white square, so suppose he tries 1 Kd8?. After 1...f1=Q White still cannot play 2 Ba4 Qxb1, but now that Black has been deprived of his b5 check, White need not pin the queen, but can block the f-file instead. 2 Rf2 opens the path for the bishop to create the terrible threat of 3 Bf3, but alas Black has a check at d3. 1 Ke7? similarly fails because the queen can check at e1. Paradoxically, only **1 Kf8!** works, allowing the check at move 1. After **1...f1=Q+** (1...f1=B/N 2 Rf2) **2 Rf2 Qxf2+** (2...Qe2 3 Bxe2 or 2...Qg2 3 Bf3) **3 Bf3** the double check finishes Black.

We finish the subject of Black checks with an elegant lightweight problem.

62 G. Latzel, 1st Pr. Deutsche Schachzeitung, 1956

≠3

Black has two checks in the diagram, but there are set mates prepared for them: 1...Qb3+ 2 Rc2+ Qb6 3 Bxb6 and 1...Qh5+ 2 Re2+ Qc5 3 Bxc5. Two other strong defences, 1...Qxa7 and 1...Qxf6, have no mates set so White's key must create a powerful threat. 1 R6f5/4/3 threatens to mate down the g-file, but Black can safely take the rook. 1 Ke1 is an interesting idea, similar to the key of the previous problem, but 1...Qxf6 2 Ra2+ Qf2+ leaves White without a mate. By a process of elimination the knight seems likely to be the key-piece. 1 Ne5/e1 threatens 2 Nf3, but the ubiquitous 1...Qxf6 foils White again. The key is **1 Nf4!** with the brutal threats of 2 Ne2 and 2 Nh3. A threat in less than the specified number of moves is called a **short threat**, and is frowned upon by composers for being too crude. In this problem the key exposes the White king to further checks along the d-file, which provides some compensation. Longer problems, of four moves and above, more often have short threats than not; it would be absurd for the key of a mate in twenty to threaten mate in nineteen, for example! The variations are 1...**Qd5+ 2 Rd2+ Kf1** (2...Qd4 3 Nh3) **3 Nxd5, 1...Qb3+ 2 Rc2+ Kf1 3 Nd3, 1...Qd7+ 2 Rd2+ Kf1 3 Ne6, 1...Rxh2 2 Rg2+** and **3 Rg1** and 1...**Qe6 2 Ne2+** (or many other moves) **Qxe2 3 Rxe2.** I haven't mentioned 1...**Qh5+**, since this is the main flaw of the problem. White can mate by **2 Ne2+** or **2 Re2+**, an unfortunate dual continuation. The other variations are very attractive, especially the way the knight shuts off Black's queen by moving to d3 and e6.

A number of three-movers and longer problems use **critical play**, either as their main theme or to add interest to the problem. This is best explained by means of an example. If you have a bishop on d3 and queen on d1, it may be a good idea to threaten mate at h7. Assuming that Qh5 isn't possible, you may decide to continue Bd3–b1 and Qd1–c2 to set up the mating threat. In this case the bishop will have crossed the critical square c2 which needs to be occupied by the queen. The next problem is solved using precisely the same manoeuvre.

≠3

In view of the above comments, it will come as no surprise that the key is **1 Bh3**, threatening 2 Qg4 and 3 Qc8. Black cannot flee with his king by 1...Kc7 2 Qg4 Kd8 as White mates at d7 instead, so the only defence is 1...a5, preparing to meet 2 Qg4 by ...a6. Unfortunately for Black, **1...a5** creates a surprising self-block at a5 which can be exploited by **2 Qa6+!** **Kxa6** (or else Qc8) **3 Bc8**.

The following problem is a much more complex example of critical play.

64 M. Vukčević, =1st Pr. Die Schwalbe, 1971

≠3

Black has just five legal moves. 1...e5 2 Bg1 and 1...Bxd3 2 e3 are immediate mate, while 1...Bxb4 2 Qxb2+ Bc3 3 Qxc3 is also set, so White only has to worry about 1...Bc2 and 1...cxb4. If Black plays 1...cxb4, he will be obliged to play 2...Bc2 because he has deprived himself of 2...Bxb4, the only other move not allowing mate in one. White can exploit this using the idea of problem 19, giving the variation 1...cxb4 2 Rh1! Bc2 3 Qg1. So 1...Bc2 is the only move with no mate set. Finding waiting moves is not easy for White, since he mustn't free the h3 pawn by moving his bishop. It follows that the rook on c1 must provide any necessary pass moves (1 K moves? cxb4 2 Rh1 Bxd3 and Black's king can move to c4). 1 Rh1 provides for 1...Bc2 since the queen can mate at g1 immediately, but after 1...cxb4 White finds himself in zugzwang, since he doesn't have a waiting move. 1 Rg1? allows 1...e5 as g1 is blocked, so what about **1 Rf1?** If now 1...cxb4 2 Rh1! leaves Black on the move, while 1...Bc2 is met by 2 Qe1 (threat 3 Qf2) **Bxd3 3 e3**. This line explains why 1 Rd1? and 1 Re1? fail.

Diagrams 77 and 78 are further examples of critical play.

We finish this chapter by examining some complex strategic problems.

65 V. Timonin, 1st Pr. Shakhmatisti Rossii, 1967

#3

Here we are faced with a crowded position and no obvious theme visible. In this situation it is often useful to ask if White can threaten mate in one? If so, why doesn't it work? Can Black be forced to weaken his position in some way which invalidates the defences to the mates in one? In this case, the moves which threaten immediate mate may occur as White's second moves in different variations. In the diagram any move of the d4 bishop creates the threat of 2 Qd4. There are three sensible squares for the bishop, namely c3, c5 and e5. In each case the bishop is immune from capture, so Black's only defences are 1 Bc3 Nc2!, since 2 Qxb3 is no longer possible, 1 Be5 Ne6! and 1 Bc5 Nc6!, where in the last two lines Black takes advantage of White's self-blocks. Focusing on the three squares c2, c6 and e6, we can see that Black's defences might be invalidated if White could persuade Black to block them by 1...Bc2, 1...Rc6 or 1...Re6. 1...Bc2 can already be met by 2 Bc3, while the other two lines would operate as planned if Black were deprived of the threat 2...Rg6+ resulting from 1...Rc6/e6. So far we haven't considered how White might make a threat which forces the three thematic defences. If 1...Bc2 is to be a

53

defence the threat must involve the d3 square and we may tie this in with the fact that so far we haven't found a function for the h4 knight. Everything suddenly falls into place, for if White moves his king at move 1, he threatens 2 Nf3 (threat Nd2) exf3 3 Qd3. Moving to the h-file avoids the possibility of 2...Rg6+ after 1...Rc6/e6 and it also explains why the rook moves defeat the threat, since 2 Nf3 would expose White's king to a check at h6. Finally we have to decide which square on the h-file is correct. 1 Kh3? g5! and 1 Kh2? Qf8! prepare second-move checks by ...g4 and ...Qd6, so the key must be **1 Kh1**!. This is a typical solving process and it is interesting that we made no attempt to find the key until after the essential logic of the problem had been uncovered. The missing links in this logic then led directly to the right move.

66 E. Zepler, 1st Pr. Olympic Tny, 1936

≠3

Black's king has two flights at b3 and b5. There is a set mate for 1...Kb3, namely 2 Qe2 and 3 Nb6, but nothing is prepared for 1...Kb5 giving the king access to a6 and c5. White can, of course, take these flights away by 1 Nxd6, but only at the cost of stalemating Black. In view of the number of squares available to the king, White's reply to 1...Kb5 must be fairly brutal and the only likely candidate is 2 Qxd7+, mating after 2...Ka6 3 Qb7 or 2...Kc5 3 Qc6. How about 1 Qg7? Unfortunately 1...Kb3 is good, when White has no mate in two (2 Qc3+ Ka4, for example). Thus White must move his king to allow Qxd7. There are only two plausible squares, e4 and g6, since he must avoid checks from Black's bishop. What happens after 1 Kg6, say, if Black just moves his bishop? Then White can safely play 2 Nd6, which is no longer stalemate, taking away Black's flights long enough to mate by 3 Qxd7. All the action takes place on the white squares so it doesn't appear to matter where Black moves his bishop. This logic seems cast-iron, but there is one tiny flaw in it. Black plays 1 Kg6 Bxf4!, so that 2 Nd6 pins the bishop and stalemates after all! Thus the key is **1 Ke4**!, anticipating the need to avoid pinning the bishop at move 2.

If the composer manages to combine a complex strategic idea with an obscure key, the solver is in for a hard time. I found the next problem especially perplexing.

67 V. L. Eaton, 1st Pr. American Chess Bulletin, 1950

‡3

Even at a casual glance, it is clear that a complex mechanism will spring into operation after the key. Two White pieces are pinned and in each case the pinning piece is itself pinned. White could mate in two if the e2 rook were free to move up the e-file, but it is constrained to move along the rank, which frees e1 for Black's king. Rather than try to identify the theme, it is easier to spot a strong Black threat. 1...Nb5 is such a move, blocking the bishop + rook battery aimed at Black's king and giving a flight at e2. Notice that White cannot unpin his pieces by a king move, since this would expose the king to annoying checks, e.g. 1 Kxa3? Bd6+, 1 Kb2? Nc4+ or 1 Ka1? Nc2+. A likely piece to make the key is hard to find, for the pieces at e2, f8, h3 and b3 are effectively immobilised. This leaves the two bishops, but even 1 Bc3 doesn't provide an adequate reply to 1...Nb5. Therefore one is led to consider **1 Bd3**, playing the bishop over the critical square b5 to nullify the defence ...Nb5 (not 1 Bc4? Nxc4, of course). At first this seems unlikely to be the key, for it creates no obvious threat. The big surprise is that Black is in zugzwang after 1 Bd3. It is hard to believe that moves like 1...c6 and 1...c5 create fatal weaknesses, but this is indeed the case. The variations are **1...c6 2 Bc3** (threats 2 Rc2/b2) **Nf2** (Black lacks the defence ...Bb5) **3 Re1, 1...c5 2 Kxa3** followed by Nd2 or R up the e-file since Black cannot now check, **1...Nb5 2 Ka1, 1...Nb1 2 Kxb1, 1...Nc2 2 Re4** is a short mate, **1...Be8 moves 2 Rxf7+** and **3 Nd2, 1...Bg3 moves** except to f4 **2 Qe3, 1...Bf4 2 Rxg2+ Ke1 3 Rxg1, 1...Q moves 2 Nd2** mate. I have left the two main defences until last. These are **1...Nc4** (unpinning the knight) **2 Nd2+** (deflecting the knight) **Nxd2+** (unpinning the rook) **3 Re6** and **1...Nf2** (unpinning the rook) **2 Re6+** (unpinning the knight) **Nxd3+ 3 Nd2.** The two main lines are perfectly symmetrical and lead to elegant mates after Black has delivered check.

68 L. Loshinsky, 1st Pr. Kubbel Memorial Tny, 1962

≠3

The final problem is by one of the greatest ever masters of the strategic three-mover, who died in 1976. Each move by the f1 knight creates twin threats of mate in one, but these always lie on the same white-squared diagonal, so that Black's bishop is able to keep everything under control, e.g. 1 Nd2? (threats 2 Re4/Nf3) Bd5, 1 Ne3? (threats 2 Rf5/Ng4) Bxe6, 1 Ng3? (threats 2 Re4/Rf5) Bc2 and 1 Nh2? (threats 2 Nf3/Ng4) Bd1. It is hard to make a threat since most of White's pieces are already gainfully occupied with important tasks. The obvious exception is the king, usefully posted within firing range of the enemy but as yet exercising no function. **1 Ke7** is logical, threatening 2 Rg4 followed by either 3 Bd4 or 3 Bd6. At first it seems that the theme will be interference of the b3 bishop by Black's knight, but Black's knight moves don't even defeat the threat. Black actually has two methods of nullifying 2 Rg4. He may prevent it directly by covering g4 with his bishop, or he may prepare to play 2...Be4, cutting off the line g4 to d4 and therefore stopping both bishop mates at d4 and d6. Each method may be implemented in two ways, so there are four defences, 1...Bd1, 1...Bc2, 1...Bxe6 and 1...Bd5. In each case White replies with a move of the f1 knight, as in the tries above. Black can still play his bishop onto the crucial diagonals, but the arrival square is now one of the squares where White is threatening mate. Thus White can mate by taking the bishop. This is how it works: **1...Bd1 2 Nd2** (f3 and e4 are the critical squares, so Black must play to the d5–h1 diagonal) **Bf3** (d5 was safe after 1 Nd2? Bd5, but f3 is not) **3 Nxf3**, **1...Bc2 2 Ne3** (g4 and f5) **Bf5 3 Rxf5**, **1...Bxe6 2 Ng3** (e4 and f5) **Bf5 3 Rxf5** and finally **1...Bd5 2 Nh2** (f3 and g4) **Bf3 3 Nxf3**. The reader is urged to work out why White's second move is unique in each of these four lines, e.g. 1...Bd1 2 Ne3? f1=Q! defends.

The last four problems in the section for solving involve interesting themes and two of them are not all that easy so be warned!

Problems for Solving

69 G. Stuart-Green, 1st Pr.
The Problemist, 1970

≠3

70 W. Shinkman,
Offiziers — Schachzeitung, 1905

≠3

71 M. Havel, 1st Pr.
Zlatá Praha, 1911

≠3

72 O. Würzburg, 1st Pr.
American Chess Bulletin, 1947

≠3

73 S. Loyd, 1st Pr.
Checkmate Tny, 1903

≠3

74 J. Cumpe, 5th Pr.
Čas. Česk. Šach, 1916

≠3

75 C. S. Kipping,
Manchester City News, 1911

≠3

76 H. Grasemann, 1st Pr.
match Baden — Berlin, 1953

≠3

77 A. Kraemer,
Deutsche Schachzeitung, 1936

≠3

78 A. Kraemer, 1st Pr.
Deutsche Schachzeitung, 1943

≠3

79 J. Scheel, 1st Pr.
BCF, 1953

‡3

80 R. Burger & R. Matthews,
1st Pr. BCM, 1962

‡3

81 G. Anderson, 1st Pr.
The Problemist, 1975

‡3

82 H. P. Rehm, 1st Pr.
Rochade, 1980/1

‡3

4 Longer problems

It might be thought that the difficulty of a problem increases in proportion to its length, but fortunately this isn't so. Few long problems are as difficult as a tricky three-mover and the great majority are much simpler. The reason is that the composer must ensure the problem is sound, so in many long problems Black has an enormous material advantage. This compels White to keep making one-move threats to prevent Black's extra material coming into play. Consequently the solver can often narrow the search down to a few moves with no more than a glance at the position.

Some of the characteristics of three-movers carry over to these more-mover problems, as they are called, but we need not examine them closely, for they only echo the points already made in Chapter 3. Diagram 94 is an example of a Bohemian four-mover, demonstrating just how hard such a problem can be to solve. Difficulties of soundness make Bohemian problems longer than four moves very rare and today almost all long problems are strategically based. This doesn't mean that they necessarily have crowded positions; the extra length allows the composer to work considerable content into even lightweight positions.

83 S. Chyrulik, 1st Pr. Zvyazda, 1975

‡5

Black has just two legal moves, ...Kb1 and ...Bb1, but White is restricted too since he must prevent the b-pawn promoting while making sure that Black's king cannot escape from the corner. White can cope with ...Kb1 if his queen is on d4, while after ...Bb1 White might mate by Qf1/g1/h1, forcing ...Ka2 allowing a mate down the a-file. So if White's king were not obstructing a7 he could mate in three by 1 Qd4 Bb1 2 Qg1 Ka2 3 Qa7. With two spare moves to play with, White has plenty of time to shift his king, but he must choose the square carefully. Not Kb6? Kb1! (not 1...Bb1? 2 Qh1 and 3 Qa8) 2 Qc3 (White must stop ...Kc1 and ...Kc2) Ka1 3 Qd4 Bb1 4 Qg1 Ka2 and the king is still blocking the vital g1—a7 diagonal, nor 1 Kb7? Bb1! 2 Qh1 Ka2, for example. The only correct square is **1 Kb8! Kb1 2 Qc3 Ka1 3 Qd4 Bb1 4 Qg1 Ka2 5 Qa7.**

Many long problems lie somewhere between problems and studies. In the next diagram, Black is well up on material and is about to promote various pawns, so if White is to win at all he has to mate quickly.

84 V. Savchenko, 1st Pr. Mattison Memorial Tny, 1970

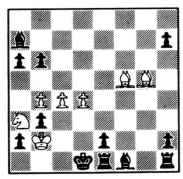

#10

Black's king is badly confined, but White must act fast or Black's pieces will emerge by ...Bh3 and ...Ref1, for example, giving Black's king a flight at e1. 1 Kxb3? (threat 2 Bc2) a1=N+! defends c2 with gain of tempo, which gives Black time to free himself. Thus White's first move is forced.

1 Nc2!

Threat 2 Ne3+ Kd2 and then either 3 Nd5+ Kd1 4 Nc3 or 3 Ng4+ Kd1 4 Nf2.

1 ...   a1=Q+!

1...h6 2 Bxh6 transposes to a line considered later, in which White can mate before move 10. If now 2 Kxa1 (2 Nxa1 Bh3) White has no threat since 3 Ne3+ would be met by 3...Kd2 *check*, so Black has time to free himself by 2...Rg1 or 2...Bh3.

2 Kxb3!

Now that the b3 pawn has gone, Black must take care that White cannot

61

capture the queen with his knight, for then Bc2 mate follows. Nor can he give up the queen on b2 or b3, for White just takes it with his king, retaining the threat of Ne3+.

2 ...   Qa4+

2...Qa2+ leads to mate in 9 as we shall see. 2...Qb1+ 3 Kc3 h6 (Black has run out of decent checks, so can only postpone mate for as long as possible) 4 Bxh6 Qc1 5 Bxc1 Kxc1 (the threat was 6 Bd2 and if 5...Rg1 then 6 Bd2 Rg3+ 7 Ne3+ Rxe3+ 8 Bxe3 and 9 Bc2) leads to mate after 6 Na1 and 7 Nb3+ Kd1 8 Bc2.

3 Kb2!

3 Kc3? (3 Kxa4? Rg1) h6! (but not 3...Rg1 4 Ne3+ and 5 Ng4+) 4 Bxh6 (4 Bd2 Qb3+ wins, as does 4 Bf4 Bb8!, fatally disrupting White's threats) Qc6 5 Bg5 (5 Bf4 Qf3+) Rg1 and White runs out of steam.

3 ...   Qa2+

3...h6 4 Bxh6 (this position would also have been reached had Black played 1...h6) Qc6 (4...Qa2+ 5 Kxa2! followed by Ne3+, Nd5+ and Nc3 mates as Black lacks the defence ...Rg1 which saves him in the next note) 5 Ne3+ Kd2 6 Nxf1+ Kd1 7 Bc2 is mate.

4 Kc3!

4 Kxa2? Rg1 5 Bf4 (not 5 Ne3+ Kd2 6 Ng2/g4+ and Black's king escapes at c3, nor 5 Bh6 h1=Q) Bb8! and once again the attack collapses.

4 ...   Qxc4+

4...h6 5 Bxh6 doesn't help to counter White's threat of Ne3+, Ng4+ and Nf2 mate.

5 Kb2!

White refuses Black's fourth queen sacrifice. 5 Kxc4 Rg1 etc. is still bad.

5 ...   Qa2+

Still Black's only defence.

6 Kxa2

At last! Now that Black has generously cleared c4 for the use of White's knight he can safely take the queen.

6 ...   Rg1

Had Black played 4...h6, he would only be able to delay mate slightly here by playing ...Rg1 or ...Bb8, to which White plays Na3 (or a1) leading to mate in 10.

7 Kb2!

The final sacrifice.

7	...	Rxg5
8	Ne3+	Kd2
9	Nc4+	Kd1
10	Bc2 mate.	

In other cases White's eventual win is not in doubt, but the task is to break down the fortress-like defences to the enemy king. Zugzwang is very often the weapon used to induce Black to create an opening in his shield.

85 I. Rosenfeld, 4th Pr. USSR Tny, 1955

#5

Here White must persuade Black to move his rook or bishop, for example he might try 1 f8=N d6 2 Bg7 g3 3 Ne6 h5 4 Nd4 forcing the rook to move, when White recaptures with mate. However, Black need not be so obliging as to allow White access to e6. After 1 f8=N? g3 2 Bg7 h5 White has no mate. Other possible zugzwangs involve f8=R and Rf3—c3, or f8=B and Bh6—c1. Each takes three moves to set up, equalling Black's supply of pawn tempi. But 1 f8=R? d6 2 Bg7 h5 and 1 f8=B? d6 2 Bh8 g3 also fail because Black prevents White moving to f3 and h6 respectively. Since all three lines involve the e5 bishop retreating, it makes sense to play this move first, waiting to see which pawn Black touches before deciding on a particular underpromotion. White must not play Bd4, blocking Nf8—e6—d4, nor Bg7, blocking Bf8—h6—c1, so the key is **1 Bh8!** with the variations:

1...d6 2 f8=N h5 3 Ne6 g3 4 Nd4
1...g3 2 f8=R h5 3 Rf3 d6 4 Rc3
1...h5 2 f8=B g3 3 Bh6 d6 4 Bc1

Underpromotions also play a role in diagrams 95 and 96.

We have already met critical play in Chapter 3 and many more-movers involve similar ideas.

86 W. Shinkman, Western Advertiser, 1872

‡4

Black's king has no moves, but mate isn't possible while he stands on c4. Hence White must use zugzwang to force the king to an inferior square. After Black plays ...d3 and ...e5, Black's king will have access to d4 so it might be helpful to see if there are any possible mating positions after ...e5, ...d3 and ...Kd4. e4 and c4 have to be defended, so the rook must operate along the rank, which gives just two possibilities. Either White's bishop is on b6 and his rook on b4, or, more fancifully, White's bishop is on a1 and White mates by discovery with Rb4. If it were Black to move in the diagram and he played 1...e5 then White could force the first mate by 2 Bd8 d3 3 Bb6 Kd4 4 Rb4, so the main problem is 1...d3. In this case White cannot move his bishop from the long diagonal at move 2, since Black would escape by ...Kd4. However, 1...d3 does open the whole length of the long diagonal and in particular permits the bishop to move to a1, as in the second mate mentioned above. If White plays 1 R along the b-file d3 2 Ba1! e5 3 Rb2 the aim is achieved, but White must be careful not to upset the other mate after 1...e5. This eliminates b6, b7 and b8, so the key is **1 Rb1!**. The variation 1...d3 2 Ba1 e5 3 Rb2 demonstrates the **Indian** theme, so-called because the first example was composed by the Revd H. A. Loveday in 1845 while he was in India. The Indian theme is a three-move idea, White's first move crosses a critical square (b2 in the above problem) on which White effects a self-interference at move 2, with the aim of lifting stalemate, to give a battery mate on the third move. The idea can be expressed with just five pieces (White: Kc1, Rf2, Ba2 Black: Ka1, Pc3 Mate in 3, solution 1 Bg8 c2 2 Rf7 Ka2 3 Ra7), but in Shinkman's problem the effect is enhanced because the rook performs a switchback onto the critical square.

Diagram 97 is another example of how the Indian theme may be elaborated by the addition of a move or two.

We have already met the pseudo-two-mover in Chapter 3. The next problem extends the task of losing a tempo to six moves.

#6

If it were Black to move, White would be able to mate immediately by Nd5 or Ng8. However, White has no suitable waiting move. If the bishop moves, Black can retain control of d5 and g8 by ...Qd8, while after 1 Re3 (other moves of the rook allow ...Qf3+), ...Qg2 serves the same purpose. In order to return to the starting position with Black to move, White has to play very accurately. The key is in fact **1 Re3** (1 B moves Qd8 really is useless, since Black has too many threats: ...Qd3+, ...Qd1+ and ...Qxe7), and after **1...Qg2 2 Bg4** (White must create one-move threats when the Black queen is not at a8, since otherwise the knight can come into play) cutting the queen off from g8. Then 2...Qxg4 3 Nd5+ Kf5 4 Re5 and 2...Qc2+ 3 Kxc2 b3+ 4 Kb2 lead to mate before move six, so Black must return by **2...Qa8**. Now White can play his tempo-losing move **3 Re5!**, the choice of square preventing Black's queen capturing at d7 or e7 after **3...Qd8 4 Bd7!**, on pain of Ng8 mate and Rf5 mate respectively. Thus Black has to return again to a8, but after **4...Qa8 5 Re4** (cutting off access to g2), White has succeeded in transferring the move to Black and mates by Nd5 or Ng8 according to Black's reply. The Black queen's desperate attempts to break White's stranglehold were to no avail.

Foreplans were mentioned briefly in Chapter 2, but as they are most commonly found in more-movers we can investigate them more deeply now. The idea is that White indulges in an introductory manoeuvre, which may be several moves long, to create one slight change in the initial position. Thanks to this almost imperceptible weakening of Black's position, White can undertake an operation which failed before.

88 V. Archakov, 1st Pr. Sputnik, 1973

≠5

Here Black's rooks control White's mating threats at b8 and d7. The g2 knight can't help because e6 is blocked, so White's best hope is to promote the g7 pawn. Unfortunately 1 Kh7/h8? fail to 1...b1=Q, either checking or pinning the pawn. Before White can move to the h-file, he has to deflect one of Black's rooks to an inferior square. Hence **1 Kf7!** (not 1 Kf8?, which carries no threat, so allows 1...b1=Q), when Black must play a rook check. After **1...Rf1+ 2 Bf3! Rxf3+ 3 Kg8 Rc3** (3...Ke8 4 Qb5+ mates next move) we have returned to the original position, but with the rook on c3 instead of c1, so that **4 Kh8!** forces mate next move since 4...b1=Q no longer pins the pawn. If Black plays **1...Rf2+** instead, the continuation is **2 Nf4!** (not now 2 Bf3? Rxf3+ 3 Kg8 Rc7! 4 Qd5+ Ke8! and there is no mate, but Black should not fall into the trap 3...Rd3? 4 Kh7! in this line) **Rxf4+ 3 Kg8 Rd4** (3...Rc7 4 Qd5+ Kc8 5 Qa8) **4 Kh8!** leading to the same conclusion. In each line White chooses his sacrifice carefully, to make sure the deflected rook ends up on the a1–h8 diagonal.

Very long problems often involve two or more foreplans and the main difficulty is to get them in the right order. It is worth mentioning that the convention laying down that White's first move should not be a check is relaxed for long problems. As the number of moves increases, the importance of the key diminishes since it forms a smaller and smaller proportion of the problem's total content. Consequently solvers should not be put off by a first move check.

89 J. Kricheli, 1st Pr. Spartakiad, 1975

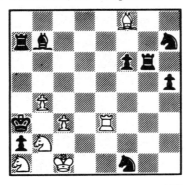

‡17

There are potential mates from both batteries aimed at Black's king, but the rear pieces are attacked, and at the moment they have no safe squares, for example, 1 Rd3? Be4, 1 Bc5? Rg5 or 1 Bd6? Ra6! (not 1...f5? 2 Bc5 Rc6 3 Rd3 mating, however). White can change the position with a series of knight checks, but how might this help him? If the b2 knight could be transferred to b6 by checks at c4 and b6, then Black would not be able to reply to Bd6 with ...Ra6. He would have to fall back on the inferior ...f5, which leads to mate as above. The immediate 1 Nc4+ Ka4 2 Nb6+ allows Black's king to slip out at b5, so White has to play a foreplan within a foreplan! First the a1 knight goes to d4: **1 Nc2+ Kb3 2 Nd4+ Ka3** (now that b5 is covered, the b2 knight can make its own move) **3 Nc4+ Ka4 4 Nb6+ Ka3** (White is aiming to play the quiet move Bd6, so the d4 knight must return to a1 to prevent promotion) **5 Nc2+ Kb3 6 Na1+ Ka3 7 Bd6!** f5 (White would like to play Bc5, as given above, but at the moment ...Rxb6 defends, so the whole preceding manoeuvre has to be played in reverse, in order that the b6 knight can return to b2) **8 Nc2+ Kb3 9 Nd4+ Ka3 10 Nc4+ Ka4 11 Nb2+ Ka3 12 Nc2+ Kb3 13 Na1+ Ka3 14 Bc5! Rc6 15 Rd3 Rxc5** (15...Nd2 also leads to mate in 17) **16 Nc2+** (covering b4) **Kb3 17 c4 mate.** The pirouettes by the knights are quite incredible. There are vivid analogies with computer programming, in which a particular task is broken down into a hierarchical structure of sub-routines or procedures, and with commutators in mathematics, in which operations are followed, after a decent interval, by their inverses.

‡25

It's quite easy for White to go round and round in circles, by **1 Be2+ Ke1 2 Bg4+ Kf1 3 Bh3+ Kg1 4 Rg4+ Kh1 5 Bg2+ Kg1 6 Bc6+ Kf1 7 Bb5+ Ke1 8 Re4+ Kd1**, but somewhere in this loop White has to find a way to break out. The immediate 1 Kb2? a3+ (or else Bxa4) 2 Kb1 a2+ deflects the king from the b-file and if White tries to remove the troublesome a-pawn by 1 Bxa4+? Kc1 2 Rc4+ Kb1 3 Bc2+, Black plays 3...Ka1! 4 Kb3 b5! 5 cxb6 Rb5+ winning. So White's preliminary manoeuvres must capture, first the b7 pawn, and then the a4 pawn. This is accomplished by moving in a spiral.

1 Be2+ Ke1 2 Bg4+ Kf1 3 Bh3+ Kg1 4 Rg4+ Kh1 5 Bg2+ Kg1 6 Bxb7+ Kf1 7 Ba6+ Ke1 8 Re4+ Kd1 9 Be2+ Ke1 (9...Kc1 10 Rc4+ Kb1 11 Bd3+ Ka1 12 Rc2 mates in 14) **10 Bb5+ Kd1 11 Bxa4+ Kc1 12 Rc4+ Kb1 13 Bc2+ Kc1** (13...Ka1 14 Kb3 mates in 16) **14 Bf5+** (a repeat performance to switch the bishop to the other diagonal) **Kd1 15 Bg4+ Ke1 16 Re4+ Kf1 17 Bh3+ Kg1 18 Rg4+ Kh1 19 Bg2+ Kg1 20 Bc6+** (not 20 Bd5+? Kf1 21 Bc4+ Ke1 22 Re4+ Kd1 23 Kb2 a4! and 24...a3+) **Kf1 21 Bb5+ Ke1 22 Re4+ Kd1 23 Kb2** (at last!) **Rxc5 24 Ba4+ Rc2 25 Bxc2 mate.**

The difficulty of a long problem is much increased if the final mating manoeuvre isn't obvious. In this case the solver may be reduced to finding ways to 'make progress', even if the nature of this progress isn't entirely clear.

91 I. Dulbergs, 1st Pr. Shakhmaty TT, 1972

≠22

In this problem Black is stalemated, so White must release his king to move to e5. This frees various Black men from their paralysis, so White will have to check immediately to force the king back to f5. Under these circumstances it isn't easy to see how White can achieve anything, for example after 1 Kc7 Ke5 White would have to play 2 Kc6+ or the king escapes to d5. The only alternative is to transfer the bishop to b2 and then play c3 Ke5 c4+, gaining control of d5 with gain of tempo. Then White can manoeuvre his king. Why he should want to do this is obscure, but the only alternative is to repeat the position.

1 Ba7 Ke5 2 Bd4+ Kf5 3 Bc5 Ke5 4 Bd6+ Kf5 5 Ba3 Ke5 6 Bb2+ Kf5 7 c3 Ke5 8 c4+ Kf5 (now the bishop returns to b8) **9 Ba3 Ke5 10 Bd6+ Kf5 11 Bc5 Ke5 12 Bd4+ Kf5 13 Ba7 Ke5 14 Bb8+ Kf5 15 Kc7 Ke5 16 Kd7+ Kf5**. Now what? There are only six moves left so White must act quickly. With the king on d7, White no longer needs the f8 knight to cover e6, but the only reasonable move with the knight is Ne6. Black must take it with the pawn, when the free e6 pawn gives Black a tempo. White can put this to good use by **17 Ne6! fxe6 18 Bf4! e5 19 Kd6 exf4 20 exf4 e3 21 Kd5 exf2 22 e4 mate**. A very tricky problem indeed.

Diagrams 98 and 99 require planning ahead, but shouldn't cause too much trouble for solvers.

Often the complexity of the diagram position is more apparent than real, since most of the pieces are immobilised for one reason or another. The play then reduces to a duel between just a few men. In the next position the white-squared bishops engage in single combat while the armies look on.

92 B. Fargette, 1st Pr. Deutsche Schachzeitung, 1969

≠8

White can't move his pieces at b4, d4, and e3 without allowing Black's king to escape, so to mate in eight he must rely on the heroics of the h3 bishop. The diagram position would be awkward for Black if it were his turn to play, since 1...Be2 is the only move to avoid Bf1, when 2 Bc8 and 3 Ba6 mates in three. Sometimes the method of corresponding squares, familiar to over-the-board players from king and pawn endings, helps to sort out this type of position, but here we can rely on common sense. After 1 Bc8 Black must play 1...Bb3 (or else 2 Ba6), but once again Black to play is quickly mated since moving to c4 or a2 allows Bh3—f1. Thus if 1 Bd7 Bb3? 2 Bc8 mates in four, so 1 Bd7 must be met by 1...Ba4!. Suppose that White can reach the c6—e8 diagonal without Black being able to play ...Ba4 in reply. Then Black is mated, since he must be on the a2—c4 diagonal to prevent Bb5; if b3 or a2 then 1 Bb5+ Bc4 2 Bd7 Bb3 (or else Bh3) 3 Bc8 wins, while if c4 White can pass on the c6—e8 diagonal and when the Black bishop moves to b3 or a2 he wins as before. So the solution runs **1 Bc8 Bb3 2 Bb7** (forcing Black to lose contact with the a4 square) **Ba2/c4 3 Bc6 Bb3** (3...Bc4 4 Bd7 loses one move more quickly) **4 Bb5+ Bc4 5 Bd7 Bb3 6 Bc8 Bc4/a2 7 Bh3 and 8 Bf1**.

In the next position White's king engages the two Black bishops.

70

‡11

Black threatens ...Bf5 and ...Bxg6, so White's first move is forced, as is Black's reply: 1 Ra8 Bc8. If White could find a haven for his king safe from bishop checks Black would be in zugzwang, for if one bishop moves away White mates in two by taking the other one. Unfortunately all the diagonals are open, so that after 1 Kf2? Bg3+ 2 Kg2 Bb8, for example, Black's bishops are able to check and go back wherever White moves his king. If the king reaches b6, White can mate but this fails on account of the time element. It takes at least five moves to reach b6, so 6 Kb6 Bc7+ 7 Ka7 Bb6+ 8 Kb8 Ba6 9 Rxa6 Bc7+ is the best White can do, but it doesn't mate in 11.

The only remaining hope is the tripled a-pawn. The king can't reach a3, but by taking the a4 pawn White gives Black a pawn move, which ruins his stalemate defence. Black's reply to Kxa4 is ...Bd7+ when Kxa5 or Kb3 a4+ restores the stalemate, so White must continue Kxa3 to make his plan effective. Thus White's moves must satisfy two rules:
1) When he plays Kb5, Black must not be able to reply ...Bd7+
2) Black must not be allowed to play ...Bd6+ and ...Bf8, or White will never be able to play Kxa3.

Rule 1 implies that when White plays Kb5, the black-squared bishop must be off the back rank, so White's king must have just come from a black square in response to a check from the b8 bishop. This square could not have been c5, as Black's check would have been at d6 and he could now retreat to f8, contravening rule 2. The only other possible square is b6. Checking the time reveals that White can just make it by 1 Ra8 Bc8 2–6 Ke1–b6 Bc7+ 7 Kb5 Bb8 8 Kxa4 Bd7+ 9 Kxa3 and mate in 11, but he cannot afford to waste a single tempo on his way to b6.

The solution is **1 Ra8 Bc8 2 Kd2!** (not 2 Ke2? Bg4+ 3 Ke3 Bc8 4 Kd4 Be5+ 5 Kc5 Bd6+ breaking rule 2, or if 3 Kd3 Bf5+ and 4...Bxg6, nor 2 Kf2? Bg3+ 3 Ke3 Bf4+ 4 Kd4 Be5+ 5 Kc5 Bd6+ and ...Bf8) **Bf4+ 3 Kd3!** (3 Kc3? Be5+ 4 Kc4 Bb8 and White cannot avoid breaking a rule after

71

5 Kc5 Bd6+ or 5 Kb5 Bd7+ 6 Kb6 Bc8, when the wrong player is to move)
Bb8 4 Kc4! (4 Kd4? Be5+) **Be6+ 5 Kc5!** (5 Kb5? Bd7+ 6 Kb6 Bc8) **Bc8
6 Kb6 Bc7+** (6...Ba7+ 7 Kb5 transposes, but not 7 Rxa7? Bb7 and 8...Be4)
7 Kb5 Bb8/d8 8 Kxa4 Bd7+ 9 Kxa3 and mates in 11.

Diagrams 100 and 101 need a clear head to avoid going round in circles,
while in Diagram 102 you may find corresponding squares a help.

Problems for Solving

94 H. von Gottschall,
h.m. Hamburg Tny, 1885

≠4

95 J. Breuer, 1st Pr.
Deutsche Schachblätter, 1949

≠4

96 A. Kraemer,
Die Welt, 1948

≠4

97 T. Siers, 1st Pr.
Die Schwalbe, 1953

≠5

98 S. Schneider, 1st Pr.
Österr. Schachb., 1953

≠9

99 M. Vukčević, 1st Pr.
The Problemist, 1980

≠13

100 B. Fargette, 2nd Pr. Thèmes
64, 1969 (version by A. Chéron)

≠16

101 G. Jahn, Sp. Pr.
Die Schwalbe, 1979

≠10

102 F. Fargette, 1st Pr. Thèmes 64, 1965

≠8

5 Studies II

In Chapter 2 we started to explore some of the most popular study themes, including mate and stalemate avoidance. Now we move on to stalemate, positional draw, domination and underpromotion. Towards the end of the chapter there are some examples of the more complex type of study common today.

Somehow stalemate seems a less exciting theme than mate, perhaps because it is always more enjoyable to win than to draw. However, these subjective impressions have no effect on the score table, where a draw snatched from apparently certain defeat is just as beneficial as an unexpected win. Many endgames familiar to over-the-board depend on stalemate resources, from the humble king and pawn v king upwards. These elementary stalemates have long been completely explored, but even simple combinations of material can produce artistic effects if handled with skill.

103 J. Rusinek, 1st Pr. L'Italia Scacchistica, 1976

Draw

White has enough material to draw but is troubled by the fork of rook and knight.

1	Rd2	Rb4+
2	Kh3	

2 e4 loses to 2...Rxe4+ and 3...Bxb1.

2	...	Ng1+

Or 2...Bf5+ 3 Kg2 when 3...Rg4+ and 3...Be4+ can be safely met by 4 Kf2.

3 Kg3!

3 Kg2? (3 Kh2? Nf3+) Rg4+ 4 Kf2 Bxb1 5 Rd1 Nh3+ 6 Kf3 Bf5 and Black consolidates his two extra pieces.

| 3 | ... | Bxb1 |

Having removed his knight from attack with gain of tempo Black is able to capture on b1, but the knight is not out of danger yet!

4 Rh2+

4 Rg2? Nf3! wins.

| 4 | ... | Kg5 |
| 5 | Kf2 | |

Now 5 Rg2 succeeds against 5...Nf3 since White takes the knight with check, but 5...Rg4+ wins, which explains Black's choice of g5 last move.

| 5 | ... | Ne2! |

Not 5...Rg4 6 Rh1 when White wins the knight for nothing.

6 Rg2+

The rook moves nearer the king with gain of time in order that White can take on e2.

| 6 | ... | Kh4 |

If Black moves elsewhere there is no mating threat at move 11.

7 Kxe2

If White continues checking then he forfeits the chance to take the knight after 7 Rh2+ Kg4 8 Rg2+ Kh3.

| 7 | ... | Rb2+ |

Black must attack at once since this material balance is in general a draw. Now 8 Kf3? loses to 8...Be4+.

8	Kf1	Bd3+
9	Kg1	Rb1+
10	Kh2	

10 Kf2? allows mate in one, thanks to Black's 6th move.

| 10 | ... | Be4 |

White's rook is pinned against the mate at h1 and if 11 Rg1 then 11...Rb2+ finishes White off. Nevertheless White can save himself.

| 11 | Rg4+! | Kxg4 |

and stalemate intervenes. The finale is straightforward, but arises only after a long struggle. Diagram 118 is another example of Rusinek's skill with this theme.

Stalemate is most surprising when White's king lies in the centre of the board. A total of eight squares must be either blocked by immobilised White pieces or covered by Black's forces. Apart from rare examples like diagram 118 this requires the presence of a Black queen.

104 U. Venäläinen, 1st Pr. Suomen Shakki, 1969

Draw

1 Kf3!

White must prevent 1...g2 so his choice is limited. 1 Bd4? e2 2 Kf3 Kf1 loses.

1 ... Kd2!

1...e2 2 Bc3+ Kf1 3 Kxg3 e5 (3...e1=Q 4 Bxe1 Kxe1 5 Kg4 is also a draw) 4 Kg4 e4 5 Kxg5 e3 6 Kf4 leads to an immediate draw, so Black plays to prevent the bishop moving to c3.

2 Bf8!

White is aiming for a skewer along the a5—e1 diagonal, taking the e7 pawn en route. 2...e2 3 Bxe7 and 2...e5 3 Bb4+ Kd3 4 Kxg3 draw easily.

2 ... g4+
3 Kg2

White must avoid being checked when Black promotes.

3 ... e2
4 Bxe7 Kc3!

Black doesn't yet threaten 5...e1=Q because 6 Bb4+ Kxb4 is stalemate, but 5...Kb3 is a threat, when promotion becomes unavoidable.

5 Bd8!

It is tempting to play 5 Bd6, threatening Bxg3 and therefore forcing Black to promote, but this allows 5...e1=R! 6 Kxg3 Re6 followed by ...Rg6 with a winning position. Black can bring his king up and any attempt by White to surround the pawn by Kf4 and Bh4—g5 fails to ...Rxg5.

| 5 | ... | Kb4 |
| 6 | Bc7! | |

Once again White must choose his square with care. After 6 Bb6? (threat 7 Bf2) e1=R! 7 Kxg3 Re6 Black brings his rook behind the pawn.

| 6 | ... | e1=R! |
| 7 | Kxg3 | |

and now this draws, for the bad position of Black's king enables White to meet ...Re7 by Bd6+. Other moves lose the pawn, for example 7...Re4 8 Bf4 or 7...Rg1+ 8 Kh4 followed by Bg3 and Kxg4.

The next study is also based on a central stalemate by Black's queen, but both the final position and the introductory play are quite different.

105 A. Herbstman, =1st Pr. 64, 1939/40

Draw

White is three pawns down and Black has a passed pawn on the seventh rank. On the plus side his own pawn presents a serious danger and Black's king is confined.

| 1 | c7 | Rf4+ |

This preliminary check is necessary as the immediate 1...Rc4 even loses after 2 Rxa4! c1=Q 3 c8=Q+ Rxc8 4 Rxh4+ and 5 Rxh6 mate.

| 2 | Kg6 | Rc4 |

If Black defends passively by 2...Rf8 White at least draws by 3 Rc1, for

77

example 3...a3 4 Rxc2 Rc8 5 Rc4 and wins after 5...Kg8 6 Rb4 or 5...a2 6 Kf7. 2...Rg4+ 3 Kf7 Rg7+ 4 Kf6 Rg8 5 Rc1 is much the same.

3	Rxa4	Rg4+!

Black has no choice as 3...Rc6+ 4 Kf7 Rf6+ (4...Kh7 5 c8=Q wins for White) 5 Kxf6 c1=Q 6 Ra8+ at least draws.

4	Rxg4	

Not 4 Kf7? Rg7+ 5 Kf6 c1=Q and Black wins.

4	...	c1=Q
5	c8=Q+!	

Surprisingly White can only draw by sacrificing his main asset — the passed c-pawn. 5 Kf7? Qf1+ 6 Ke7/e8 (6 Kg6 Qa6+ and now 7 Kg5 Qa5+ or 7 Kf7 Qe6+ 8 Kf8 Qxg4 9 c8=Q Qg8+) Qe2+ 7 Kf6 (7 Kd8/f8 Qxg4 or 7 Kd6 Qe6+ 8 Kc5 d6+ and ...Qxg4) Qe6+ 8 Kg5 Qe5+ and 9...Qxc7 wins for Black.

5	...	Qxc8
6	Kf7	Qd8

All the checks are covered and this is the only way to defend h4. 6...Qc2 7 Rxh4+ Qh7+ 8 Rxh7+ Kxh7 9 Kf6 and 10 Ke5 draws.

7	Rg6!	Kh7

Black's queen has a hard time in this study — still no checks and no way to defend h6.

8	Rh6+!	Kxh6

with stalemate.

The solving section at the end of the chapter contains two especially fine stalemate studies, Diagrams 119 and 120. In both cases Black's queen plays a major part in the final manoeuvres (this is a hint for one position!).

It isn't safe to assume that once you have found a stalemate the solution is at an end. Composers sometimes try to incorporate two or more different stalemate positions in the same study.

106 A. Avni, 1st Pr. Israel RT, 1978

Draw

Black has a winning material advantage but his king is exposed to attack.

1 Rg1

Threatens mate and if 1...Nf5 then 2 e4 R moves 3 Rxg6 (but not 3 exf5 Bd5+ winning) and Black's last pawn disappears.

1 ... Nf3!

Best as 1...Ng2 leads to stalemate after 2 Rxg2! Rd1+ 3 Bg1 Bd5 4 e4 Bxe4 5 f3 Bxf3.

2 Rg3+

If White takes the pawn Black has a decisive attack, for example 2 Rxg6? (2 e4? Rg5 saves the pawn) Rd1+ 3 Bg1 Bd5 4 e4 (trying for stalemate – 4 Rh6+ Nh4+ and 4 Rg3+ Kh4 are no better) Bxe4 5 Rg3+ (the alternatives 5 Re6 Ne5+, 5 Rh6+ Nh4+ and 5 Rg2 Nxg1 also lose) Kh4 6 Rh3+ Kg4! 7 Rg3+ Kf4 and White is helpless to prevent ...Nxg1+.

2 ... Kh4
3 Rxf3!

3 Rxg6? is still tempting, but loses to 3...Rd1+ 4 Kg2 (4 Bg1 Bd5 is like the last note) Bd5 5 Rh6+ (Black threatened 5...Nxh2+ 6 Kxh2 Rh1 mate and 5 Bg3+ Kh5 6 R moves Nh4+ also leads to mate) Kg4 6 Rg6+ Ng5+ 7 f3+ Bxf3+ (four consecutive checks!) 8 Kf2 Rd2+ 9 Kg1 Rg2+.

3 ... Rd1+
4 Bg1

4 Kg2? Bd5 followed by ...Kg4 wins since White can't set up the stalemate of the main line (5 Bg1 loses to ...Rxg1+ or ...Bxf3+).

4 ... Bd5

79

5 e4!	Bxe4
6 Kh2	

The point of White's defence. He can safely unpin the rook as 6...Bxf3 is stalemate. Black has one last attempt to win.

6 ...	Rxg1

So that 7 Rf4+ Rg4 wins.

7 Rh3+	Kg4
8 f3+!	

Again White must eliminate a pawn which would ruin the stalemate.

8 ...	Bxf3
9 Rg3+!	Rxg3

with another stalemate. To achieve three from such a natural initial position is quite a triumph for the composer.

Diagram 121 conceals no less than six stalemates, the final one being highly unusual.

In over-the-board play draws by perpetual check arise mainly in the middlegame, the few endgame examples being restricted to queen and pawn endings. However, under special circumstances perpetual check can be delivered by a couple of minor pieces, as in Diagram 122. Draws by repetition don't necessarily involve checks, of course, but they are hardly more subtle in most cases. A White piece moves between two squares creating continuous threats which can only be met with a similar oscillation by Black. The following study contains a quite different mechanism giving rise to repetition.

107 V. Korolkov & L. Mitrofanov, 1st Pr. Tuvinsk Committee T, 1958

Draw

At some stage White will have to bring his rook back to the first rank to stop Black's pawn, but first he makes sure that his knight is not attacked.

1 Ne6+

Not 1 Rh6? f2 2 Ne6+ (2 Rh1 Nf3 wins) Kd7 3 Nf8+ (3 Rh1 Nf3 4 Rd1+ Kxe6 wins) Ke8 4 Rh1 Nf3! threatening 5...Ng1. If 5 Rf1 then 5...Nd2+ while if the rook moves further to the left it is shut off by ...Ne1.

| 1 | ... | Kd7 |

Or 1...Kc8 (1...Kd6 2 Nd4+ and 3 Nxf3) 2 Rf8+ Kd7 3 Rd8+ Ke7 4 Rd2 Kxe6 5 Rf2 Kf5 6 Rf1 and the f3 pawn falls.

2 Nf8+

2 Rh6? f2 transposes to the first note.

| 2 | ... | Kc8 |

2...Kc7 3 Ne6+, 2...Kd8 3 Rd6+ and 2...Ke7/e8 3 Re6+ are trivial.

3 Rc6+!

Before White brings his rook back Black's king must be driven to the b-file. 3 Rh6? f2 4 Rh1 Nf3 5 Ne6 (5 Rc1+ Kb8 doesn't help) Ng1 6 Rh8+ Kd7 7 Rd8+ Kxe6 8 Rd1 Nf3! 9 Kc2 Ne1+ (9...Nh2 also wins) 10 Kd2 f1=Q 11 Rxe1+ Qxe1+ 12 Kxe1 Kf5 and Black wins by one tempo.

| 3 | ... | Kb7 |

3...Kb8 (3...Kd8 4 Rd6+ and 5 Rd2) 4 Rh6 f2 5 Rh1 Nf3 transposes to the main line.

| 4 | Rh6 | f2 |
| 5 | Rh1 | |

5 Rh7+? Kc8 6 Rh1 Nf3 transposes to 3 Rh6?.

| 5 | ... | Nf3 |
| 6 | Ne6! | |

Not 6 Rh7+? Ka8. Other moves don't meet the threat of ...Ng1.

| 6 | ... | Ng1 |

6...Kc6 also leads to a draw after 7 Nd4+! Nxd4+ 8 Kxb4 Nc2+ (or else Rf1) 9 Kb3 Ne3 10 f5! f1=Q (10...Nxf5 11 Rf1) 11 Rxf1 Nxf1 12 f6 Kd7 (12...Nd2+ 13 Kb4) 13 Kb4 Ne3 14 Kxb5 Nd5 15 f7 Ke7 16 Kc6 winning Black's last pawn.

| 7 | Rh7+ | Kc8 |

7...Kc6 8 Rc7+ Kd5 (8...Kd6 9 Rc1 Nf3 10 Ng5 is a draw as 10...Ne1 fails to 11 Ne4+) 9 Rc1 Nf3 10 Ng7! Ke4 (10...Ne1 11 Nf5) 11 Nh5 is at least a draw for White. 7...Ka8/b8 8 Rh8+ repeats so 7...Kc8, aiming to meet 8 Rh8+? by 8...Kd7, is Black's only winning chance.

| 8 | Rc7+ | Kb8 |

81

9 Rc1	Nf3
10 Rh1!	

The only way to answer the threat of ...Ne1. 10 Nd4? Ne1 11 Nc2 f1=Q 12 Nxe1 Qxf4 leaves Black with a slow but sure win on material.

10 ...	Ng1
11 Rh8+	Kb7
12 Rh7+	

and the position after 7 Rh7+ has been repeated. Thus White can force a threefold repetition by move 17, with the White rook running rings (or at least squares) round Black's pieces.

We now consider the topic of the 'positional draw'. It is hard to give a clear definition of this term, because it embraces a wide range of phenomena. Perhaps the simplest to understand is the blockade. In this case Black has enough extra material to win, but because his pieces are imprisoned behind a barrier he cannot bring the extra material to bear. In practical play this sometimes happens when there are interlocking pawn chains across most or all of the board, but in studies it can happen in other situations.

108 A. Gurevich, 1st Pr. Dagestan Tny, 1952

Draw

1 Rh8!!

White has bishop and rook attacked in such a way that one will be lost in a couple of moves. B+N+P v R is a win for Black, so under normal circumstances losing either piece will also lose the game. In fact White can almost draw by offering the bishop, but Black can win by precise play: 1 Rh4 (1 Re5? Bf4 loses at once) Kxg8 2 Rg4 Kg7! (2...g5? 3 Kb7! removes the check at f4 and threatens Rg3 against which Black has no defence since knight moves lose a piece to Rg3 or Re4) 3 Kb7 (the threat is to draw by perpetual attack on Black's bishop, for example 4 Rg3 Bf2 5 Rg2 Bd4 6

Rg4 Nf3 7 Rf4 or 6...Ne2 7 Re4) and now:

1) 3...Kf6? (3...g5? 4 Rg3) 4 Rg3 Bd4 (4...Bc5 5 Kc6 Ba7 6 Kb7 and 4...Bf2 5 Rg2 repeat as 5...Nh3 in the latter line drops a piece to 6 Rh2) 5 Rg4 Bc5 (5...Ne2 6 Re4 or 5...Nf3 6 Rf4+) 6 Kc6 Kf5 7 Rxg6 draw.

2) 3...Kh6! 4 Rg3 (4 Kc6 Kh5 5 Rg3 Bf2 6 Rg2 Nh3 and Black disentangles and wins) Bc5! 5 Kc6 Bd4! 6 Rg4 (6 Kd5 Ba7 7 Ra3 Bf2 8 Ra2 Nh3 and once again Black frees his pieces) Nf3 7 Rf4 (not check with the king on h6) Ne5+ 8 Kd5 Bg1! (8...Be3? 9 Re4 draws immediately while 8...Bc3? 9 Rh4+ Kg5 10 Rh3 Bb2 11 Rb3 and 8...Ba7 9 Ra4 Bb8 10 Rb4 lead to perpetual attack on the bishop) 9 Rh4+ (9 Kxe5 Bh2 wins the pawn ending and 9 Rf1 Bh2 10 Rh1 Ng4 is no better) Kg5 10 Rh1 Nf3 11 Ke4 Kg4 and wins.

1	...	Kg7

1...Bd4 2 Bh7+ wins the pawn.

2	Bh7!

2 Rh4? transposes to the first note.

2	...	g5

It seems that White's resources are at an end and that he must now suffer a fatal loss of material, but he can draw by unexpectedly giving up the rook.

3	Bf5!	Kxh8
4	Bg4	

Suddenly Black's knight is trapped and his bishop can achieve nothing by itself as it can only operate on the dark squares. Everything depends on whether Black can activate his king.

4	...	Kg7
5	Kc7	Kf6
6	Kd6	

Just in time! If Black could have reached e5 he would have won.

6	...	Bc1

Since White cannot move his bishop it might seem that he is in danger of zugzwang. Fortunately White always has two squares available to his king when Black threatens to cross the g4–c8 diagonal, e.g. with Black's king on e7, White can be on d5 or c6. Thus he cannot become movebound.

7	Kd5	Ba3
8	Ke4	Ke7
9	Kd5	Kd8
10	Kc6	Bf8
11	Kb7	

and so on. Black cannot make progress.

Now try to solve Diagram 123. White has to play with great subtlety to prevent Black arriving at the above positional draw.

Another type of positional draw arises when White deliberately heads for a position which, according to all normal rules, should be lost for him. At the eleventh hour he is saved by some quirk in the positioning of the pieces which prevents Black from exploiting his material superiority.

109 A. Troitsky, 2nd Pr. Shakhmaty v SSSR, 1935

Draw

Can White's lone passed pawn counterbalance Black's trio?

1 e6!

Every move must be exact. 1 Rg7? Rd3+ 2 Kc5 (the lines 2 Ke7 g3 3 e6 g2 4 Kf8 Rd6 5 e7 Re6 6 e8=Q Rxe8+ 7 Kxe8 c3 and 2 Kc7 g3 3 e6 c3 4 e7 c2 5 e8=Q c1=Q+ 6 Kb8 Rb3+ 7 Rb7 Qf4+ win for Black) g3 3 Kxc4 (3 e6 c3 or 3 Rg4 g2 4 Rxe4 Kf2 5 Kxc4 Rg3! with a Black win) g2 4 e6 Rd8 5 e7 Re8 6 Kd4 Kf2 7 Rf7+ Ke1 8 Rg7 Rxe7 9 Rxg2 e3 10 Kd3 e2 and White loses his rook.

1 ... Rd3+

As usual passive defence is bad in rook endings: 1...Ra3 2 e7 Ra8 3 Rxc4 draws straight away.

2 Ke5!

Or *1*) 2 Kc5? Rd8 3 Rg7 c3 4 Rxg4+ (or 4 e7 Rc8+) Kf2 5 Rxe4 Rc8+ and 6...c2 promotes.

2) 2 Kc6? Rd8 3 e7 Re8 4 Kd7 Rxe7+ 5 Kxe7 e3 6 Rxc4 g3 and White loses in two symmetrical variations: 7 Rg4 e2 8 Rxg3+ Kf2 and 7 Re4 g2 8 Rxe3 Kf2.

3) 2 Ke7? blocking the pawn looks bad and sure enough Black wins by 2...e3 3 Rxc4 g3 4 Kf7 Rd8 and Black's pawns are too strong.

| | 2 ... | e3 |

2...Rd8 3 Rxc4 is still a draw.

3 Rxc4

3 Rg7? e2 4 Rxg4+ Kf2 wins.

| | 3 ... | e2 |
| | **4 Rxg4+** | |

The immediate 4 Re4? gains a tempo, but in this position the g-pawn is more important than one tempo and Black wins by 4...Kf2 5 e7 e1=Q 6 Rxe1 (6 e8=Q Qxe4+) Kxe1 7 Kf4 Rf3+.

| | 4 ... | Kf2 |
| | **5 Re4** | |

5 Rf4+ Rf3 6 Re4 amounts to the same thing.

| | 5 ... | Re3 |

5...e1=Q 6 Rxe1 Kxe1 7 e7 followed by Kf6 draws easily.

| | **6 Rxe3** | **Kxe3** |
| | **7 e7** | **e1=Q** |

White has been aiming for this position but it isn't clear why! 8 e8=Q Kf3+ loses, while otherwise White has a pawn on the seventh against a queen, which is only a draw if the pawn is an a-, c-, f- or h-pawn. The present position reveals one of the few exceptions to this rule.

8 Ke6!

Not 8 Kd6 Qb4+ or 8 Kf6 Qh4+ when Black wins by the usual method. After 8 Ke6! Black cannot cover e8 with his queen so he must give a discovered check. However, **8...K to the d-file+** is met by **9 Kd7!** and thanks to the bad position of Black's king he has no check, so White can promote next move. Similarly **8...K to the f-file+ 9 Kf7!** draws.

Diagram 124 is another paradoxical position along similar lines.

Now it is time to turn again to studies in which White is hoping to win. One of the most popular study ideas is that of domination, in which the lesser force unexpectedly traps the greater. The effect is improved if the board is open, so that Black's pieces have great apparent mobility.

110 A. Gurevich & G. Kasparian, 1st Pr.
All-union Physical Culture and Sport T, 1955

Win

The analysis in this study is rather more complex than most, but it is worth following through to appreciate the stunning finale.

1 Bd4+!

White has five plausible checks, so even the first move presents difficulties. The alternatives are refuted as follows:

1) 1 Rxf2? (1 Ra1? and 1 Ke2? are met by 1...hxg2) Nxf2 2 gxh3 (2 Kxf2 h2) Nxh3 3 Bxh6 (or else ...Ng5 and the knight escapes) Kd5 (intending ...Ke5–f5 and ...Ng5) 4 Kf3 (4 Nb3 Ke5 and now 5 Nd4 Kf6 6 Nf3 Kg6 7 Bf8 Ng5 or 5 Nd2 Kf5 6 Nf3/e4 Kg6 and the knight comes out) Ke5 5 Kg3 (5 Nc4/c6+ Kf5 followed by ...Kg6) Ng1 6 Kf2 (or else ...Ne2+) Nh3+ draws.

2) 1 Nb3+? (giving random checks isn't likely to help White) Kb4 2 Rb2 hxg2 or 2 Nd2 hxg2.

3) 1 Nb7+? Kc6 2 Nd8+ (2 Na5+ Kb5) Kd7 3 Rd2+ Kc8 4 Rxf2 Nxf2 5 gxh3 Nxh3 and 6...Ng5.

4) 1 Rc2+? and 1 Bf8+? are both met by 1...Kb5 and after 2 Rxf2 Nxf2 3 gxh3 Nxh3 Black's knight escapes via g5.

1 ...	Kd5!

Black must keep the bishop under observation.

2 Ke2

Now Black has problems, for example 2...hxg2 3 Bxf2, 2...Kxd4 3 gxh3 or 2...Ng3+ 3 Kxf2 h2 4 Ra1 h1=Q 5 Rxh1 Nxh1+ 6 Kg1 (or 6 Ke3) and wins.

2 ...	h2!

If Black can't promote on g1, he'll aim for h1 instead! The threat is 3...Ng3+.

3 Ra1

3 Bxf2 (3 Rd2 Ng3+ 4 Kxf2 Ne4+) Nxf2 4 Ra1 h1=Q 5 Rxh1 Nxh1 6 Kf3 h5 followed by ...h4 and ...Ng3 is safe for Black.

3 ...   f1=Q+!

Black has to play resourcefully to stay in the game. 3...Ng3+? is no different from 2...Ng3+?.

4 Kxf1

4 Rxf1? Ng3+ wins for Black.

4 ...   Kxd4

Finally Black genuinely threatens ...Ng3+.

5 g4!

Not 5 Ra4+ (5 Nb3+ Ke3) Ke5 6 Rh4 Ng3+ 7 Kf2 h1=Q 8 Rxh1 Nxh1+ 9 Kf3 h5 with a draw nor 5 Nc6+ Ke3 6 Ra3+ Kd2 7 Ra2+ (7 Rh3 Ng3+ 8 Kf2 h1=Q 9 Rxh1 Nxh1+ 10 Kf3 Ke1 and ...Nf2) Ke3 8 Re2+ Kf4 and Black has the advantage.

5 ...   Ng3+
6 Kg2   h1=Q+

Now 7 Rxh1 Nxh1 8 Kxh1 (delaying this capture doesn't help) Ke4 9 Kg2 Kf4 10 Kh3 h5 11 gxh5 Kg5 wins the last pawn and draws. Having seen this, many solvers would search for an improvement earlier, but it always pays to have one last look around to see if there is something unexpected.

7 Kxg3!

and Black's queen is trapped! 7...Qxa1 8 Nb3+ Ke5 9 Nxa1 Kf6 10 Kh4, 7...Qe4 8 Ra4+, 7...Qd5 8 Rd1+ and 7...Qa8 8 Nb3+ are the variations. The only slight flaw in this magnificent study is that 6 Kf2 also wins.

Black's queen is also humbled by a rook and a knight in Diagram 125.

In the most extreme cases a single minor piece can outgun a queen, usually aided and abetted by a passed pawn.

Win

White is a piece and a pawn down but Black's forces are very badly placed for the fight against White's c-pawn.

1 c5

1 Kg6? (1 Be5+? Kh7 2 c5 f4 3 c6 f3 4 exf3 Nh6+ and 5...e2) f4 2 Be5+ Nf6 3 c5 (3 Bxf6+ Kg8 4 c5 Kf8) Kg8! 4 Bxf6 (4 Kxf6 f3) Kf8! 5 c6 Ke8 and the pawn is neutralised.

1 ...   f4

1...Nh6+ 2 Ke6 f4 3 c6 f3 4 c7 promotes with check and 1...Bh2 2 Bxh2 f4 3 c6 f3 4 exf3 e2 5 Bg3 wins.

2 c6

2 Kg6? Nf6! 3 Be5 transposes to 1 Kg6?.

2 ...   f3
3 exf3

3 c7? (3 Kg6? Bh2! 4 c7 Ne7+) f2 4 Kg6 Bh2! 5 c8=Q (5 Bxh2 Ne7+ and ...f1=Q) f1=Q and Black defends.

3 ...   Ne7!

3...Nh6+? (3...e2? 4 c7 Nh6+ 5 Kg6 e1=Q 6 c8=Q+ Ng8 7 Qh3+ Qh4 8 Be5+ Nf6 9 Qc8 mate) 4 Kg6 Nf5 (4...e2 5 Be5+ Kg8 6 c7) 5 Be5+ Kg8 6 Kxf5 e2 7 c7 e1=Q 8 c8=Q+ Kf7 9 Qe6+ Kf8 10 Bd6+ wins Black's queen.

4 Bxe7

4 Kxe7 e2 5 Bg3 (5 c7? e1=Q+ 6 Kf7 Qc1 and 5 Bb4 Bh2 are bad) Bb6 6 Kf6 (6 Kd7 Kg7 7 c7 Bxc7 8 Kxc7 Kf6 9 Kd6 Kf5 10 Kd5 e1=Q 11 Bxe1 Kf4 wins White's last pawn) Bc7 7 Be1 Bf4 and White cannot make progress since if he brings his king back to round up the e2 pawn, he loses

his own pawn at c6, for example 8 Kf5 Kg7 9 Ke4 Kf6 10 Kd3 Ke6 11 Kxe2 Kd5 drawing.

4 ...   Bh2

Black has succeeded in preventing the advance of the c-pawn, but by a sacrifice White can get it moving again.

5 f4!

5 Bxg5 e2 6 Bd2 Kh7 (Black's bishop is well placed on the h2–b8 diagonal where it can hold up both pawns) 7 Kf6 (7 Ke6 Kg6 8 Kd7 Kf5 9 c7 Bxc7 10 Kxc7 e1=Q 11 Bxe1 Kf4 draws) Kg8 8 Kf5 (8 Ke6 Kg7 9 Kd7 Kg6 10 c7 Bxc7 11 Kxc7 Kf5 followed by ...e1=Q) Kf7 and White cannot win after 9 f4 Bxf4 10 Kxf4 Ke6 11 Bb4 e1=Q or 9 Bb4 Bd6 or 9 Ke4 Ke6.

5 ...   Bxf4

5...e2 6 c7 e1=Q 7 c8=Q+ mates.

6 Bxg5   e2

6...Bc7 7 Bxe3 is a technical win by 7...Kh7 8 Ke6 Kg6 9 Kd7 Ba5 (9...Bh2 10 Bc5 and 11 Bd6) 10 Bc5 Kf5 11 Be7 and 12 Bd8 promoting his pawn.

7 Bxf4   e1=Q
8 c7

The crucial moment. White's bishop shields his king from checks, covers c1 and stands ready to deflect Black's queen away from c3.

8 ...   Qc3

After 8...Kh7 9 c8=Q White threatens Qh3 and Qg8, while Black cannot exploit the potential stalemate.

9 Be5+   Qxe5
10 c8=Q+   Kh7

and White mates in two by 11 Qg8+ or 11 Qh3+.

In the last two studies, and in Diagram 126 at the end of the chapter, the domination comes like a thunderclap after a long introductory struggle. In complete contrast, the domination process in the next two studies is more like the gradual squeezing of a boa constrictor.

Win

Black's queen must not be allowed to escape from the back rank since in general 2R v Q is a draw. Thus 1 Rf7? Qd6 and 1 Re7? Qg8 throw the win away by allowing the queen to start checking. White must also avoid 1 Rd7? Qg8 2 Kf3 Qa8 followed by check, 1 Ke1? Qg8 2 Kf1/f2 Qf8+ 3 Rd7 Qd6/c5+ and 1 Ra7? Qe8+ 2 Kf2 (2 Kd2 Qg8 or 2 Kf1/f3 Qb5/h5+) Qf8+ 3 Kg2 (3 Rf7 Qc5+) Qg7+! forcing stalemate. This last line proves that White will have trouble escaping from the queen checks by playing his king to the g-file since by playing ...Kh8 Black will always be able to set up this trick.

1	Rh7+	Kg8
2	Rhe7!	

Now that g8 is blocked White can play his rook to e7. Other moves fail, for example 2 Rhc7 Qe8+! (Black need not repeat moves and risk White finding the win second time round) 3 Kf1/f2 (3 Kd2 Qf8) Qf8+ 4 Kg1 (4 Kg2 Qa8) Kh8 and White cannot make progress because of the threat ...Qg7+. Even if White continues 5 Rh7+ Kg8 6 Rhe7/c7 Black just renews the threat by 6...Kh8. If 2 Rhd7 instead White still wins, but only by transposition to the main line after 2...Qe8+ 3 Kd2/f1/f2 Qf8 (+) 4 Ke1! Qe8+ 5 Re7 Qf8 6 Ke2 Kh8 7 Rbc7.

| 2 | ... | Kh8 |

White wins immediately if Black loses control of g7 and f7, e.g. 2...Qd8 3 Rg7+ Kh8 4 Rh7+ Kg8 5 Rcg7+ Kf8 6 Rh8+.

3 Rbc7!

The purpose of this move is to cover c4 so that White's king can go to f1 when Black's queen is on g8. The alternatives are:
1) 3 Rbd7? Qg8 4 Kf3 Qb3+ 5 Re3 Qb8 draws.
2) 3 Ra7? (3 Rec7? Qg8 and 3 Ke1? Qg8 are much the same) Qg8 4 Kf2 Qf8+ 5 Ke1/e2 (once again K to the g-file allows ...Qg7+) Qg8 draws.

	3	...	Kg8

After 3...Qg8 4 Kf1! Qf8+ 5 Rf7 Qg8 any waiting move by White leaves Black in zugzwang.

	4	Ra7

Or 4 Rcd7, but not 4 Rb7? Kh8, 4 Red7? Qe8+ or 4 Ke1? Kh8.

	4	...	Kh8
	5	Rf7	

Other moves are met by 5...Qg8 6 K to the f-file Qf8+ and White has lost time.

	5	...	Qe8+

5...Qg8 6 Kf2 is zugzwang.

	6	Kf2	Kg8

Black has little choice since ...Qg8 leads to zugzwang as before.

	7	Rg7+	Kf8
	8	Rh7	Kg8
	9	Rag7+	Kf8
	10	Rh8+	

winning the queen. The peculiar shuffling moves by the rooks are hard to understand, even though the idea behind them is simple enough. When one rook is on b7 and the other is on f7, Black has the defence ...Qd6. White seeks to prevent this by moving the b7 rook elsewhere. This is only possible when Black's king is on g8, or else ...Qg8 defends. White's third move covers c4 and thus prevents ...Qg8, so forcing the king to the crucial square. White's first two moves were independent of this plan and are designed solely to stop Black's checks.

Here is another example of constriction.

113 G. Kasparian, 2nd Pr. Tidskrift KNSB, 1959

Win

91

The first few moves are forced.

| 1 | a6 | Nb6 |
| 2 | a7 | Na8 |

Black's only way to meet the threat of Rxb6.

3 Rb8

How can Black continue? 3...Nc7 4 Rc8 is no good, so Black's only hope is to answer Rxa8 by ...Kb6 followed by ...Kb7 winning the a-pawn. In order that this defence should operate Black's bishop must be immune from attack by the a8 rook.

| 3 | ... | Ba1! |

The only suitable square. White cannot make immediate progress, but can still hope for victory based on zugzwang. Neither bishop nor knight may move and Black's king is restricted to c5, c6 and c7 to be within range of b6. However, White is also limited by the necessity to stop ...Bd4 when Black's king is on c6 or c7 (for otherwise ...Bd4 Rxa8 Kb7 draws). Can White force Black into zugzwang while at the same time avoiding ...Bd4?

4 Ke2

White must head for d3. After 4 Kf2? Kc6 5 Ke3 (or else ...Bd4) Black can escape by 5...Nc7! 6 Rc8 Kb7 7 Rxc7+ Ka8 8 Ke4 (8 Kd3 Be5 followed by ...Bh2–g1) Bf6 9 Kd5 Bg5 followed by ...Be3 with a draw. The problem is that White's king takes too long to reach a6 from e3, so that Black has enough time to round up the a7 pawn. If White doesn't play to win the knight immediately at move 6, Black still draws, e.g. 6 Kd3 Be5 or 6 Ke4 Bf6! 7 Rc8 Kb7 as before.

| 4 | ... | Kc6 |
| 5 | Kd3! | Kc5 |

Or 5...Nc7 (5...Kc7 6 Ke3! Kc6 7 Ke4 wins as in the main line) 6 Rc8 Kb7 7 Rxc7+ Ka8 8 Kc4 Be5 9 Rd7 Bg3 10 Kb5 Bf2 11 Ka6 and wins.

6 Ke3!!

White is aiming for the position Kd3 v Kc5 with Black to move, so he must lose a tempo. 6 Ke4?! is met by 6...Kc6 and now White can only win by returning to the previous position after 7 Kd3 Kc5 8 Ke3!!. After **6 Ke3!!** there are two variations:

1) 6...Kc6 7 Ke4 Nc7 (7...Kc5 8 Kd3 Kc6 9 Kc4 Kc7 10 Kb5 and 11 Ka6 wins) **8 Rc8 Kb7 9 Rxc7+ Ka8 10 Kd5 Bf6 11 Kc4!** (not 11 Kc5? Bd4+ nor 11 Kc6? Bd4 with a draw in both cases) and now Black's can't play ...Bd8 (to reach b6 with gain of tempo) because of Rc8+, so he has to spend two more moves reaching the g1–a7 diagonal, giving White time to bring his king to a6.

2) 6...Bf6 (6...Bd4+ 8 Ke4 threatens Rxa8, so Black must play 8...Ba1

92

when 9 Kd3 wins) **7 Ke4!** (7 Rxa8? Kb6 and now 8 Rf8 allows ...Bg5+ while if White cuts out the check by 8 Ke4 Black draws by ...Ba1 followed by ...Kb7) **Ba1** (with his king on a white square there was a threat of Rxa8, so the bishop has to scurry for shelter again) **8 Kd3! Kc6 9 Kc4** winning.

We end this brief look at the world of endgame studies by presenting three compositions involving more complex analysis. Such studies are difficult to solve because neither side has strong threats, so there seems to be no particular motivation to play one move rather than another. It is often necessary to penetrate to a considerable depth to uncover the reasons why only one move leads to success.

114 V. Kivi, 1st Pr. Tidskrift för Schack, 1945

Win

1 g7	Rc8

1...Rc1+ 2 Ka2! (not 2 Kb2? Rc8 3 g4 Rb8+ with a draw) Rc2+ 3 Ka3 Ra3+ 4 Ka4 Rc8 5 g4! is essentially the same as the main line.

2 g4!

Black was threatening 2...Kf6 3 g8=Q Rxg8 4 Bxg8 Kf5 followed by ...Kg4 drawing. 2 Be6? failed to 2...Ra8+ and 3...Kf6 so White's move, exploiting the bad position of Black's rook, was forced.

2 ...	Rb8

Now ...Kxg4 is threatened. Black chose b8 to keep White's king cut off for as long as possible.

3 Be6

The Black king must remain next to the g4 pawn or else White wins by g8=Q. The rook is also tied to the back rank and will remain on b8 until driven away.

93

If Black ever plays ...Kh6, White can win without problems by replying g8=R!, but it is interesting to note that here White can also win by promoting to a queen, for example 3...Kh6 4 g8=Q Rb1+ 5 Ka2 Rb2+ (trying to keep the king pinned to the a-file) 6 Ka3 Rb3+ 7 Ka4 Rb4+ 8 Ka5 Rb5+ 9 Ka6 Rb6+ 10 Ka7 Rb7+ 11 Ka8 Ra7+ 12 Kb8 Rb7+ (12...Ra8+ 13 Kc7 Ra7+ 14 Kd6 Rd7+ 15 Ke5 Rd5+ 16 Kf6 Rf5+ 17 Ke7 Rf7+ 18 Qxf7 wins) 13 Kc8 Rc7+ 14 Kd8 Rd7+ 15 Ke8 Re7+ 16 Kf8 Re8+ 17 Kf7 Re7+ 18 Kf6 and the checks come to an end. In a line like this it isn't practical to give every variation as there are two possibilities for Black at each move, but the reader can quickly convince himself that White's king can always find shelter at f6.

4	Ka2	Kg5
5	Ka3	Kf4
6	Ka4	Kg5
7	Ka5	Kf4
8	Ka6	Kg5
9	Ka7	Re8

The only other square is d8, but in that case White could continue by 10 Kb7. After 10...Re8, on the other hand, Black threatens ...Re7+ and White cannot play Kb7 or Kb6.

10   Bf7!   Rd8

Black has another defence by 10...Re7+ 11 K moves Kh6, when 12 g8=N+! is the only move to win. Here 12 g8=R fails to 12...Rxf7 and after 12 g8=Q Black delivers perpetual check by 12...Re6+ (if White's king is on a8 or b8 it is even simpler — Black checks along the 7th rank until the king reaches f8 and then plays ...Re8+) 13 Kc5 Rc6+ (Black can always ensure that White's bishop is not able to interpose) 14 Kb4 Rb6+ 15 Kc3 Rb3+ 16 Kd4 Rd3+ (not 16...Rb4+? 17 Bc4, for example) 17 Ke5 Re3+! (avoiding White's last trap — 17...Rd5+? 18 Kf6! Rf5+ 19 Ke7! wins) 18 Kd6 (18 Kf6 Re6+) Re6+ and so on. With the bishop on f7 rather than e6 there is no place to hide from the barrage of checks.

11   Kb6!

A precise move avoiding a fork by ...Rd7+. After 11 Kb7? Kh6! 12 g8=R (12 g8=Q Rd7+ draws as in the last note, 12 g8=N+ Kg7 wins material and finally 12 Kc7 is answered by 12...Kxg7) Rd7+ Black picks up the bishop. 12 Ka6? fails to 12...Kxg4. After 11 Kb6! White wins in all lines:
1) 11...Kh6 12 g8=R! wins.
2) 11...Kxg4 12 Kc7 Ra8 13 Be6+ K moves 14 Bc8 Ra7+ 15 Bb7 and the pawn promotes.
3) 11...Ra8 12 Be6 (White has freed his king to come over to support the g-pawn) Re8 13 Kc5 Rd8 14 Kc6 Kf4 15 Kc7 Re8 (15...Ra8 16 Bc8) 16 Kd7 Ra8 17 Ke7 Kg5 18 Bf7! (White must still play accurately — not

18 Bd7? Kg6 nor 18 Kf7 Ra7+ 19 Kf8 Ra8+ when White loses time) and now:

3a) 18...Kxg4 19 Be8 Ra7+ 20 Bd7+ promotes.

3b) 18...Ra7+ 19 Kf8 Ra8+ (19...Kh6 20 g5+) 20 Be8 wins.

3c) 18...Kh6 19 g8=R is simplest although 19 g8=Q also wins as 19...Ra7+ 20 Kf6 Rxf7+ 21 Ke5 eventually leads to a position in which Black's rook can be captured by White's queen. The difference between this line and the note to Black's tenth move is that thanks to the initially unfavourable position of Black's rook White can force Black to take the bishop, opening a diagonal for the queen.

3d) 18...Rb8 19 Be8 Rb7+ 20 Bd7 Rb8 21 Kf7 and 22 g8=Q wins.

4) 11...Rb8+ 12 Kc6! Rd8 (12...Kh6 13 g8=R! — in this position promoting to a queen only draws, or 12...Kxg4 13 Kc7 Ra8 14 Be6+ etc) 13 Be6 and wins as in line 3.

Tricky to solve, but combining rook and knight promotions in a study containing just six pieces is a fantastic achievement.

Sometimes it is easier to work backwards from the end of a study, especially if it isn't clear what White should be aiming for.

115 P. Perkonoja, 1st Pr. Suomen Shakki, 1971

Win

White can't win by supporting his pawns with his king, for example 1 Kf4? d2 2 Nc3 Kh7 3 Kg5 Kg8 4 Kg6 Kh8 5 h7 d1=Q 6 Nxd1 c3 7 Ne3 c2 forcing stalemate. So the knight must be used to defend the kingside pawns while White's king blockades the c- and d-pawns. But how then is White to win? He cannot take the c4 pawn with his king, while otherwise he is doomed to move his king between c3, d2 and e3 for ever. The only hope is to stalemate Black's king using only the knight and the h-pawns, forcing Black to commit suicide by pushing his own pawns. However, 1 Nf6? turns out to be premature after 1...c3 2 Ng4 (2 Kxd3 c2) d2! (not 2...c2? 3 Kd2 Kh7 4 Kc1 Kh8 5 Ne5 Kh7 6 Nxd3 Kxh6 7 Nf4 and wins) 3 Ke2 Kh7 with a draw since if White stalemates the king again, Black can easily sacrifice both pawns. Clearly e3 is a bad square for the king in this line. If White's king were on c3 instead, then Nf6 would work, since after ...d2 Kxd2 c3+ Kc1 c2 Ng4 White would win easily. In fact, this line works even without the h5 pawn. Where should White put his knight while he transfers his king from e3 to c3? It must defend the h6 pawn and be ready to jump to f6, so the knight should be stationed at g4. Now let's consider a position with WNg4, WKc3 and BKh7. With Black to play White wins: 1...Kg8 (1...Kh8 2 Nf6 d2 3 Kxd2 c3+ 4 Kc1 wins as above) 2 Nf6+ Kf7 (2...Kh8 3 h7 is the same) 3 h7 Kg7 4 h8=Q+! Kxh8 5 h6 with the familiar zugzwang. With White to play there is no way to make progress as only Kd2 is feasible. Once White's knight is on g4 Black can only oscillate between h7 and h8 with his king, since 1...Kg8 2 Nf6+ Kf7 3 h7 Kg7 wins for White no matter where his king is — he simply plays it to c3 and then continues with either h6 or h8=Q+ Kxh8 h6, depending on whether Black's king is on h8 or g7. Thus with White's king on e3, knight on g4 and Black's king on h7, Black to play loses by 1...Kh8 (1...Kg8 2 Nf6+ as above) 2 Kd2 Kh7 3 Kc3 Kh8 4 Nf6 etc. This is the position White must aim for. In general, White cannot win this type of position as Black can arrange to be on the right square (h8 or h7) when White's knight arrives at g4. The win exists here only because White has a forcing sequence of moves leading to the required position.

1 Ne7

As 1 Nf6? doesn't work this is the only way to defend the h6 pawn.

1	...	Kh7
2	Nf5	Kg8

2...Kh8 meets with the same reply.

3 Nd6

White must keep playing forcing moves. 3 Kd2? Kh8! 4 Ne3 (4 Kc3 Kh7 is also a draw) Kh7 5 Ng4 Kh8 draws, as the wrong player is to move.

3	...	Kh7

3...Kh8 4 Nxc4 Kh7 5 Kf4 Kxh6 6 Kg4 Kh7 7 Kg5 Kg7 8 h6+ Kh7 9 Kh5 Kg8 (or 9...Kh8 10 Kg6 Kg8 11 h7+ Kh8 12 Ne5) 10 Kg6 Kh8 11 h7 d2 12 Ne5 leads to mate.

4	Nf7	Kg8
5	Ne5!	

Not 5 Ng5? Kh8 6 Kd2 Kg8 7 Kc3 Kh8 8 h7 Kg7 9 h6+ Kh8 with a draw, even if it were Black to move.

5	...	Kh7

5...Kh8 6 Nxc4 wins as above.

6 Ng4

96

reaching the required zugzwang position. The finish might be **6...Kh8 7 Kd2 Kh7 8 Kc3 Kg8 9 Nf6+ Kh8 10 h7 Kg7 11 h8=Q+ Kxh8 12 h6 d2 13 Kxd2 c3+ 14 Kc1 c2 15 Ng4** and wins.

116 G. Kasparian, 2nd Pr. Shakhmaty v SSSR, 1948

Win

White is even a pawn down in the initial position so he must attack immediately.

	1 c6	Ne5!

Or *1*) 1...Nf6 2 Bh3+ Kb8 3 Nc5 Ne8 (else 4 Nxa6+, 5 Bc8 and 6 Bb7 mate) 4 Bd7 Nd6 5 Nxa6+ Ka8 6 Nxc7+ Kb8 7 Na6+ Ka8 8 Be6 followed by 9 Bd5 with decisive threats.
2) 1...Nb6 2 Bh3+ Kb8 3 Nc5 Bg3 (if Black doesn't defend c7 White wins as in line 1) 4 Nxa6+ Ka8 5 a4 followed by a5 winning a piece as the knight must stay at b6 to prevent Bc8-b7.

	2 Bh3+	Kb8
	3 Nc5	Nxc6

3...Bd8 (3...Ka8 4 Bc8) 4 Nxa6+ Ka8 5 Kc3 is zugzwang, for example 5...N moves 6 Bc8 or 5...Bf6 6 Nxc7+ Kb8 7 Na6+ Ka8 8 Bg2 winning.

	4 Nd7+	Kb7

4...Ka8 5 Bg2 Kb7 6 Ne5 and 4...Kc8 5 Ne5+ Kb7 6 Bg2 lose at once.

	5 Bg2	

Threat Ne5.

	5 ...	Bg3

The introductory play is over and White has to consider his next step. He can only win by attacking the pinned knight with his king. Black controls the dark squares and his pawns can cover b5, so this attack can only come from d7. Thus White must free d7 by transferring the knight to a4 by means of checks at c5 and a4, but at the moment Nc5+ Kb6 Na4+ allows ...Kb5. White's next move is designed to prevent this defence.

6 Kc4   a5!!

At first sight Black is defenceless against the plan of Nc5—a4 and king to d7, as all the action takes place on the white squares over which Black has no control. However, he has an extremely subtle stalemate defence based on burying his bishop at b8. If Black delays he will be too late, for example 6...Bh2 7 Nc5+ Kb6 8 Na4+ Kb7 9 Bd5 a5 10 Kd3 a6 11 Ke4 Bg1 12 Kf5 Ba7 13 Ke6 Bb8 14 Kd7 Ka7 and White is just in time to take the knight with his king, avoiding the stalemate.

7 Nc5+

If White delays this Black draws, for example 7 Bd5 a6! and now 8 Nc5+ (8 Kd3 is completely pointless since even when his king reaches e6 there is no real threat) Kb6 9 Na4+ Kb7 transposes to the note to White's 9th move.

7 ...   Kb6
8 Na4+   Kb7

In order to understand White's next move it is necessary to consider the following position, which is central to the whole study:

117

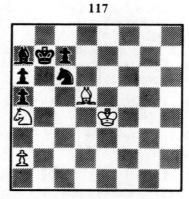

Black to play loses because his bishop must make up its mind whether it is going to b8 or not. After 1...Bb8 2 Nc5+ (or else ....Ka7 draws) Ka7 (2...Kb6 3 Nd7+ Kb5 4 a4+ wins) 3 Bxc6 Kb6 4 Kd5 White emerges with a clear extra piece, while 1...Bg1 2 Kf5 Ba7 3 Ke6 Bb8 4 Kd7 Ka7 5 Kxc6 loses too much time. On the other hand, if White is to play in Diagram 117, he cannot win. Suppose he plays his king to the f-file, 1 Kf5 say. Then 1...Bb8! 2 Nc5+ Ka7! 3 Bxc6 Kb6 4 Nd7+ Kxc6 5 Nxb8+ Kb5 leaves the White king too far away to come back to defend the a-pawn. In order to reach b1 in this line, White's king must start on the e-file (or further left, of course). 1 Kd3 is possible, but Black just replies 1...Bg1 and waits for the king to go to e2 or e4 before returning to a7. There are no waiting moves with bishop or knight and 1 a3 exposes the pawn to attack from Black's bishop after 1...Bg1 2 Kf5 Be3 3 Ke6 Bc1 with a comfortable draw.

From this analysis it becomes clear that the win depends on whether White's king can reach the f-file before Black's bishop arrives at a7. If, for example, White's king is on f3 when Black's bishop is still on g1, White wins. The reason is that ...Ba7 is met by Ke4 with the above zugzwang, so Black must wait by ...Bb2. White then plays Kf4 and Kf5, always being prepared to meet ...Ba7 by Ke4, by which time it is too late for Black and White can simply take the knight by Ke6 and Kd7. In other words the arrival of the king at f3 seals off a7 from Black's bishop.

9 Kd3!!

The obvious 9 Bd5? draws after 9...a6! 10 Kd3 Bf2 11 Ke2 Ba7! and Black has set up his defence in time (12 Kf3 Bb8!). By moving the king first Black is forced to spend an extra tempo bringing his bishop to the a7–g1 diagonal and this costs him the game.

9	...	Bf2

9...a6 10 Ke3! Bh2 (10...Be5 11 Ke4! Bd4 12 Kf5 Ba7 13 Ke6 and Kd7 wins) 11 Bd5 (threat Ke4) Bg1+ 12 Kf4 wins after, for example, 12...Ba7 13 Ke4!.

10 Ke2!

Not 10 Bd5? a6! throwing away all the good work.

10	...	Bg1
11	Bd5	

White must clear e4 for his 14th move so 11 Be4? is bad.

11	...	a6
12	Kf3	Bd4
13	Kf4	

Of course, not 13 Ke4? Ba7 draw.

13	...	Ba7

Or else Kf5–e6–d7 wins out of hand.

14 Ke4!

reaching Diagram 117 with Black to move and therefore winning for White.

Ambitious solvers may now like to tackle Diagrams 131 and 132, which should provide a couple of evenings entertainment, at the very least!

Problems for Solving

118 I. Rusinek, 1st Pr.
Peckover Jubilee Tny, 1976

Draw

119 V. Pachman, 1st Pr.
The Problemist, 1980/1

Draw

120 L. Kubbel, 1st Pr.
Shakhmaty, 1925 – I

Draw

121 L. Kubbel & A. Herbstman,
1st Pr. Troitsky Memorial T., 1937

Draw

122 V. Yakimchik, 1st Pr.
Shakhmaty v SSSR, 1957

Draw

123 A. Gurevich, 1st Pr.
Shakhmaty v SSSR, 1952

Win

124 V. Korolkov, 1st Pr.
Spartak, 1962

Draw

125 V. Pachman, 1st Pr.
Česk. Šach. 1972

Win

126 V. Bron, 2nd Pr.
IV FIDE Tny, 1965

Win

127 J. Gunst, 1st Pr.
A. Hinds Tny, 1946

Win

128 V. Evreinov, 1st Pr.
Zaporoshkia Pravda, 1962

Win

129 V. Halberstadt, 1st Pr.
Thèmes 64, 1958

Win

130 I. Bilek, 1st Pr.
Magyar Sakkelet, 1971

Win

131 Y. Afek, 4th Pr.
Thèmes 64, 1976

Win

132 E. Puhakka, 3rd comm., Problem 1958/9

Win

6 Helpmates

In the first five chapters White was attempting to give mate and Black was trying to stop him, the normal situation in over-the-board play. This familiar situation doesn't hold for most of the problems in the rest of the book. At one time such problems were considered unorthodox and were consigned to the realm of 'Fairy Chess', a rather unfortunate term used to describe non-directmate problems.

Now, however, despite a certain reluctance in some quarters, problems such as helpmates and selfmates are considered as legitimate as the more conventional types, a happy situation since solvers can obtain a great deal of pleasure from them. I have found that over-the-board players easily take to the concept of a helpmate, although this could be just a case of wish-fulfilment! The basic rule governing play in a helpmate is that both sides co-operate to help White mate Black. Although the two sides are working in concert, the moves must still be legal, so that neither player is allowed to move into check, for example. The only competition involved is that between composer and solver! There is a convention that Black moves first in a helpmate, so a helpmate in two consists of four half-moves; Black plays, White plays, Black plays again and finally White mates. There is no special reason why Black should move first in helpmates and not in any other type of problem. This convention is just one of those historical accidents which nobody dares change. There is a second convention, concerning the method of writing down solutions, which is even more confusing for the over-the-board player. The solution of a helpmate in two is written 1 x y 2 z a, where x and z are the Black moves, while y and a are the White moves. This is the reverse of normal practice and it takes a long time to inhibit the reflex which insists that the move immediately after a number must be a White move. Once again, there is no particular reason for this and I only adhere to it to keep in line with other problem books and magazines. It's time to look at our first helpmate:

133 H. Forsberg, 1st Pr. Revista Romana de Sah, 1936

a) Diagram b) BRa6 c) BBa6 d) BNa6 e) BPa6 h≠2

This is a five-in-one problem. After solving the diagram position, replace the piece at a6 with black rook, bishop, knight and pawn in turn to make four more helpmates. The solver's first aim in a helpmate is to find the mating position. Once this is done, the method of reaching the final position from the diagram can be tackled. The second part of the solving process is usually easy in a two-move helpmate, so the main task is to spot the mate. Typically the solver will visualise a series of potential mating positions based on the material in the diagram and check each one to see if it can be reached in the given number of moves.

In Diagram 133 the White king is too far away to take part in a mate, so White is restricted to the use of his rook and knight. These two pieces can mate on their own, but only in a corner, and White's knight is too far from c3 to arrange a corner mate. It follows that all the mates involve a self-block of Black's king. If we imagine a series of mating positions with one self-block, we can work out afterwards which part of the problem we are actually solving! For example, White can mate by Nc1 and Rb3, provided a4 is blocked. The blocking piece can't be a rook or a queen, since the White king would be in check, while a bishop or pawn could take the rook. It follows that this is part d, with a knight at a6, and the solution runs **1 Nc5** (remember that this is a Black move) **Nc1 2 Na4 Rb3**. The White pieces can also mate with Rb4, Nc2 and a block at a2. The piece at a2 must be a bishop (a knight is impossible because it can't reach a2 while b4 is occupied by White's rook), so this solves part c by **1 Bc4 Ne1 2 Ba2 Nc2**. A third position has Nc5 and Ra4, with a block at b2, which could be a rook or a queen. The rook can't reach b2 in two moves with the b-file blocked, so this gives the solution **1 Qf6 Nc5 2 Qb2 Ra4** to the diagram position.

There are just two parts left, b and e. With BRa6, the self-block can't be at a4 or b4 (check to WKg4) and the rook can't reach a2, so it must be at b2 or b3. A mate is certainly possible with BRb3 and White's rook on the

104

a-file, but can this be arranged? After 1 Rb6, White's rook must clear the way from b6 to b3, so the solution runs **1 Rb6 Rb1 2 Rb3 Ra1**. Finally with BPa6, no mates are possible in two moves with BKa3 and BPa4, but Black's king is not obliged to stay at a3 during the solution. Helpmates involving Black king moves are generally tricky to solve, because even a shift of one square completely alters the potential mating nets and makes it hard to guess the final position. In this case, Black's king and pawn can meet halfway at a4 and a5, allowing White to mate by **1 a5 Rb3+ 2 Ka4 Nc5**. Notice that this mate was impossible with any other Black man at a6; a rook or a queen could take at c5, while a bishop or a knight couldn't reach a5 in two moves.

134 L. Lindner, 1st Pr. São Paulo, 1955/6

h≠2

White is powerfully equipped with a queen and bishop; moreover, Black's king is virtually mated already. It seems incredible that White has trouble mating in two moves with Black's help. There are several tantalising tries which fail because one side or the other can't find a decent waiting move, such as 1 e1=R pass 2 Re3 fxg3, or 1 e1=B/N Qe2 2 pass Qe3, or even 1 e1=anything Qxe1 2 pass fxg3. In each case no move can be substituted for pass and still preserve the mate. Aiming for fxg3 seems the most promising idea, which leads us to investigate how else Black can block e3. One possibility is by exd1=N and Ne3, but once again White lacks a waiting move. The solution is to replace exd1=N by cxd1=N, which opens a flight for White's king and leads to the mate **1 cxd1=N Kb1 2 Ne3 fxg3**.

Mate seems close in Diagram 147, but the solution is well hidden. The answer to Diagram 148 will acquaint the solver with an unusual property of pinned pieces.

Helpmates are handicapped by their lack of variations. Since the scope for composing original two-movers with just one variation is obviously very limited, it might appear that composers would quickly exhaust the creative potential of the helpmate. There are various ways round this difficulty. The simplest is to compose helpmates with more than one solution. This sounds like another name for cooks, but one must distinguish between intended and unintended solutions. If a problem is designed to have multiple solutions, the number of solutions must be specified under the diagram along with the condition. If there are more solutions than the specification, the problem is cooked and must be discarded. There should be a close thematic relationship between the solutions, just as there is often a connection between the variations in a directmate problem. Sometimes one comes across a helpmate with no such connection and this makes life hard for the solver, since finding one solution gives no clue to the others. In general, however, uncovering one solution provides a useful hint. Occasionally the thematic link is so strong that one can immediately write down the other solution(s).

135 B. Schauer, 1st Pr. Die Schwalbe, 1974

3 solutions h≠2

White would like to give mate along the third rank, but first Black's rook is in the way, and secondly the bishops at b8 and g8 cover b3 and g3. The idea is to unpin the BRg3 so that it can move off the third rank to interfere with one of the bishops. Since White's b3 rook is itself pinned, White can only do this by playing one of his other pieces to the third rank. After Black's rook moves away, this piece can give a battery mate, simultaneously shutting off the other Black bishop. There are three solutions and three possible unpinning moves, Bf3, Be3 and Nf3. It is a reasonable guess that each solution will contain a different unpinning move. Suppose one solution starts 1 R moves Bf3 2 R moves. The final move must be Bd5. Because Black's rook must be on the b8—f4 diagonal and yet be unable to play back to the third rank, it can only stand at d6. This gives the solution **1 Rd3 Bf3 2 Rd6 Bd5**. Applying the same logic to the other moves reveals the solutions **1 Re3 Nf3 2 Re6 Ne5** and **1 Rf3 Be3 2 Rf7 Bf4**.

106

136 G. Yacoubian, 2nd Pr. Sinf. Scacchist., 1974

2 solutions h≠2

There are two batteries aimed at Black's king and two solutions, so we may suppose a symmetrical relationship between the batteries in the two solutions. The Black queen can take the front piece of each battery and it is worth noting that the BBh7 and RRe1 control both batteries. Guessing that one solution starts 1 Qxc6, White can mate by playing c4 provided that e4 is blocked, the WNf4 moves and the two Black pieces lose control of the battery. The knight can shut off one piece while departing from f4 and e4 can be blocked by the queen moving along the pin-line from c6. This also shuts off the Bh7, which leaves the Re1 to be dealt with by the knight. The solution runs **1 Qxc6 Ne2 2 Qe4 c4.** No further thought is required to find the other solution **1 Qxc3 Ng6 2 Qe3 c7.** since there is an exact symmetry between the pairs of lines a3−f3, a8−f3 and e1−e4, h7−d3.

Cooks are the helpmate composer's worst enemy and he is frequently obliged to add Black pieces which serve no active function, but are present solely as cook-stoppers. Yacoubian's problem is particularly well constructed in that all the pieces except the BBh4 play an essential role in the solution.

If you can find one solution of Diagram 149, the other will follow because the squares c4 and c5, together with the pairs of White men bearing down on them, are used symmetrically in the two solutions. Diagram 150 isn't too hard, but Kricheli's Diagram 151 could take a bit longer.

It is a convention that each solution of a multiple-solution problem should start with a different move. This can lead to useful elimination of possible Black first moves when you have found some of the solutions. If the composer wishes to indicate that his solutions diverge at a later point, he must use a special notation under the diagram. For example, if one finds h≠2, 1.3.1.1 under the position, this means that there are three solutions, with the same first Black move but with three different White first moves. One more example should make this clear: h≠2, 1.2.2.1 would lead the solver to expect the pattern

$$1 \, x \, y \, 2 \, a \, b$$
$$1 \, x \, y \, 2 \, c \, d$$
$$1 \, x \, z \, 2 \, e \, f$$
$$1 \, x \, z \, 2 \, g \, h$$

of moves amongst the four solutions, where a≠c and e≠g, but otherwise the moves a—h may not be distinct. The problems in this book don't use this notation, but you may meet it elsewhere.

137 A. Kárpáti, 1st Pr. Tipografia National T., 1968

2 solutions   h≠2

The White queen is well placed to mate by playing c7, but the g2 pawn must be shifted first. The pawn can't be freed by a bishop move because of the first rank pin, but White can release it by offering his rook at f1. This suggests a solution 1 pass Rf1 2 gxf1=N (the only suitable promotion) c7. Pass must be a queen move, but after most moves she displays a persistent habit of interposing on the long diagonal. In fact h8 is the only satisfactory square. The second solution is similar. If the pawn at h2 disappeared, White could mate by Qh7, so once again White must offer his rook, this time at g1. 1 pass Rxg1+ 2 hxg1=R (again an accurate promotion) Qh7 solves, except for the awkward Black queen! This time she has to flee to a8 to avoid inconveniencing her colleague.

108

138 J. Kricheli, 1st Pr. Priokskai Pravda, 1968

2 solutions h≠2

The connection between the two solutions may be more subtle than the straightforward examples we have seen so far. In this problem the link is between the strategy involved rather than the moves themselves. If Black can block e4, White will mate by Nf4. The knight is the only piece which can reach e4 in time, but Black must take care to choose the correct path. After 1 Nxg5 pass 2 Ne4 Nf4, his aim is achieved, but in taking the g5 pawn Black has deprived White of his only waiting move, gxh6. It follows that the knight must go via d2, as follows: **1 Nd2 gxh6 2 Ne4 Nf4**. In the second solution Black unpins the queen by 1 Ne1. White can then choose between Qc2 followed by Nf4 mate or Qc8 followed by Nf6 mate. In the first case, Black has no waiting move since he must either check or cover f4, so White has to choose **1 Ne1 Qc8**, leaving Black with the waiting move **2 hxg5** allowing **Nf6**. In each solution one player is obliged to decide between two candidate moves, and the wrong one denies the other player a pass move. The roles of White and Black are reversed between the two solutions.

Diagram 152 contains similar strategy.

Twin positions provide another method of introducing variety into a helpmate. Diagram 133 is a good example, so we shall only look at one more twin.

139 B. Ostrukh, 3rd comm. Problemist, 1977/8

a) Diagram   b) g1→b5   h≠2

If White's knight were transparent, a Black queen move would allow
mate by Nc4 or Nf1. In reality this shuts off the bishop or rook. White
must make one of his men redundant by creating self-blocks, either at d3
and e2, or at d1 and e1; then the knight can mate. **1 Qd1** is a good start,
but how can White block e1? The answer is to play **1...Re1 2 fxe1=N** (not
bishop as this gives check) **Nf1.** In the twin we have the analogous solution
1 Qe2 Bd3 2 exd3 Nc4. The capture of White pieces in a helpmate is
paradoxical, because there seems to be no reason why Black should reduce
White's attacking forces. Consequently White sacrifices are often hard to
see in helpmates.

The twin of Diagram 153 is also the result of a queen shift. The solver
must sort out a bewildering array of pins to deliver mate.

The final method of incorporating more than one line of play into a
helpmate is a device known as set play. This is related to the set play of
Chapter 1, but the helpmate form is far more precise. The idea is that in
addition to there being a unique solution to the diagram position when
Black moves first, there is also a unique solution when White moves first.
This second solution is called the set play and it is half a move shorter than
the other one. The composer indicates the presence of set play by an
asterisk under the diagram. Readers may be wondering why it isn't
possible to derive a solution to the helpmate by playing an initial Black
waiting move and following on with the set play. The reason is that in
helpmates with set play, all Black's legal first moves must disrupt the set
mate or there will be cooks.

110

140 N. Petrović, 1st Pr. Feenschach 8TT, 1953

h≠2*

Mate by the a8 bishop is overwhelmingly likely, but the g2 pawn blocks the diagonal. In the set play, with White moving first, he must interfere with the bishop to allow the pawn to move. Sinie the rook is pinned, the set play must be **1...Kd5 2 g1=B** (to avoid being able to interpose on the diagonal) **Kd6** (to prevent d7—d5). Black to play has no waiting move to preserve this variation. 1 Bg1 is the only plausible first move; now the rook is unpinned, but there is no point releasing the pawn by Rf3 if the pawn can't advance. The other way to remove the pawn is by **1 Bg1 Rxg2**. If Black had a pass move White could mate by moving along the rank, but there is no such move, so he must play **2 Bh2+ Rg3**. The switchback by the king in the set play is echoed by the rook in the solution.

There are two situations in which set play is particularly effective. The first occurs when there is an echo between the two final positions; often the pieces are all shifted in the same direction by one square, so finding the set play helps to find the solution. The second situation is when Black's lack of a waiting move forces a total change of plan, when the solution and the set play have no connection whatsoever. The next position is a particularly dramatic example.

141 P. Leibovici, 1st Pr. Revista Romana de Sah, 1948

h≠4*

Symmetrical positions always pose the question as to why a solution which works on one side of the board fails on the other. Because the chessboard has an even number of squares, it isn't possible to have perfect lateral symmetry. There is always an extra file on one side and the extra squares will allow a move which invalidates one potential solution. Often the crucial move will be buried deep in a side-variation which the solver might have overlooked but for the symmetrical diagram. See position 214 for an unusual symmetry-breaking mechanism. Returning to Diagram 141, there is an obvious mating position with BKh8, WPh6 and WNf7. Black's king takes three moves to reach h8, so this provides the set play **1...h4 2 Kf8 h5 3 Kg7 h6+ 4 Kh8 Nf7.** Black can't lose a tempo because his king is confined to the snaky path e7−f8−g7−h8 by the knights. Maybe the king heads in the opposite direction in the solution? If Black takes a knight, mate is virtually impossible, so the first move must be Kd8. Black will want to use the White pawns, but from d8 the closest he can approach in three moves is to a5. As it happens this is sufficient, since there is mating position with Pc3, Nc4 and Nc7. The move-order is **1 Kd8 c3 2 Kc7 Nfe8+** (not Nd5+ as the king must move to b6) **3 Kb6 Nc7 4 Ka5 Nc4.**

Solvers are warned that in Diagrams 154 and 155 the solution differs dramatically from the set play.

The previous position provides a link with the rest of the chapter, which deals with longer helpmates. As the length increases so does the difficulty, but only to a limited extent. Long helpmates usually contain few pieces, since with Black's co-operation any decent White force can deliver mate within a few moves. Finding the solution usually depends more on logic than intuition and the main interest for the solver lies in working out why the **order** of moves is unique. Sometimes knowing that it must be unique is itself a valuable clue, as in the next position.

142 K. Ébersz & P. Takács, 1st Pr. Magyar Sakkvilag, 1934

h≠5

There is no hope of mating the king near its present square, so his majesty must go for a little walk. But where? If there is no special clue, one should examine diagonal paths first. The reason is that if the king were to be mated, say, at e4, then there would be three possible routes enabling the king to arrive in four moves, namely d7–e6–e5–e4, d7–d6–e5–e4 and c7–d6–e5–e4. There is no visible reason why he should have to traverse one particular path. In contrast, there is just one way for the king to arrive at h3 in five moves, so the uniqueness problem has been solved automatically. Positions with a White R+B combination often lead to double checkmates from a battery. With the king on h3, for example, White could arrange Bd7, Rf5 for Rf3 mate, or Rb3, Bd3 for Bf5 mate. Thus h3 is a promising destination, but there is the problem of crossing the f5 square. After 1 Kd7, White has two moves to remove both guards from f5, but the bishop presents difficulties. One try is 1 Kd7 R along rank 2 Ke6 Bg8+ 3 Kf5. Indeed, if the d5 pawn were absent, White could finish off by 3...Bb3 4 Kg4 Ra3 (having chosen a2 at move 1) 5 Kh3 Be6. As it is the g8 bishop can't come to the third rank in one move. The other formation requires Be6 and Rf5, but the rook was forced to quit the f-file at move one so this takes too many moves. There is just one other possibility, which is to shield the bishop by 1 Kd7 Bb1 2 Ke6 Rc2 3 Kf5. From b1 the bishop **can** reach the third rank in one move, so White mates by 3...Rc3+ 4 Kg4 Bd3 5 Kh3 Bf5. The theme is clear enough; first the rook eclipses the bishop, then the roles are reversed and the bishop eclipses the rook. This is an example of critical play closely related to the Indian theme of Chapter 4.

Despite its age, Diagram 156 is well worth solving. Sam Loyd's original position had both extraneous pieces and cooks, but one of the cooks was far more attractive than the intended solution, so it has been rearranged to turn the cook into the solution!

2 solutions h≠4

A mate is possible with just three Black and four White moves, for example 1...Ne6 2 Nc4 Nc5 3 Na3 Ne4 4 Nc2 Nc3 or 1...Ne6 2 Nd3 Nf4 3 Nc1 Ng2 4 Ne2 Ne3. In each case there are several possible paths for the White knight, but there is always the same problem — no Black waiting move. The b2 knight **must** take three moves to reach the white squares c2/e2; a rook or king move would destroy the mating net so the Na8 offers the only hope. However, White can't afford a Black knight check forcing his king to move and wasting a tempo when there are none to spare. The only way of resolving this dilemma is to take the knight when it delivers its check. There are two solutions and two possible checks:

1) c7: White can't reach e3 from c7 in two moves, so this leads to a position with BNc2 and WNc3. White's path must be e6—c7—b5—c3 and Black's is uniquely determined to avoid giving a check, so the solution is **1 Nc4 Ne6 2 Nc7+ Nxc7 3 Na3 Nb5 4 Nc2 Nc3**.

2) b6: The a4 pawn prevents the knight reaching c3, so White must mate by Ne3. The solution is **1 Nd3 Nd7 2 Nb6+ Nxb6 3 Nc1 Nc4 4 Ne2 Ne3**.

The problem in Diagram 157 is the lack of **White** waiting moves.

In very long helpmates the mating position must be found before tackling anything else.

144 E. Albert, 2nd Pr. IV FIDE T. 1967

h≠5

It is possible to mate in the corner, with the Black knight standing next to the king, but this takes too many moves. Hence the mate must be on the edge of the board and there is only one type of mating position, that with BKe1, BBd1, BNe2 and WKg2, WNf3. It takes too many moves for the knight to reach f3, but d3 is more accessible and we can reflect the mate to give BKe1, BBf1, BNe2 and WKc2, WNd3. White needs five moves and Black needs four to reach this position, so there is one spare Black move. However, White's king must cross d3 to reach c2 (notice the diagonal path again) and the Black bishop stands at e2 or f1 the whole time, covering d3. If the bishop moves off the f1—a6 diagonal Black wastes two moves, when arranging BBf1, BNe2 takes too long. The solution is to use the reserve tempo to play the bishop to a6, when the knight can interfere at b5. The move-order is easily found to be **1 Ba6 Ke4 2 Nb5 Kd3 3 Nc3+** (not 3 Nd4+? and the king can't go to c2) **Kc2 4 Bf1 Nf2 5 Ne2 Nd3.**

145 G. Neukomm, 2nd Pr. Magyar Sakk. Társaság, 1945

h≠7

There are two possible mating positions, first, WKb6, WBb7 v BKa8, BNb8, and secondly WKc7, WBb7 v BKa8, BNa7. In either case there may also be a Black rook on the board somewhere. We leave it to the reader to discover why the first mating position cannot arise as a solution to the problem and concentrate on the second possibility.

Even though we know the destination, it's still easy to get lost! White requires seven moves, so he can't afford to waste a single tempo. Assume first that Black doesn't castle. He needs four king moves, two knight moves and a rook move to make way for the king to go to a8, so he too has just enough tempi. The rook can't reach b7 in one move, so White's final move Bb7 isn't a capture. The last move must be Bc8—b7, so White must play Kc7 by move six at the latest. Black's king must be on a8 by his sixth move, so he has already made four king moves and one rook move. It follows that Black's last move is a knight move, 7 Nb5—a7 in fact. But in this case White's Kc7 was illegal.

This proves that Black castles in the solution, so the first move is 1 Nb5. There is a temptation to allow castling by playing the White king to the h3—c8 diagonal, but this costs a tempo, hence the bishop must move to allow castling. Since it must reach b7 in two moves the solution begins 1 Nb5 Bg2, so White's final move is Bg2xRb7. It takes two moves for the rook to travel from d8 to b7, accounting for all Black's moves. As the White king is on c7 by move six, Black's final move must be Rb8-b7+. White's sixth move must be Kc6-c7+, or else Black's king would have stood in check, hence Black's previous move was Nb5—a7+. In particular, Black mustn't play Na7 too early. We now have enough information to write down the solution: **1 Nb5 Bg2 2 0—0—0 Kf3!** (not 2...Ke3 3 Kb8 Ke4 4 Ka8 and White is stuck because his king can't move to d5) **3 Kb7! Ke4 4 Rb8** (just in time to allow access to d5) **Kd5 5 Ka8 Kc6 6 Na7+ Kc7+ 7 Rb7+ Bxb7.**

I have included Diagram 158 as an example of how hard a helpmate can be to solve, even if there aren't many pieces on the board. The Dutch grandmaster John van der Wiel solved it in 15 minutes — can you do better? Diagram 159 is a promotion fantasy.

The final helpmate was composed by a computer which compiled a database of K+N v K+N positions, searching for sound helpmates. Dr Mertes was the programmer, so until computer's lib arrives his name appears over the diagram.

146 Dr. H. Mertes, 3rd Pr. Schach-Echo, 1974

h≠7

Mate is only possible with the Black king in a corner and the knight standing next door. a8 looks a likely spot since it takes exactly seven Black moves to bring the K to a8 and N to a7. Thus Black's last move must be Kb7/b8—a8 or Nb5—a7. After Black's seventh move White's king must be at c7 with his knight about to arrive at b6, but in this case the three moves mentioned above were all illegal, proving that the mate cannot be arranged at a8. The only other possible corner is a1, since the others require too many Black moves. It takes six moves for the Black men to take up their positions at a1 and b1, but what is Black's first move? It looks like Nb1, but in this case the same logic that we applied to the a8 corner proves that mate is impossible. Black cannot afford to lose more than one tempo, so the first move must be 1 Ke6!. The White king must move out of the way to allow Kd5, but the obvious attempts don't work, for example 1 Ke6 Ke3 2 Kd5 Nd4 3 Kc4 Ke4 4 Kc3 Kd5 5 Kb2 Kc4 6 Ka1 Kb3 7 Nb1 Nc2 requires an illegal fifth move by White, while 1 Ke6 Ke3 2 Kd5 Kd2 3 Kc4 pass 4 Kb3 Nd4+ 5 Ka2 Kc3 6 Ka1 Kb3 7 Nb1 Nc2 would be fine except that White has no pass move. Nevertheless, this second line provides the necessary clue, for White can lose a tempo by choosing a different first move. The solution runs **1 Ke6! Kd3! 2 Kd5 Ke3 3 Kc4 Kd2 4 Kb3 Nd4+ 5 Ka2 Kc3 6 Ka1 Kb3 7 Nb1 Nc2**.

Problems for Solving

147 Z. Zilahi,
Magyar Sakkélet, 1956

h≠2

148 S. Eberle, 1st Pr.
Problem, 1960

h≠2

149 C. Feather, 1st Pr.
Mat, 1976

2 solutions   h≠2

150 V. Schneider, 1st Pr.
Schach-Echo, 1966

2 solutions   h≠2

151 J. Kricheli, 1st Pr.
Shakhmaty v SSSR, 1972

2 solutions   h≠2

152 J. Kricheli, 1st Pr.
WCCT, 1970

2 solutions   h≠2

153 K. Gandew, 1st Pr.
Novi temi, 1972

a) Diagram b) e7→f6 h≠2

154 P. Benko,
Berliner Morgenpost, 1970

h≠3*

155 P. Takács, 3rd Pr.
Chess Amateur, 1923

h≠3*

156 S. Loyd,
Chess Monthly, 1860 (version)

h≠3

157 G. Páros, =1st Pr.
Magyar Sakkvilag, 1945

h≠3

158 E. Masanek, 3 h.m.
Die Schwalbe, 1962

h≠3

159 T. Kardos, 1st Pr. Budapester Sportbunda Th. Ty., 1956

h≠7

7 Selfmates and reflexmates

As was the case with helpmates, these problems feature the same familiar pieces moving in the same way as usual; only the objective has changed. In a selfmate White is trying to force Black to deliver mate, while Black is doing his best to frustrate White's suicidal tendencies.

A simple example will make this idea clear.

160 L. Ugren, 2nd Pr. Makuc-Moder M. T., 1970

s≠2

Black can only move his queen, so if White is to force Black to mate him, the most likely method is to deflect Black's queen by a forcing sacrifice, for example if 1...Qh8 then 2 Qb2+ forces 2...Qxb2 mate. Similarly 1...Qh6 2 Qc1+ forces 2...Qxc1 mate. Are there any safe squares for the Black queen? 1...Qh1/h5/g4 are met by 2 Qd1+, 1...Qh2/f6/h8/d4 by 2 Qb2+, 1...Qh6/g5/f4 by 2 Qc1+ and 1...Qxg3 by 2 Qxd3+, so the only two safe squares are h3 and e4. Even these bolt-holes would vanish if the g3 rook were absent, since White could then play 2 Qxd3+. This suggests a rook move along the g-file as the key. It doesn't matter that this allows the Black queen access to two more squares, f2 and e1, since these are already dealt with by 2 Qb2+ and 2 Qc1+ respectively. The only problem is that White must be careful not to move his rook to a square which interferes with one of the set mates. g1 and g2 can be eliminated at once since they destroy the set mates at c1 and b2. 1 Rg4? fails to 1...Qh5! and the next three squares have the same defect of blocking a crucial diagonal from the h-file, i.e. 1 Rg5? Qh6, 1 Rg6?

Qh7 and 1 Rg7? Qh8. Thus only **1 Rg8!** is correct, putting Black in zugzwang.

Although a selfmate in two is half a move longer than a directmate in two, Black's last move is usually completely forced, so the complexity is just about the same. We have already seen some rather simple try-play in the very first problem, and it is common for short selfmates to contain tries. The next example is more subtle.

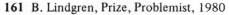

161 B. Lindgren, Prize, Problemist, 1980

s≠2

Black has a half-battery aimed at the White king, but the first point to note is that Black has pass moves such as ...Bg3 and ...h3, so the key must carry a threat. The only plausible threat is a sacrifice at g6, so we can immediately reduce the possible keys to 1 Bg8 (threat 2 Qg6) and 1 Qh1/h2/f2/e3 (threat 2 Bg6).

1 Qf2 is ridiculous as Black just takes the queen, and 1 Bg8 allows 1...Ref2 giving the White king a flight at h4. Deciding between the other three moves is more tricky. In general, Black has four defences to the threat of Bg6+. He has two ways of giving the White king a flight, by 1...Ref2 or 1...Rff2, and two ways of covering g6 with his rook, 1...Rg2 and 1...Re6. Let's look at 1 Qh2 first. This deals with 1...Rg2/e6 since White can reply 2 Rxf3+ forcing 2...Bxf3, and 1...Ref2 gives White a choice of moves, since both 2 Qf4+ and 2 Qh3+ force Black to take the queen and mate. Unfortunately 1...Rff2! refutes 1 Qh2, since White cannot deflect the e2 rook to a square covering h4. 1 Qh1 doesn't suffer from this problem, as 1...Rff2 2 Qe4+ forces 2...Rxe4 mate, while the variation 1...Ref2 2 Qh3+ is preserved. 1...Rg2 interferes with the queen's guard of f3, allowing 2 Rxf3+ Bxf3, but Black can improve by 1...Re6! and White has no reply.

Thus **1 Qe3!** is correct, physically preventing the defence 1...Re6, and leading to the three variations **1...Ref2 2 Qf4+**, **1...Rff2 2 Qe4+** and **1...Rg2 2 Qg5+**, the last line being a surprising change.

In Diagram 169 the action centres on the various lines leading to g2, while Diagram 170 features changed play.

Long selfmates can be very hard indeed to solve and in fact this is probably the most difficult type of problem, particularly if the mating position is obscure. Even three-movers can be tricky, as the next position illustrates.

162 E. E. Westbury, 1st Pr. BCF Tny, 1930

s≠3

Black has just five legal moves, but it is very unlikely that 1...Bg2 will seriously weaken Black's position, so we are looking for a key with a threat. Where does one start with a position like this, where there is no obvious theme, idea or mating position? Often the only way to make progress is to explore the effect of any forcing moves at White's disposal. We have already seen that sacrificial deflections play a major role in self-mates, so it is helpful to see if any are possible. 1 Qd5+ forces 1...Bxd5+, which suggests the idea of playing a3, taking away the flight and preparing this sacrifice. Alas, there is a major objection in that the knight at b6 stands ready to capture Black's bishop at d5, and if the knight moves away then Black can take the sacrificed queen with his king. 1 Bf5+ is another forcing move, unpinning Black's bishop to take at c1, but at first sight this looks even less hopeful, since it is hard to see how ...Bxc1 could deliver mate. At this point a small flash of inspiration is necessary to see that if White plays 1 Ka3 and 2 b3, then Black is powerless to prevent 3 Bf5+ forcing a mating reply. So **1 Ka3** is a candidate, threat 2 b3. Black only has two moves to meet this threat, 1...Rxg3, so as to interpose at c3 after 2 b3 Rxf3 3 Bf5+, and 1...Bxf3, to meet 2 b3 by 2...Be4. The first leads to the variation **1...Rxg3 2 Bf5+ Bxc1 3 Qc3+ Rxc3**, while the second is answered by **1...Bxf3 2 b4+ Kc6 3 Bb3+ Bxc1.**

This problem was composed over half a century ago, and typically for older problems, much of the merit lies in its surprising key. Diagrams 193 and 200 in Chapter 9 show a more modern style of selfmate com-

123

position, in which classical directmate themes are transferred to the new domain.

Selfmates are particularly suitable for underpromotion effects. It is possible to show various extreme tasks, such as eight underpromotions to a knight, in selfmate form, but it is questionable whether the mere striving after numerical achievement can be truly artistic. The next problem displays a purely formal effect in an open, attractive setting.

163 W. Jørgensen, 1st Pr. Feenschach, 1968

s≠3

White must try to induce the Bg1 to move, without at any stage being able to interpose a piece on the first rank himself. Black can only move his pawn and it has four possible first moves. The e7 pawn is about to promote and there are four choices of promotion piece. We can guess that the theme will be the four moves of the f7 pawn met by the four promotions of the e7 pawn. The only Black move capable of allowing e8=Q+ is 1...fxe6, freeing the c7 square for Black's king. After 1...fxe6 2 e8=Q+ Kc7, what can White's final move be? Not a capture at e6, aiming to put Black in zugzwang, for then White could interpose at e1, while otherwise White cannot prevent ...e5. So White's third move cannot be a waiting move and is therefore a forcing check deflecting the Bg1. The only possibility is 3 Qc5+, which works provided the key covers b7. This indicates **1 Rb8** and we only have to check the variations

    1...fxe6 2 e8=Q+ Kc7 3 Qc5+
    1...fxg6 2 e8=R g5 3 g4
    1...f6 2 e8=B+ Kxe6 3 Rb5
    1...f5 2 e8=N f4 3 Nxf4

to verify that this is correct.

The promotions in Diagram 171 take quite a bit of sorting out!

Moving on to long selfmates, many of the comments in Chapter 4 apply here. Systematic manoeuvres, foreplans, etc., are just as popular in long

124

selfmates as in more-movers and we need not cover the same ground again. Two examples should suffice.

164 G. von Broecker, London Chess Fortnightly, 1892

s≠9

This is an entertaining study in the field of corresponding squares. The only pieces which will move in the course of play are the white-squared bishops and the rook. White wants to make Black play BxB mate or PxB mate, but he must take care to keep his rook at h8, or to the left of his bishop, otherwise Black can take the bishop with impunity. It is easy to see that the final position must have WBc6, BBb7 and WRh8, with Black to move, but how can this be forced?

First of all, suppose that the rook is at h8. Then any position in which the bishops lie on adjacent squares, with Black to move, will lead to selfmate in 5 at most. For example, with WBg2 and BBf3 play runs 1...Be4 2 Bf3 Bd5 3 Be4 Bc6 4 Bd5 Bb7 5 Bc6 Bxc6 mate.

Now suppose that we have WBd5 and BBb7. Where must the WR be, with Black to move? The rook must be prepared to move to h8 after ...Bc6 by Black, so it cannot stand at h8 now. It follows that the rook must lie at c8. So with WRc8, any position in which the bishops are separated by one square leads to selfmate in 6 at most, for example, WBg2 and BBe4 might run 1...Bd5 2 Bf3 Bc6 3 Be4 Bb7 (if Black moves to the square adjacent to the WB, the reply is always Rh8) 4 Bd5 Bc6 5 Rh8 Bb7 6 Bc6 Bxc6 mate.

With WBe4 and BBb7, White needs to reply to ...Bc6 with Rc8 and to ...Bd5 with Rh8, so d8 is the only square. Any position with two squares between the bishops and WRd8 leads to selfmate in 7 at most. The same logic applies to prove that with WRe8 and three squares between the bishops, we have selfmate in 8, while finally with four squares between and WRf8, it is selfmate in 9 at most.

Thus the key is **1 Rf8** and although there are many variations, the following two are typical: **1...Bc6 2 Re8 Bd5 3 Rd8 Be4 4 Rc8 Bf3 5 Rh8**

125

etc., and **1...Bc6 2 Re8 Bb7 3 Bf3 Bc6 4 Rd8 Bb7 5 Be4 Bc6 6 Rc8 Bb7 7 Bd5 Bc6 8 Rh8 Bb7 9 Bc6 Bxc6 mate**.

165 M. Zucker, 1st Pr. Schach, 1975

s≠13

If only d3 were blocked by the rook, White could force immediate selfmate by 1 Qb5+. How can the rook be transferred with gain of tempo? A suitable foreplan is necessary. White must alternately lift his guard of a3 and check, since if Black is allowed to play ...a4 the mating net vanishes. The only way a rook move could do either of these things is by playing to e7, cutting off the guard of a3 from a bishop at f8. The first step is thus to move the bishop to f8, by **1 Be3 Ka3 2 Bc1+ Ka4 3 Bh6 Ka3 4 Bf8+ Ka4** (now the rook can zigzag to d3) **5 Re7 Ka3 6 Rd7+ Ka4 7 Rd6 Ka3 8 Rd3+ Ka4** (finally the mating net must be restored by reversing the initial bishop manoeuvre) **9 Bh6 Ka3 10 Bc1+ Ka4 11 Be3 Ka3 12 Bc5+ Ka4 13 Qb5+ axb5 mate**. Compare this with Diagram 91.

You may find Diagram 172 quite a challenge, but once you have discovered the tempo-gaining mechanism of Diagram 173, the rest shouldn't be too hard.

Readers may have noticed that selfmates often have ugly, congested positions. This is an inevitable consequence of the need to control the freedom of both kings. The same necessity introduces many constructional difficulties for the composer and makes it hard for him to incorporate a large number of interesting variations. Therefore a new type of problem has been devised called the reflexmate, designed to keep the best features of the selfmate while allowing more open positions. The aims of the two players are exactly the same as in the selfmate, but there is an extra rule, namely that if either side can mate in one then he must. Thus White's objective is to reach a position where Black can (and therefore must) mate in one, without at any stage allowing Black to put him in a position where he can mate in one himself.

Here is an example.

166 E. Visserman, 1st Pr. Problem, 1956

r≠2

There is no danger that White will be able to mate Black, so we can concentrate on arranging for Black to be able to mate White. The most promising potential mating move is ...c1=Q, which is capable of trapping the White king on a variety of squares, such as e1, e2, e3, f1 and g1. There are two ways White can set up this mate. He can either play his king to the mating square, threatening to move the bishop away (to allow the Ra2 to cover f2), or he can move the bishop first. Thus there are several candidate keys, such as 1 Ke1 (threats 2 Bf1/d3/d1/xc4), 1 Ke3 (threat 2 Bf1), 1 Kg1 (threat 2 Bd1), 1 Bf1 (threats 2 Ke1/e2/e3), 1 Bd1 (threats 2 Ke1/f1/g1/e3), 1 Bd3 (threats 2 Ke1/f1), 1 Bf3 (threat 2 Ke2), 1 Bg4 (threat 2 Ke2) and 1 Bh5 (threat 2 Ke2). Deciding which one is right requires a good deal of patience!

First, 1 Bh5 unpins the Black knight to allow 1...Nf1! (not 1...Nf3/g4 interfering with the Bh5 to allow 2 Kf1 c1=Q). In all the other cases Black's only possible defence is to promote prematurely at move 1, often to a minor piece. In this way Black avoids being forced to make a queen by the operation of the reflex rule at move 2. For example, 1 Ke1? is met by 1...c1=B! (not 1...c1=N? 2 any Rxe2) and White cannot arrange a mate. Similarly 1 Ke3? c1=B+! (not 1...c1=N and Black will still have to play 2...Rxe2), but on the other hand 1 Kg1 c1=B? allows 2 B any Be3, so the refutation of 1 Kg1? is 1...c1=N!.

Turning now to the bishop moves, 1 Bf1? c1=N+! (1...c1=B+? 2 Kg1 Be3 and 1...c1=R+? 2 Kg1 Rxf1 are wrong) leaves White with no good reply. 1 Bd1? copes with 1...c1=R+ 2 Kg1, 1...c1=B+ 2 Kg1, 1...c1=N+ 2 Ke1 and 1...cxd1=B+ 2 Ke3, but not with 1...cxd1=N+!. 1 Bd3? c1=R+! (not 1...c1=Q+? 2 Kg3 Qf4, nor 1...c1=N+? 2 Ke1 Nxd3, nor 1...c1=B+? 2 Kg1 Be3) is adequate. 1 Bg4? is surprisingly refuted by 1...c1=Q+! (not 1...c1=R+? 2 Ke3 Rxc3, while the bishop and knight promotions are answered as before) since 2 Kg3 Qf4 isn't mate now that Black has lost control of h3. Thus Black has been forced to resort to five different

127

promotions to demolish the various White tries, but **1 Bf3!** leaves him with no resource, for example **1...c1=Q+ 2 Kg3 Qf4**, **1...c1=R+ 2 Ke3 Rxc3**, **1...c1=B+ 2 Kg1 Be3** or **1...c1=N+ 2 Ke1 Nd3**. The manner in which the tries induce unique refutations is well worth studying.

In some reflexmates the condition that White must mate in one if he can assumes major importance.

167 J. Trillon, 1st Pr. Thèmes 64, 1975

r≠8

White has to allow Black to mate on the b1–g6 diagonal, without at any stage giving Black the chance to allow a mate on the b3–g8 diagonal! There is a choice of first moves, but **1 Bc2** is the most plausible because the threat of 2 Bf5 severely restricts Black's options. 1...Bc6 2 Be4, 1...Bf5 2 Bd3 and 1...bxc2+ 2 Ka2 all lead to immediate mate, so **1...Be8** is forced. White must be careful, for example 2 Bf5? Bc6 forces 3 Be6 mate. Once again White can confine Black's choices by **2 Be4** preventing 2...Bxg6 3 Bf5, 2...Bc6 3 f5 and 2...Bd7 3 Bf5. **2...Bf7** is the only move. Black's defence is based on oscillating between f7 and e8. Since ...Bxg6 is never mate because of the f4 pawn, it is hard to see how this defence can be broken down. The only method is to answer ...Bf7 by Be6, forcing the sequence ...Bxe6 f5 ...Bxf5. In order to reach e6 in reply to ...Be8–f7, the bishop must have come from d7, since if it had come from c8 or f5 Black could have played ...Bc6 forcing Be6 mate. Thus White's bishop must head for d7, but by a roundabout route, since White must first deal with Black's threat of 3...Bd5. The solution is to play **3 Bd3!**, utilising the pawn at b5 to prevent 3...Bc4 (met by 4 f5). Black is forced to continue **3...Be8**, when White approaches d7 by **4 Bxb5**. Now 4...Bd7/c6 5 Ba4, 4...Bxg6+ 5 Bd3 and 4...Bxb5 5 f5 must be avoided, so **4...Bf7** is forced, threatening 5...Bc4. Fortunately White can hide by **5 Ba4!**, and after **5...Be8** (5...B elsewhere 6 f5) arrive at the required position by **6 Bd7 Bf7 7 Be6 Bxe6 8 f5 Bxf5 mate**. The duel between the two bishops is reminiscent of Diagram 92. You may like to check that 1 Be2? fails to 1...Be6! when 2 Bxb5 is

128

impossible because of 2...Bc4, and that 1 Bf3? Bc8! forces White to retreat his bishop to meet the threat of ...Bxa6.

Finally, just as with any other sort of problem, constructional defects can give the key away immediately.

168 J. Burbach, 1st Pr. Probleemblad, 1978

r≠2

Black has the terrible threat of ...Rg6, forcing Qxg6 mate. White has very few legal moves which nullify ...Rg6 and only one carries a plausible threat, namely **1 d3** intending 2 Rb4 axb4. The variations are 1...Kc2 2 Na1+ bxa1=Q, 1...Rb5 2 Na1 (not 2 Nc1? as the queen covers c1) bxa1=Q and 1...Rb7 2 Nc1 (not 2 Na1? as the bishop can interpose at a2) bxc1=Q. It is surprising that a problem with the reflexmate equivalent of an unprovided check and a couple of mundane variations should be awarded a first prize.

Diagram 174 doesn't have any such defects and may prove quite a challenge.

Problems for Solving

169 E. Ivanov, 1st Pr.
Mattison Memorial Tny, 1970

s≠2

170 S. Seider, 1st Pr.
Israel Ring Tny, 1975

s≠2

171 H. Bettmann, 1st Pr.
Babson-Task T. 1926

s≠3

172 F. Prokop, 1st Pr.
Tidskrift för Schack, 1952

s≠5

173 N. Ivanovsky & E. Harichev,
1st Pr. Problemista TT, 1973

s≠40

174 G. Anderson, 1st Pr.
The Problemist, 1976/7

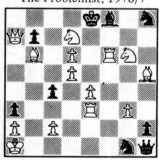

r≠2

130

8 Series problems

In this chapter one of the basic rules of chess is modified. Normally White and Black move alternately, but until the end of the chapter one of the players makes a whole series of consecutive moves, while his poor opponent only gets to make a single move at the end. By far the most common type of series problem is the serieshelpmate, so we shall concentrate on these and give the other types just a brief mention near the end. A serieshelpmate in n moves consists of n consecutive Black moves designed to reach a position in which White can mate in one. Apart from the usual requirement that all the moves must be legal, there is only one restriction on Black's freedom during his series; he mustn't give check, except possibly on the last move of the series.

175 J. Mortensen, 5th comm. BCF Tny, 1962/3

sh≠13

If White were to play then he could mate in one by Bxf3. However, Black has to make thirteen consecutive moves first and he must destroy the set mate with his very first move, since 1 fxe2 is forced. Solving a series problem requires two steps; first, the final position must be determined and then the method of reaching it must be found. Some problems have obvious final positions, but the sheer length can still pose difficulties. In Mortensen's composition almost all the work lies in the first part, since the method of arriving at the final position is clear enough. After 1 fxe2 Black needs three further moves to free the Black king from the h5 square, which leaves nine. It takes ten to journey to d1, so this cannot be the mating square. h1 requires even more, so the most promising squares are h5 and h6, with suitable Black blocking men on the g-file. In this case the mating moves would be Qh3 and Qh4 respectively. A Black piece must play to g5 to free the king, but if the mate is to be at h6 the blocking pieces must be at g6 and g7. It seems more economical of time to mate at h5, since the g5 piece, which must be a rook, doesn't have to move for the mate. So we start by **1 fxe2 2 e1=R 3 Re5 4 Rg5 5 Kg6 6 h5 7 h4 8 h3 9 h2**, but now we have to decide which piece to promote to. Just to set up the mate gives Black a choice between Q, R or B at g6, but a queen or bishop would give an illegal check to the White king from g6, so the solution must finish **10 h1=R 11 Rh6 12 Kh5 13 Rhg6 Qh3**.

Two main themes stand out in series problems. These are systematic manoeuvres and underpromotions. A typical manoeuvre involves a redeployment to protect one or other king from check at the crucial moment, followed by the reverse of the manoeuvre to set up the final mate. Alternatively, pieces may perform lengthy tours before returning to their original squares by a different route.

176 K. Smulders, 2nd Pr. Feenschach 24 TT, 1969

sh≠14

If Black's king were at a5, White could mate by Rb5. It takes fourteen moves for Black to complete the journey by circumnavigating the White rook. At each stage the knight has to shield the king from check. The solution runs **1 Nc5 2 Nb7 3 Kb8 4 Kc7 5 Na5** (the composer has used the White king to make sure that the knight's path to the next square is unique, so that here, for example, the knight cannot reach c6 via d8) **6 Nc6 7 Kd6 8 Kc5 9 Na7** (here uniqueness is forced because Black cannot take at d4) **10 Nb5 11 Kb4 12 Ka5 13 Nc7 14 Na6** (returning at last!) **Rb5**. Note the WPf6, which prevents a cook by playing the king to h8 and mating by Rh6.

The next example is similar, but more elaborate.

177 J. Kricheli, 1st Pr. Feenschach, 1966

sh≠25

The c-pawn can promote to a bishop or knight without checking the White king. There must be at least one blocking piece on the h-file to shield the king from the rook, so we are looking for a mating position with Q+N v K+B or N. There is in fact just one such position (although it is not easy to find), with BKa5, BBb4 and mate by Qa6. A black-squared bishop in the final position implies that the c-pawn will promote to a bishop. To reach a5, Black's king must first be freed from the top right corner by the interposition of a shield at f7. Therefore Black must free the h3 bishop by a shield at h2 in order to reach f7. The solution starts **1 c5 2 c4 3 c3 4 c2 5 c1=B 6 Be3 7 Bg1 8 Bh2 9 Bf1 10 Bc4 11 Bf7 12 Kf8 13 Ke8** (now the king must go to d8, so a shield is needed at e7; the bishop must return to h3 to free the Bh2) **14 Bc4 15 Bf1 16 Bh3 17 Bg1 18 Bc5 19 Be7 20 Kd8 21 Kc7 22 Bd6** (the final shield) **23 Kb6 24 Ka5 25 Bb4 Qa6.** The elaborate bishop manoeuvres were needed to shield both kings.

Diagrams 181 and 182 involve this type of plan. In each case you should decide on the final position before moving the pieces. Diagram 183 is rather different. Once again the final position is fairly obvious, but the solver is in serious danger of going round in circles!

We move on to consider series problems depending on promotions. Many of these are designed to show an extreme combination of promotions, such as six promotions to a bishop or five to a rook. In most cases the final position stands out clearly, and the main problem lies in promoting to the correct pieces and getting the move-order right. The solver's main weapon is arithmetic. Knowing the length of the problem and how many moves the pawns will take to promote, it is easy to work out the number left for the promoted pieces to reach their destination squares. It is usually possible to work out exactly which moves will be played before you touch the pieces on the board. This only leaves the move-order, but by working out which moves have to be postponed until near the end it usually drops into place quickly enough.

133

The following example, which holds the length record for a series-helpmate with White having just K+P, should make the method clear.

178 C. Jonsson, 1st Pr. BCM TT, 1972/3

sh≠35

The Black king will be mated on c6 by axb5, with Black men on b7, c7, d7, d6, d5, c5 and b5. The piece at b7 must be a bishop, so Black must promote a pawn on a white square, which has to be d1. Thus the only Black man which could have blocked a square without moving does, in fact, promote, and so all the pawns promote. This takes twenty moves. Three are needed for the king to reach c6 and two for the Re3 to reach its destination. Thus ten moves are left for the pieces at c1, d1, e1, e1, e1 and e5 to reach their destinations. The e1 men will need two moves each, at least, and the d1 piece is the bishop which needs two moves to reach b7. Thus if the c1 and e5 pieces take just one move, we have a total of thirty-five moves with none to spare.

The Re5 cannot end up at c5, or the final position isn't mate, so it must end up at d5. For the c1 piece to arrive in one move, it must be a rook which plays to c7 (not a queen as it would check from c7). By a process of elimination the c5 piece, which must be a bishop or knight, has to come from e1. This eliminates the bishop, as it would have checked from e1 (Black doesn't have any spare moves to arrange a shield for the White king). So it is a knight. Now the Bd1 must play to b7 before the king arrives at c6, so the Pe4 must move before the king arrives at c6 to make way for the bishop. How is the White king shielded to allow Pd5 to move? This cannot be accomplished by playing the Black king to c5, since Black could then never play Kc6 (remember Re5 only moves once, to d5). Thus the Ne1 must arrive at c5 to free the Pd5. The BK must move to allow the knight to d3, but not to d4 where it blocks the advance of the d-pawn. The sequence must be: promote c-pawn and play Rc7, play Kc4 to free Re3 and Pe4, promote Pe4 to N and play to c5, promote d-pawn to B and play to b7, then Kd5, Kc6 and Rd5 freeing the other two e-pawns to promote.

The solution runs **1 c3 2 c2 3 c1=R 4 Rc7 5 Kc4 6 Rb3** (not d3, blocking the d-pawn; thus this rook will end up at b5) **7 e3 8 e2 9 e1=N 10 Nd3 11 Nc5 12 d4 13 d3 14 d2 15 d1=B 16 Bf3 17 Bb7 18 Kd5 19 Kc6 20 Rd5 21 e5 22 e4 23 e2 24 e2 25 e1=R** (mustn't check) **26 Re6** (the rook has been allotted two moves, so this is the only way to reach a blocking square) **27 Red6 28 e5 29 e4 30 e3 31 e2 32 e1=R 33 Re7 34 Red7 35 Rb5+ axb5**.

A systematic approach is essential with long series problems. Even if it seems to take the fun out of solving, it is far quicker than any other method.

You can try for yourself with Diagrams 184 and 185.

In recent years there has been a growth in other types of series problem, notably the seriesselfmate and the seriesreflexmate. In both of these it is **White** who plays the series, while Black waits for his moment of glory at the finish. In the next problem, for example, White plays thirty-five consecutive moves (without checking, except possibly on the last move), to reach a position in which Black **must** mate in one.

179 A. Lehmkuhl, =1st Pr. Feenschach, 1978

ss≠35

As in an ordinary selfmate, there are two ways in which Black's final mating move may be forced; by a sacrificial deflection, or by zugzwang. Owing to the position of Black's king a deflection is unpromising, because most of the likely mating squares lie in the lower half of the board. Indeed, the positions of the Re4 and Ba5 lend support to the zugzwang theory, because these pieces can be immobilised by pinning. This still leaves the question of mating square open, but we can use an idea from the helpmate chapter; if the king must move, look first at diagonal paths. This suggests f1. White cannot force ...Nxg3 mate, since the knight could go to f2 instead, but ...g2 mate looks possible. However, this requires the pawn on f2 to shift (or else Black could play ...gxf2 rather than ...g2). The pawn on f2 can move only if the f3 pawn is captured, but then ...g2 isn't mate. No other zugzwang-based mates are possible at f1.

135

If a Black knight is to give mate (we are assuming the rook and bishop will be pinned, so it must be the Nh1, since the other has too many squares available. The mating move has to be ...Nf2. How about WKd1? For example, remove b7, d4, f3, h3 and place the king at d1. We need one piece to pin Re4 (e.g. WBg2), one to pin Ba5, one to confine the Black king (e.g. WQc7) and two to self-block at c1 and c2. So to arrange a mate at d1 needs five White pieces, one too many. Finally, we should consider WKd3. This also allows mate by ...Nf2 and it satisfies the diagonal criterion. Again remove b7, d4, f3, h3. Then the selfmate can be arranged by having WBg2, WNc2, WQc7 and WR (or Q) at a1, a3 or a4. Promotions to rook or queen require special arrangements to avoid checking the Black king. Since the BNh3 needs to be captured and a White bishop will finish at g2, a bishop promotion at c8 to shield the Black king seems likely. Since the Re4 and Pg3 stay on the board, the f- and h-pawns don't change files, so all the other promotions are on black squares, which implies that c8 has to be the bishop in any case. The knight which ends up at c2 could come from d8 or f8, taking the BPd4 en route.

The first problem is that although the c-pawn can promote unobstructed, all the other pawns are blocked at the moment. The quickest way to release one is to play Bc8xh3, but then the bishop has to return to c8 to provide a shield, a waste of time. Then the h-pawn can become a rook and play Rf8xf3–a3, freeing the f-pawn to become a knight. This takes at d4 to release the d-pawn to promote to a queen, which moves to c7 allowing Bh3–g2. An excellent plan, with just one flaw – White hasn't taken the pawn at b7! By playing Rh8–h7xb7 the rook can take the b7 pawn as well, but at the cost of two more moves. We must check whether we have exceeded the thirty-five: **1 c4 2 c5 3 c6 4 c7 5 c8=B 6 Bxh3 7 Bc8 8 h4 9 h5 10 h6 11 h7 12 h8=R 13 Rh7 14 Rxb7 15 Rf7 16 Rxf3 17 Ra3 18 f4 19 f5 20 f6 21 f7 22 f8=N 23 Ne6 24 Nxd4 25 Nc2 26 d4 27 Kc4** (the White king's last chance to cross the 4th rank without loss of time; on the other hand, any earlier would have blocked the d-pawn) **28 Kd3 29 d5 30 d6 31 d7 32 d8=Q 33 Qc7 34 Bh3 35 Bg2 Nf2**. Just in time!

The final position in Diagram 186 may come as a surprise.

180 C. Jonsson, 4th Pr. 2nd WCCT, 1982

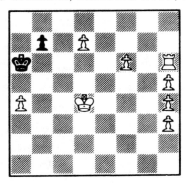

sr≠24

In this case White must play twenty-four consecutive moves (usual rule on checking) to reach a position in which Black can (and therefore must, by the reflex rule) mate in one, without at any stage being able to mate in one himself. In this type of problem underpromotions frequently arise because White could mate himself if he promoted to a queen.

Black's mating move must be ...b6, so we need WKc5 and blocking men at c6, d6, d5, d4, c4 and b4. Thus all the White pawns apart from the Pa4 will promote. This takes fifteen moves, to which we must add one king move. Eight moves are left for d8, f8, h6, h8, h8 and h8 to reach their destinations. One of the h8 promotions can travel to d4 in one move, but the other two will require two moves. With five of the eight gone, we can conclude that d8, f8 and h6 move just once each. The piece ending at c6 must be a B or N, but as all promotions take place on dark squares we can narrow this down to a knight, which arrives from d8. Thus the only square left for the Rh6 is d6. This in turn takes a potential square away from the f8 promotion, so there is only one possibility left; f8 ends up at b4. We may begin by **1 d8=N 2 Nc6 3 f7 4 f8=B 5 Bb4 6 Rd6,** but now White must take care. Two h8 promotions will end at c4 and d5. These must be rooks or queens, hence the White king cannot be at c5 at this stage, or R/Qa8 mate will be possible. White must delay Kc5 until the rook/queen promotions are safely out of the way. We continue **7 h6 8 h7 9 h8=R** (not Q, for if the queen goes to d5, she can mate by Qb5/a5) **10 Rh5 11 Rhd5 12 h5 13 h6 14 h7 15 h8=R** (this is heading for c4, so again a queen is impossible) 16 Rh4 (now the king can move to c5) **17 Kc5 18 Rc4 19 h4 20 h5 21 h6 22 h7 23 h8=B** (not Q to avoid mate at a8) **24 Bd4 b6.**

137

Problems for Solving

181 J. M. Rice, 2nd Pr.
BCM Tny, 1971

sh≠13

182 H. P. Rehm & H. Helledie,
1st Pr. Feenschach, 1971

sh≠14

183 L. Ugren, 2nd Pr.
Mat, 1976

sh≠19

184 B. Lindgren, 3rd Pr.
The Problemist, 1977

sh≠33

185 C. J. Morse, The
Serieshelpmate, 1978 (2nd edn)

sh≠44

186 J. Tomson,
The Problemist, 1984

ss≠22

9 Novotny, Grimshaw and Plachutta

The wide scope of this book has made it impossible, for reasons of space, to examine many of the deeper aspects of chess problems. In particular, there has been virtually no mention of themes. Almost all problems are composed to demonstrate a particular idea, or theme, but a catalogue of problem themes would require another book if it were to be reasonably comprehensive. In any case, it is quite possible for solvers to enjoy the interplay of pieces in a problem without knowing that the composer has been elucidating an aspect of the Somov 'E' theme.

Composers need to have a good grasp of problem nomenclature in order to be reasonably sure that they are doing something new, and not simply reinventing the wheel. To a large extent solvers can do without this detailed knowledge, but it is nevertheless helpful to have a basic knowledge of problem themes. A particular arrangement of pieces may indicate the problem's theme and allow the solver to converge on a likely key far more rapidly than otherwise. This chapter gives a brief survey of three closely related problem themes and aims to show how the same ideas can occur in many different types of problem from two-movers to helpmates. Those who are interested in expanding their knowledge of problem terminology can easily do so from such excellent books as *Chess Problems: Introduction to an Art* by Lipton, Matthews and Rice (1963) and *An ABC of Chess Problems* by Rice (1976).

The first of the three themes is the **Novotny**, which is based on the following idea. If a Black bishop on a1 is covering a mate at g7, and a Black rook on a4 is covering a mate at h4, then White can cause a disaster by playing a piece to d4, the intersection of the two guard lines. Whichever piece Black chooses to take the intruder, the other is interfered with and White can execute one of the mates. This idea occurs from time to time in over-the-board play, as in the following example.

187 Sigurjonsson—Øgaard, Esbjerg, 1978

It seems that White must win by 1 Qf5, but 1...g6 is a satisfactory reply because the rook at b6 prevents a Rxg6+ sacrifice.

1 d6!   **Rxd6**

After 1...Bxd6 2 Qf5 g6 3 Rxg6+ White forces mate. If Black tries to exchange queens by 1...Qg5, White mates by 2 Rxf7 Bxd6 (or 2...Rxf7 3 Qc8+) 3 Qe6 with overwhelming threats. After 1...Rxd6 the other half of the Novotny appears, because White can make use of the fact that the rook at f8 is unguarded.

2 Qf5   **g6**

In the game Black played 2...Qxd3, but resigned after 3 Qxd3 Rxf6 4 Rxf6 gxf6 5 Qg3+ Kh8 6 Qc7, since his bishop is trapped.

3 Qxg6+!   **fxg6**
4 Rxf8+   **Kg7**
5 R1f7 mate.

Although a single Novotny makes an attractive game combination, it is a little mundane for a problem, so composers usually add something extra. In the next position the Novotny is multiplied by four, but which is the right one?

188 C. Mansfield, 1st Pr. Die Schwalbe, 1956

#2

Each of the Black pieces lying from h2 to h5 has a responsibility. The Bh2 prevents mate by Bxb3, the Rh3 and Rh4 prevent mates by Qe3 and Qxe4 respectively, while the Bh5 covers Qd1 mate. Thus there are four potential Novotny interferences, at f3, f4, g3 and g4. The White pawns at f2 and g2 are poised to take advantage of these, so the experienced solver can at once narrow his search down to four moves (possibly five, including Bf4). There is an unprovided flight at d4, but this matters little since all the potential key moves cope with it. There is no short cut, we just have to try them all!

1 g3? (threats 2 Qe3 and 2 Bxb3) copes with 1...Kd4 2 Qxc3, but fails to 1...Nc2! 1 g4? (threats 2 Qd1 and 2 Qxe4) arranges 1...Kd4 2 Qxe4, but allows 1...Nxf2!. 1 f4? (threats 2 Qxe4 and 2 Bxb3) is defeated only by 1...e3! (this also defeats 1 Bf4?), which leaves the key **1 f3!** (threats 2 Qe3 and 2 Qd1). 1...Kd4 is again met by 2 Qxc3, but quite apart from the thematic Novotny variations, there are additional defences 1...Bf4 and 1...Rf4, stopping both threats. These are answered by 2 Qxe4 and 2 Bxb3, so the other pair of threats reappear as variations after the key. These two lines are similar to the Novotny in that they are based on the mutual interference of Black pieces playing to the same square, but different in that a White piece isn't captured in the process. This is the **Grimshaw** theme, the second of the three themes to be examined in this chapter.

Many three-movers feature ideas based on the Novotny theme, but the extra move allows more variety and creates extra difficulty for the solver, since he usually has to find the right key to set up a Novotny at move two.

≠3

A potential Novotny stands out clearly at b4 and White would like to play Nb4, meeting ...Bxb4 by Qd4. This requires control of e6 and **1 Rf6** is the obvious candidate, particularly as the rook move provides the reply 3 Qd6 after 2 Nb4 Rxb4. Most of the moves which meet the threat of 2 Nb4 are defeated fairly simply, e.g. 1...Kxd5 2 Qc6+ (or 2 Qb5+) Ke5 3 Nf3, 1...Rg4/h4 2 Nf3+ Ke4 (2...Kxd5 3 Qc6) 3 Qd4, 1...Rf4 2 Nf3+ Rxf3 3 Qd4, or 1...Bc5 2 Qc7+ Kxd5 3 Qxc5. The last few lines are typical defences to a Novotny threat, in that Black plays one of his pieces across the critical square. The main defence **1...Bf8** is based on the same idea, but unluckily for Black it is a case of out of the frying pan into the fire, since he crosses a second critical square, e7, allowing **2 Ne7!**, with mates by Qc6 or Qd6 after Black takes the knight, or by Qd4 after 2...Ra6.

The composer has also managed to incorporate two different Novotny interferences into Diagram 202.

Perhaps the most economical rendering of the Novotny idea occurs in endgame studies. In this case the rook and bishop are usually preventing pawn promotions rather than mates, but the idea is the same. The following study is special in that there are a number of tempting tries.

190 P. Benko, 1st Pr. Magyar Sakkélet, 1977

Win

1 e7

The move-order is important. After 1 g7? Rg3 (not 1...Rd8? 2 Rd6 Rg8 3 Rxd1 Rxg7 4 Rd7+ and the pawn promotes) 2 e7 Bh5 3 Rg6 (a false Novotny) Rxg6! (3...Bxg6? loses to 4 Kf2!) 4 e8=Q Rf6+ 5 Ke1 (5 Kg1 Bxe8 6 g8=Q Rg6+) Bxe8 6 g8=Q Bd7 Black draws, since White cannot exploit the loose Black pieces (7 Qg7 Rd6 or 7 Qd8 Re6+ 8 Kf2 Bc6).

1 ... Re3

After 1...Rf3+ there are three moves, but only one wins:
1) 2 Kg1? Rg3+ 3 Kh2 (3 Kh1? Bf3+ 4 Kh2 Rg2+ and ...Bxc6, or 3 Kf1/2 repeating) Re3 4 g7 Bb3 and White cannot win after 5 Rc7+ Ka6 or 5 Rc3 Rxe7 or 5 Re6? Rxe6 6 g8=Q Re2+.
2) 2 Kg2? Re3 3 g7 Bb3 4 Rc7+ Kb6! (4...Ka6? 5 Kf2 transposes to the main line) 5 Rc3 Bd5+ and 6...Rxe7.
3) 2 Ke1! Re3+ 3 Kxd1 Rxe7 and now:
3a) 4 Rf6? Re5! (4...Re3? 5 Kd2 Rg3 6 Ke2 Kb7 7 Kf2 Rg5 8 Kf3 Kc7 9 Kf4 Rg1 10 Kf5 Kd7 11 Rf7+ and 12 Kf6 wins, as does 4...Re4? 5 Rf7+ Kb6 6 g7 Rg4 7 Ke2 Kc6 8 Kf3 Rg1 9 Kf4 Kd6 10 Kf5, since in both cases White can reach the Lucena position) 5 g7 Rg5 6 Rf7+ Kb6 7 Ke2 Kc6 8 Kf3 Kd6 9 Kf4 Ke6! 10 Kxg5 Kxf7 11 Kh6 Kg8 draws.
3b) 4 Kd2? Re4! (4...Re5? 5 Rc7+ Kb6 6 Rh7! Kc6 7 g7 Rg5 8 Ke3 Kd6 9 Kf4 Rg1 10 Kf5 wins) 5 Rc7+ Kb6 6 Rh7 (6 g7 Rg4 7 Rf7 Kc6 8 Ke3 Kd6 9 Kf3 Ke6 also draws) Kc6 7 g7 Rg4 8 Ke3 Kd6 9 Kf3 Rg1 10 Kf4 Ke6 and the king arrives in time.
3c) 4 Rc5! (yet another demonstration of the fact that rooks belong behind passed pawns) Rg7 5 Rg5 Kb6 6 Ke2 Kc6 7 Kf3 Kd6 8 Kg4 Ke7 9 Kh5 Kf8 (9...Kf6 10 Kh6) 10 Kh6 Ra7 11 Rb5 wins.

This R+P v R ending could almost be a study in itself!

2 g7

Not 2 Rc7+? Kb6 3 g7 Kxc7 4 g8=Q Be2+ and 5...Rxe7.

2	...	Bb3
3	Rc7+	

3 Re6? Rxe6 (3...Bxe6? 4 Kf2) Rxe6 4 g8=Q Bc4+ 5 Kf2 Re2+ 6 Kf3 Bxg8 7 Kxe2 Bf7 is a draw.

3	...	Ka6

3...Kb6 4 Rc3! wins as the bishop drops with check.

4 Kf2!

White's king is vulnerable to a bishop check on a white square, so he moves it away with gain of tempo.

4	...	Re4
5	Rc6+	Ka5

For other king moves see the note to White's ninth move.

6 Re6!

White finally finds the right moment for his Novotny.

6	...	Rxe6

6...Bxe6 7 e8=Q wins since the bishop has no check.

7	g8=Q	Rf6+
8	Kg3	

Not 8 Ke3? Bxg8 9 e8=Q Re6+.

8	...	Bxg8
9	e8=Q	

If Black had played 5...Kb5, his king would now be in check, while if he had played 5...Ka7/b7, then White would win the rook after 9...B moves 10 Qe7+.

9	...	Be6
10	Qd8+	

and wins. The threats of Qxg8, Qe5+ and Qd8+ were too much for Black.

Diagram 203 is a straightforward example, but Diagram 204 shows a type of Novotny which can only occur in a study.

Even if the Novotny occurs on the second move of a three-mover, it often provides a strong pointer to the key.

191 L. Loshinsky, 1st Pr. 50th Anniversary T., USSR, 1969

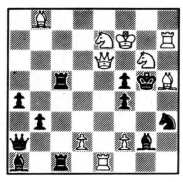

‡3

The rook at c5 covers Qxf5 mate, while the bishop at a1 prevents the queen mating at f6. These lines cross at e5, so there are possible Novotnys by Be5 and Re5. At the moment, however, 1 Be5 fails to 1...Bd5! pinning the queen, while 1 Re5 doesn't work because of the similar defence 1...b2!. Notice that Black must be careful which pin he chooses, i.e. 1 Be5 b2? 2 Bf6, or 1 Re5 Bd5? 2 Rxf5; in these lines the rook and bishop can replace the pinned queen in the mating position. It is tempting to search for a way these defences might be invalidated. There are potential interferences by ...f3 and ...R1c4, which prevent one or other of the pins. If these could be induced at move one, the correct choice of Novotny at move two would force Black to play the wrong pin and White could mate as above.

The only problem is to find a threat which can be met by ...f3 and ...R1c4. The clue is provided by ...R1c4, which suggests that the threat involves the move Bxf4+. Then it isn't hard to see **1 Re3!** (threat 2 Bxf4+ Nxf4 3 Rg3). There are two thematic lines **1...f3 2 Be5! b2 3 Bf6** and **1...R1c4 2 Re5! Bd5 3 Rxf5**, and the less interesting variations 1...fxe3 2 f4+ Nxf4 3 Bxf4 and 1...Bxf3 2 Bxf3 followed by 3 Rh5. Loshinsky's problem has crystal-clear logic.

Diagram 205, by the same composer, involves the same careful choice of Novotny in different variations.

As one might expect, the Novotny is also popular in more-movers, usually in combination with other motifs. Here is one example.

#6

The White battery will obviously play a major role, but there must be some way the extraneous White pieces at f1 and h6 can participate. There are potential mates by 1 R along b-file+ Ka3 and now 2 Bf8 or 2 Rxf3, but each mate is covered twice, the Bf8 mate by the Rg8 and the Bh2, and the Rxf3 mate by the Bc6 and the Rh3. White can deflect either c6 or g8 by playing a8=Q, followed by cutting off the capturing piece by Rb7+ or Rb8+, while a Novotny at g3 will take care of one of the other two pieces. However, in both cases the choice as to which piece will lose control is Black's, so he can arrange to lose one guard from each mate.

White can play with more finesse, however, and force Black to take at a8 with a piece of White's choice. The idea is to continue Rb7+, for example, and only then a8=Q, when Black must take with the rook. Then White returns to check again at b3. Similarly Rb8+ and a8=Q forces the bishop to take. It follows that White must play g3 first, forcing Black to make a decision. Then White will know which piece he wants to bury at a8.

Thus **1 g3!** (many threats, including 2 a8=Q) and now:

1) **1...Bxg3** (now the target is the Bc6) **2 Rb8+ Ka3 3 a8=Q** (threat Qxa5 and if 3...a4 then 4 Rb3) **Bxa8 4 Rb3+ Ka4 5 Rb7+ Ka3 6 Rxf3.**

2) **1...Rxg3 2 Rb7+ Ka3 3 a8=Q Rxa8 4 Rb3+ Ka4 5 Rb8+ Ka3 6 Bf8.**

The Novotny theme is not confined to directmate problems. Here is a selfmate example.

193 M. Vukčević, 4th Pr. Schach–Echo, 1976

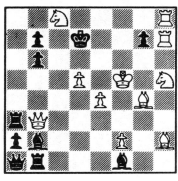

s≠3

The White king is very open, with three legal moves, so a mate by Black seems a long way off. However, there is a bishop and king battery aimed at the enemy monarch. The king battery is a popular device in selfmates to enable White's king to be mated on different squares, since by giving check White's king can reach the correct destination while severely restricting Black's options. The White queen is underemployed at the moment, so she must be brought into the action. Finally, White would like to play 1 Rxg7+ Bxg7 2 Nf6+, but Black doesn't have to take with the queen since the bishop isn't pinned. All these ideas point to **1 Qc3!**, threatening 2 Qxg7+ Bxg7 3 Nf6+ Qxf6, and creating an unusual Novotny at c3. Whichever piece takes at c3, the White king is allowed access to a square which was forbidden before. The main lines are **1...Bxc3 2 Kf4+ Kc7 3 Kf3+ Be5** and **1...Rxc3 2 Ke5+ Kc7 3 Kd4+ Rg3**. There is also one side-variation, 1...Bc1 2 Qc6+ bxc6 3 Nf6+ Qxf6.

The second of the three themes is called the Grimshaw. This has already been mentioned in the commentary to Diagram 188. Because the Grimshaw lacks a direct element of compulsion, there has to be a motive for Black's self-interferences, since he isn't likely to perform them voluntarily. In Diagram 188, the motive was the closure of an important White line, but there are other possibilities. In the next position zugzwang provides the necessary stimulus.

194 L. Loshinsky, comm. Tidskrift v.d. KNSB, 1930

≠2

Black's pieces are already burdened with important duties; the Ra7 stops mate at e7, the Ba8 mate at c6, while on the other side of the board the pieces at h7 and h8 cover f7 and e5 respectively. In fact Black is already in zugzwang, as the following lines prove: 1...Bb7 2 Re7, 1...Rb7 2 Rc6, 1...Bg7 2 Qxf7, 1...Rg7 2 Qe5, 1...Bf6 2 Qg4, 1...f6 2 Qe4, 1...Bxd4 2 Nxd4, 1...f5 2 Qd6 and 1...Rxc7 2 Nxc7. The first four variations are of the standard Grimshaw type, but the next two are rather less common, since they feature a type of interference between a bishop and a pawn. This is called a pawn Grimshaw, and it is only possible when the pawn is on the second rank. The last three lines are non-thematic. White only needs a waiting move to solve the problem, and the only one available is **1 Bb3!**. Note that 1 Ba2? fails to 1...Rxa2, unpinning the knight to cover e7.

The Grimshaw arises far less frequently in longer problems than the Novotny, but it does sometimes occur in helpmates.

195 M. Myllyniemi, 1st Pr. Stella Polaris, 1967

a) Diagram   b) g8→g5   h≠2

The B, R, R, B line-up is familiar from Diagram 188, so we may expect self-interferences to take place. Taking the diagram position first, White could mate down the e-file by Bxe5 and B moves or Nxe5 and Nd3/g6 (to cover f4), were it not for the four Black pieces which stand ready to move to the e-file. A co-operative effort is needed to nullify all four pieces in just two moves. All Black's interferences take place on the g-file, because a piece played to the f-file could still interpose between rook and king. With the king at g8, Black's Rg7 isn't possible, so he must play Bg7. This means that a White piece must prevent Black's Be5 by moving to f6, so White's two moves are Bxe5 and Bf6. The Bh5 must be dealt with by the remaining Black move, which is thus Rg6. The solution is **1 Bg7** (the move-order is unique as Rg6 would be check if played first) **Bxe5 2 Rg6 Bf6.**

Moving the king from g8 to g5 prevents Rg6 and by the same logic as above Black must play Bg6, so a White piece is needed at f7. White has to play Nxe5 and Nf7, possible now since the White king covers f4. Black's remaining move is Rg7 to neutralise the Bh8, and the solution runs **1 Bg6 Nxe5 2 Rg7 Nf7.** The two Black Grimshaws are spread over the two parts of the problem, necessary in a helpmate because there are no variations.

Diagram 206 combines the Grimshaw with other interferences, while in Diagram 207 the Grimshaw and Novotny themes are combined.

So far, all the self-interferences have been between a rook and a bishop. Other combinations of pieces can interfere with each other, but it is easy to see that the self-interference of two rooks, for example, cannot be exploited in a two-mover unless one of the rooks is already pinned.

The self-interference of like-moving pieces (usually two rooks or queen and bishop) most commonly occurs by means of the so-called **Plachutta** interference. The next position provides a simple example.

196 T. Gorgiev, 1st h.m. Moscow Tny, 1936

Win

1 d7	g2+

A surprising move designed to speed a rook to the d-file. 1...Rd3 2 Bxd3 Rd5 fails to 3 Rf4+ and now 3...Kg5 4 Rf5+ or 3...Kh3 4 Bf5+.

$$2 \quad \text{Kxg2}$$

Not 2 Bxg2? Rd3.

$$2 \quad ... \quad\quad\quad\quad\quad \text{Re2+}$$

2...Rg5+ 3 Kf2 wins.

$$3 \quad \text{Kf3}$$

Not 3 Rf2? Rg5+ 3 Kf1/f3 Rxf2+ 4 Kxf2 Rg8 with a draw.

$$3 \quad ... \quad\quad\quad\quad\quad \text{Rd2}$$
$$4 \quad \text{Kf4}$$

Threat Rh1+. Black's has only one defence.

$$4 \quad ... \quad\quad\quad\quad\quad \text{Rc3}$$

The characteristic set-up for a Plachutta interference. Each rook has one duty to perform, and the lines of action necessary for the duties cross. By depositing a piece on the intersection point, White cracks Black's defence.

$$5 \quad \text{Bd3!}$$

and whichever rook takes, it is deflected away from its original defensive role by the execution of the other threat: 5...Rdxd3 6 Rh1+ Rh3 7 d8=Q+, or 5...Rcxd3 6 d8=Q+ Rxd8 7 Rh1+.

Although the Plachutta is basically a three-move theme, it finds its best expression in longer problems, which give scope for some additional finesses.

197 A. Cheron, Le Temps, 1973

$\neq 7$

The rook at c7 prevents Nxc3 mate, while the rook at d6 prevents Nb6 mate, a perfect arrangement for a Plachutta at c6. At the moment no

White piece can take advantage of this circumstance, but the bishop at f1, which at present has no function, can arrive at c6 in three moves.

1 f4!

White prepares 2 Bg2 and 3 Bc6+. 1 Bg2? first is a mistake because of the reply 1...f4!.

1 ...   Rc4

Black's best defence is to play his rooks to the other side of the c6 square. The other main defence is 1...g5 (1...Ra6 2 Bg2 Rc4 transposes to the main line, while 1...Rxe6 2 Bg2 Rc4 3 Bd5! Rh6 4 Bxc4 Rxh5+ 5 Kg2 Rg5+ 6 fxg5 mates next move) 2 Bg2 g4+ (2...Rc4 3 Bd5 and 2...Ra6 3 Bb7 transpose) 3 Kh4! (3 Kg3? Rdxd7 4 exd7 e5 5 d8=Q exf4+ saves Black) Rc4 (3...Ra6 4 Bb7 Rd6 5 Bc6+ and 3...Rdxd7 4 exd7 Rc4 5 d8=Q also mate in seven) 4 Bd5! Rc7 5 Bc6+ and mates in two more.

2 Bg2   Ra6

2...Rxe6 3 Bd5 and 2...Rxd7 3 exd7 g5 4 d8=Q are as in the last note.

3 Bd5!

Black's poor rooks, after having carefully crossed c6, are now wretchedly forced to go back to the wrong side. White does have to take care with his move-order, since 3 Bb7? Rxe6! 4 Bd5 Rh6! 5 Bxc4 Rxh5+ and 6...Rg5+ delays the mate.

3 ...   Rc7
4 Bb7

Not 4 Bc6+? Rcxc6.

4 ...   Rd6
5 Bc6+

and the Plachutta operates as planned after **5...Rcxc6 6 Nb6+ Rxb6 7 Nxc3** or **5 Rdxc6 6 Nxc3+ Rxc3 7 Nb6**.

You may be wondering how the names Plachutta, Novotny and Grimshaw came to be attached to these themes. The answer is that, like many problem themes, they are named after the composers who first investigated them. These three were all mid-nineteenth century composers.

Diagram 208 shows another extended Plachutta idea, while Diagram 209 gives you the chance to sort out various different types of self-interference.

Perhaps the most satisfying type of self-interference problem is one which combines interferences by White and Black.

198 W. Tura, 1st Pr. Europe Echecs, 1962

≠2

Black's rooks and bishops are all occupied preventing mates. The Ra4 and Ba5 stop queen mates by Qxd4 and Qe1, while the Rg6 and the Bf7 prevent Bd6 and Rb5 respectively. 1 Ne6? isn't possible because of 1...Nf5+, so there are three possibilities for a Novotny key, 1 Bb4, 1 Rb4 and 1 Be6. 1 Bb4? threatens 2 Qe1 and 2 Qxd4, but prevents Rb5, so that Black can defend by 1...Re6! cutting off White's guard of f5. Similarly 1 Rb4? allows 1...Be6! and 2 Bd6 is impossible. In other words, White's attempted Novotny interferences at b4 fail because they constitute the two halves of a White Grimshaw. The key is **1 Be6!** (threats 2 Bd6 and 2 Rb5), leading to Grimshaw defences at b4 allowing the original queen mates: 1...Bb4 2 Qxd4 and 1...Rb4 2 Qe1.

More elaborate schemes are possible in three-move problems.

199 M. Vukčević, 2nd h.m. Probleemblad, 1971

≠3

There is a potential Novotny at d6, since the Bb8 prevents Rf4 mate, and by playing 1 d6 White introduces the second threat of 2 Be6. However,

152

the lines of the Rb4 and the Ba2 themselves cross at c4, so Black can retaliate with his own Novotny 1...Qc4!. Whichever way White takes the queen, Black can make the appropriate capture at d6, thus: 2 Rxc4 Bxd6 or 2 Bxc4 Rxd6.

White can introduce a different Novotny at d6 by 1 Rd6, with threats 2 Rf4 and 2 Nh6. 2 Nh6 mate depends on the Bc3 controlling e5, and the lines of the Rb4 and the Bd4 cross at d4, so Black can play 1...Qd4! followed by 2 Rxd4 Bxd6! or 2 Bxd4 Rxd6!. White needs to make a preliminary deflection to invalidate these defences. The Qb2 has played no part in the variations so far, and the Re1 stopping mate at e3 is a vulnerable spot in Black's position, so we might try to create confusion by 1 Qe2. This has the crude threats of 2 fxg4 and 2 Qxd3, so Black is forced to take the queen. After 1...Qxe2, the queen loses contact with d4, so White replies 2 Rd6!. On the other hand 1...Bxe2 leaves the queen with the extra duty of guarding e3, so she cannot now move to c4. Thus 2 d6!. If it were not for the blunt threats this fine problem would doubtless have been placed much higher by the judge.

Diagram 210 is a flawless exposition of interacting White and Black Grimshaws.

There is a good deal of similarity between Diagram 210 and the next position, although one is a directmate and the other a selfmate.

200 W. Tura, 1st Pr. Szachy, 1966

s≠3

White's aim is to play one or other knight to e2 in order to force ....Bxe2 mate. At the moment this is out of the question, since Nd4–e2+ actually delivers mate, while Nf4–e2+ allows the Rf7 to interpose at f1. However, the lines of action of the Rf7 and Bh8 cross at f6, so White can carry out a preliminary interference at f6 to prepare one of the knight checks, e.g. 1 Bf6 (threat 2 Nfe2+) or 1 Rf6 (threat 2 Nde2+). Nevertheless, Black meets 1 Bf6 by 1...Rf5! and 2 Nfe2+ can be met by 2...Kd3, while on the other hand 1 Rf6 allows 1...Bxd4!. The lines of the two

153

Black defensive pieces cross at c5. No White piece can move to c5, so a Novotny isn't possible, but White might be able to induce a Grimshaw. Black must have some potent reason to want to play a piece to c5, and that reason is provided by the key **1 Qc8!**, with the threat 2 Rc2+ Nxc2 3 Qxc4+ Bxc4. Black's only defence is to block the queen's path to c4 by moving to c5. This creates a Black Grimshaw allowing White to execute his own Grimshaw at f6: **1...Bc5 2 Bf6!** or **1...Rc5 2 Rf6!**. Note that 1 Qc6? fails since the queen can take at h1.

The final problem is one of my personal favourites.

201 T. Siers, 1st Pr. Schachspiegel, 194ż

≠6

White can create two mating threats, by Bg8 intending Bb3 or by Rg7 intending Ra7. Black can meet the first by ...Qxg3 and the second by ...g1=Q. These defensive lines cross at e3, so White can cause a Plachutta by advancing his pawn to that square. Unfortunately Black can throw a spanner in the works by the Novotny move ...Nf7. If Black can force White to decide which piece will take at f7, then he will know how to take at e3; on the other hand, if Black commits himself to taking at e3 with a particular queen, White will know which piece to play to f7. The key question is who has to decide first.

The following moves fail:

1) 1 Bg8? Nf7 (1...Qxg3 is also possible, transposing after 2 e3 Nf7!) 2 e3 (2 Bxf7 Qxg3 3 Rg7 g1=Q 4 e3 Qg3xe3! defends, and 2 Rg7 leads to variation 2) Qxg3! (not 2...Nd6+ 3 Kf8 Nc4 4 Rg7 nor 2...g1=Q 3 Bxf7 Qxe3 4 Rg7 Qhxg3 5 Bb3+, since in this case Black ends up with the wrong queen at e3) 3 Bxf7 Qxe3 4 Rg7 g1=Q and Black defends. When the bishop is on f7, Black wants the h3 queen at e3, so he must make haste to play ...Qxg3 and ...Qxe3, even before ...g1=Q. 1 Bg8? fails precisely because White is then committed to taking on f7 with the bishop.

2) 1 Rg7? Nf7 2 Bg8 (with this move White attempts to provide himself with the option of taking at f7 with either piece, but the damage has

154

already been done; other moves also fail, for example 2 e3 g1=Q 3 Rxf7 Qxe3 4 Bg8 Qhxg3 or 2 Rxf7 g1=Q 3 Bg8 Qhxg3! 4 e3 Qg1xe3) g1=Q (2...Qxg3 also works) 3 Rxf7 (White has no choice but to take the knight, since there is a threat of ...Qg2 and ...Qxc6+, so he still has to make his decision first; if 3 Bxf7 Qxg3 4 e3 Qg3xe3) Qhxg3 4 e3 Qg1xe3!.

The correct first move is **1 e3!**, which works precisely because 1...Nf7 fails to the non-thematic line 2 Kxf7 hxg3 3 Rg8 Qh5+ 4 Ke6/e7 and mates on a8 at move six. Deprived of his most flexible move, Black has no choice but to play ...g1=Q or ...Qxg3, both of which commit him to take at e3 with one queen or the other. The lines run:

A) **1...g1=Q 2 Bg8!** (2 Rg7? Nf7! leads to variation 2 above) **Qxe3** (2...Nf7 3 Bxf7 Qxe3 4 Rg7 transposes) **3 Rg7 Nf7 4 Bxf7!** (choosing the correct piece) **Qhxg3 5 Bb3+ Qxb3 6 Ra7.**

B) **1...Qxg3 2 Rg7!** (not 2 Bg8? Nf7!) **Qxe3 3 Bg8 Nf7 4 Rxf7! g1=Q 5 Ra7+ Qxa7 6 Bb3.**

A marvellous problem resembling a superbly engineered piece of machinery, requiring only the touch of a button to spring to life. The inner gearwheels are obscured unless the solver takes the cover off the machine to see what makes it all tick, a task well worthwhile.

Diagram 211 is another staggering achievement.

Problems for Solving

202 H. Pruscha, 1st Pr.
Deutsche Schachzeitung, 1959

≠3

203 V. Bron, 2nd h.m.
Kubbel Memorial Tny, 1946

Win

204 A. Kazantsev, 1st Pr.
Chigorin Mem Tny, 1949/50

Draw

205 L. Loshinsky, 1st Pr.
64, 1974

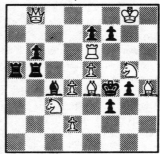

≠3

206 V. Karpov, 1st Pr.
Tungsram, 1980

2 solutions h≠2

207 E. Rukhlis, =1st Pr.
Sverdlovsk KFC Tny, 1946

≠2

208 H-P. Rehm, 2nd Pr.
Probleemblad, 1962

≠6

209 L. Kubbel, 1st Pr.
Swjesda Minsk, 1928

≠3

210 W. Whyatt, 1st Pr.
BCF Tny., 1961

≠3

211 M. Vukčević, 1st Pr.
Themes 64, 1981

≠8

10 Retro-analytical problems

So far we have been concerned with what happens after the diagram position, but the problems in this chapter depend, to a greater or lesser extent, on the play leading up to the diagram. Although the positions in chess problems are generally unlikely to have occurred in a game, it is nevertheless assumed that they have arisen from the starting array of a game via a sequence of legal moves. Thus illegal positions are strictly forbidden. A position with a White bishop on a1 and a White pawn on b2 could never have arisen from the initial position, for example, so a problem with such an arrangement is not permitted. Two further simple examples are (*1*) White pawns on g2, h2 and h3 and (*2*) White king on a1, White pawns on a2, b3 and c2, and a Black rook on b2. In each of these three cases the configuration described renders the position illegal regardless of the positions of any other pieces. The illegality may be far more subtle and depend upon seemingly irrelevant facts about the position, so composers have to be very careful to make sure their problems have legal positions. Sometimes quite innocuous positions lead to trouble and the author who wrote that with WKc7, Pb5 v BKa8, Pa7, 'White wins with or without the move', fell into just such a trap, for this position cannot arise with White to move. These difficulties are of more concern to the composer than the solver, however, so we may move on to other aspects.

Problems involving retro-analysis are very diverse and there is not enough space to consider all the types which the solver may encounter. I have divided the chapter into three main parts. The first deals with problems having a small retro-analytical content, but which are otherwise orthodox. The second deals with the pure retro problem, while in the third we shall look at a mixed bag of problems with assorted conditions.

A chess diagram gives a great deal of information about the position on the chessboard, but this information may not be complete. There are two situations in which the range of legal moves available to a player depends not only on the present positions of the pieces, but also on what has happened before. These two situations are castling and the *en passant* capture. Since problems have no previous play there have to be conventions to deal with these two exceptional moves. The convention with regard to castling is that castling is always considered legal, except if it can be proved illegal. This makes sense, because it is never possible to prove that castling is legal (the game might have started 1 Nc3 Nc6 2 Rb1 Rb8 3

Ra1 Ra8 4 Nb1 Nb8 5 Nf3 etc.), so castling can only occur at all in problems if it is assumed to be legal. Composers have played upon this convention for well over a century. A favourite trick is to have, say, BKe8, Ra8, Pa7, Pc7 and no other Black men. Then if White is to play, Black must have just moved his king or rook, so cannot castle. If we add WKe6 and WQa6 to this position we have a mate in two by Sam Loyd in which the key **1 Qa1** (threat 2 Qh8) only appears to allow castling.

The convention on *en passant* captures is that they are considered illegal, except where it can be proved that Black's last move was the double pawn push allowing the *e.p.* capture. Thus is a diagram with WPh5 and BPg5, White can only continue 1 hxg6 if Black's last move must have been ...g7—g5. Here is an example.

212 F. Amelung, Düna-Zeitung, 1897

≠2

The last move must have been by the g5 pawn or the Black king. If by the king, it must have come from g7, but in this case White's f6 pawn has no square from which it could have departed to deliver check to the king. Thus the last move was made by the g5 pawn; it could not have come from g6, in which case White's king was in illegal check, so the last move was indeed ...g7—g5. Thus the solution **1 hxg6 Kh5 2 Rxh7** is perfectly valid.

Here is a more complex position which leads to the same conclusion.

213 M. Caillaud, The Problemist, 1983

≠2

A swift examination shows that all Black's moves have mates set, with the single exception of 1...exd5. It would be quite easy to try to solve this problem without noticing that retro-analysis might be involved, but the generally congested appearance of the diagram and the many apparently irrelevant White pieces (b2, f2 and so on) would give the game away to an experienced solver. Two White men are missing and this balances the number of pawn captures Black must have made. Black must have played ...d7xe6 and ...f7xg6 at some stage in the past. Since neither of these could have been the last move, it follows that Black's last move was not a capture. A quick check shows that it must have been ...c7−c5 or ...h7/6−h5. Let us suppose for the moment that the latter case holds. Then Black's h8 rook could never have escaped from the top right corner since it would have been permanently trapped behind the h-pawn, g-pawn and the f8 bishop, which has never moved. On the other hand, White's pawns must have made at least three captures to reach their present positions, which, together with the h8 rook and the twelve Black men in the diagram, accounts for all sixteen Black men. Thus White's h-pawn has never made a capture. Nor can it have promoted, since the way was always blocked by Black's h-pawn. Yet the pawn is not present in the diagram, so it must have been one of the two pieces taken at e6/g6. This is clearly contradictory, so we have proved that the last move was ...c7−c5, hence White can play **1 dxc6**, with the variations 1...Qxg8 2 dxe8=N, 1...Rxe5+ 2 Nd5, 1...Rxf4 2 Rxf4 and 1...Bxd7 2 Qxf7. Readers will have noticed the similarity between the arguments needed for retro-analysis and the style of mathematical proofs. Indeed, in many cases the actual solution of a retro problem is completely trivial and the content lies entirely in the argument necessary to prove some fact about the position. Diagram 223 will allow readers to cut their retro-analytical teeth.

The following position has superficial similarities with the last problem, but introduces a new phenomenon.

160

214 T. R. Dawson, Falkirk Herald, 1914

#2

What was Black's last move? Not ...Kd8/f8—e8, for then Black's king stood in an impossible double check, nor ...Kd7/f7—e8, since White's e6 pawn has no previous move. It follows that the last move must have been ...d7—d5 or ...f7—f5. In the first case White can mate in two by 1 c5xd6 followed by 2 d7, while in the second 1 g5xf6 and 2 f7 is equally effective. So it appears that although White can guarantee to mate in two, one cannot tell from the diagram which move he should play! This paradox can be resolved by a more subtle retro-analysis. The White pawns have made at least ten captures to reach their present positions, so they have taken all the missing Black men, including in particular the c8 bishop. Thus the last move could not have been ...d7—d5, since that would imply that the c8 bishop had been captured on its original square, by something other than a pawn. So the key is **1 g5xf6**.

Diagram 224 features an unusual twin combining orthodox two-mover strategy with retro-analysis.

Solvers should also be on the look-out for retro tricks in helpmates. The following position is typical.

h≠3*

Remember that the star means set play. Normally set play in a help-mate can only be invalidated in the actual solution by the lack of a Black waiting move, but a different mechanism is possible if retro-analysis is invoked. A mate on the a-file seems possible and White gains a vital tempo by castling, bringing the rook into play and covering b2 at the same time: **1 0–0–0 2 Ka4 Rd5 3 Ka3 Ra5.** However, the solution starts with a Black move, so White must have moved last. This move was with the rook or the king, so White cannot castle. Thus Black cannot simply lose a tempo by playing ...Kb5–a4. The actual solution is strikingly different from the set play and does not employ the White king at all: **1 Na6 Rb1 2 a1=R c4 3 Ra4 Rb5.**

Diagrams 225 and 226 revolve around the question of whether or not Black's *en passant* capture is legal.

Moving on now to pure retro problems, the first point to make clear is that it may not be White to play in the diagram. Often the first step in the logical process of unravelling the position is to determine whose move it is. Sometimes, indeed, the condition under the diagram is just 'Who is to play?' The conventions applying to problems with orthodox conditions (Black to play in helpmates, otherwise White to play) are relaxed in just this one respect if the problem has a retro condition. Perhaps the most basic question is, 'What was the last move?' The following position is of this type.

216 W. Keym, Feenschach, 1977

Last move?

It isn't hard to see that White has just moved. If Black had moved, he could only have played ...c7–c6, but in this case White's king could never have reached f8, since all the squares on the sixth rank would have been permanently guarded by Black's pawns. What are the possibilities for White's last move? It could not have been Ra8–b8, for the same logic which proved that White has just played would apply to the position with the rook on a8, leading to an impossibility. So the last move must have been Ra8xb8, a7xb8=R, c7xb8=R or c7xd8=R. Each of these cases represents four possibilities, since in order to describe the last move completely, we also have to specify whether the captured piece was a queen, rook, bishop or knight. Suppose the last move was c7xd8=R. Then the move Black made prior to this must have been with the piece White uncaptured at d8. A queen, rook or bishop would have no move, while a knight must have come from e6, impossible as this would give check to the White king. Therefore the last move was a capture at b8.

In order to eliminate some of the other candidate moves we must analyse the pawn captures made by White. As the bishop at c8 has never moved, the rooks at d8 and e8 are promoted pawns which arrived via captures at c7 and d8. This accounts for four missing black pieces, to which we may add the BBf8, taken on its original square, and the BRh8, which could not have been captured by a WP at d8, since the WK entered before the pawns promoted at d8 and Black's rook could not have jumped over the king to reach d8. Not counting the BBf8 and BRh8, we have proved that of the five other missing Black men, two were taken at c7, two at d8 and one at b8. We can now deduce the identity of the piece just captured at b8, since the BRa8 could not have reached c7 or d8, the two other potential capture squares. We can eliminate c7xRb8=R as the last move since this implies White has made six pawn captures, which is too many, and Ra8xRb8 can be dismissed because this leaves Black with no feasible previous move (...c7–c6 is impossible, as before). So by a process of elimination, the last move was a7xRb8=R. For a position with just thirteen men, we had to work quite hard!

In Diagram 227 the condition is, 'Who mates in 1?' It is easy enough to see that if Black is to move he can mate by ...Nh1–f2, while if White is to move he can finish the game by Qa7–e7. This is a thinly disguised 'Who is to move?' problem.

The only limitation on the variety of conditions which may appear under the diagram is that set by the composer's imagination. The following problem sets the solver an unusual task.

217 G. Donati, The Problemist, 1980

Path of Rb1?

The question 'Path of Rb1?' means that we have to determine the history of the b1 rook. Clearly the answer will not be unique, since at any stage the rook might have oscillated, so what we are being asked for is a 'minimum path' for the rook, i.e. which squares the rook **must** have visited during the course of the game.

This is the first position in which it will be necessary to make extensive retractions, so we shall have to settle on a method of writing retractions. The simplest is to use normal (forward) chess notation for the moves, but to write them in reverse order. When writing the moves, full algebraic notation must be used. It is no good to say, for example, that Black's last move leading up to the diagram was ...h5, since this doesn't tell us whether the pawn came from h6 or h7. We have to write ...h6–h5 or ...h7–h5, as appropriate. Similarly if a capture takes place, we must specifiy the captured piece, so that if Ra1xNb1 is encountered, the reader knows that the rook on b1 must be moved to a1 and a Black knight added at b1.

Starting the retro-analysis, we note that the BPf2 is Black's a-pawn, which has made a series of captures at b6, c5, d4, e3 and f2. Together with the WBf1, which was captured on its home square, this accounts for all the missing White men. At first glance one cannot see how to advance the argument further, since there aren't any other obvious obstructions to the disentanglement of the position. As a tip to solvers, if you get stuck in a retro problem, it is often helpful to try to reach the diagram from the initial position, just to see what goes wrong. Here the difficulty is the arrangement of pieces in the centre of the board. The d6 pawn cannot have come from c5, for in this case either the d4 pawn or the c5 pawn is White's f-pawn and it would have collided with Black's a-pawn, since both pawns have to move on the same diagonal to reach their destinations. The White king can't have come from f5, since Black's previous move would have been ...d7xe6+ (too many Black P captures) or ...e7–e6+ (how did f8 bishop get to d2? – Black still has eight pawns so BBd2 is not a promoted P). Black's king has no previous moves and the only WP retractions, a2xb3 and d3–d4, don't help a bit. The central formation seems locked solid and it requires considerable imagination to find any way the pieces could have reached their present positions.

The key idea is to replace the BBd2 by a White piece (i.e. the sequence W piece moves from d2 +, BB moves to d2 occurred), so that the BB can retract to f8. Then Black can take back ...e7–e6 and the WK is freed, which unlocks the position. The rest is trivial. No White men can be uncaptured until the BPf2 is freed, which only comes at the end of the above sequence, so the only available piece to perform the changing of the guard at d2 is the WRb1, and it must play to d2 from d1. However, Black's pawns form a barrier to the WR. There are only two ways it can retract to d1: either (1) W retracts d3–d4 and Ra1-a4-h4-h1-d1, or (2) W retracts his rook via a1, a8, h8, h6, g6 (or f6), g4, h4, h1 and d1. When the R reaches d1 the BB retracts to a5 to bury itself on f8 via d8 and e7. But all this time the WR is held paralysed at d2, so the crucial question is whether White has enough reserve retrotempi to avoid running into retrostalemate (a self-explanatory term – just as normal stalemate is when you have no legal next move, so retrostalemate is when you have no legal previous move; of course, this implies that the position is illegal) while the BB moves to f8. There are just two available, namely a2xb3 and d3–d4, and these provide just enough time, e.g. (with WR on d1) 1...Ba5–d2 2 Rd2–d1+ Bd8–a5 3 d3–d4 Be7–d8 4 a2xb3 Bf8–e7 5 Kf5–e5 e7–e6+ (these moves are retractions, as explained earlier) and the position frees itself.

Black's apparent lack of retrotempi as the WR journeys to d1 presents no problem, since White can immediately uncapture a piece at b1 to provide the necessary spare moves. However, this logic proves that (1) above isn't possible, since it prematurely consumes the retrotempo d3–d4 and W runs out of moves before the BB gets to f8. After all that, we can prove that Black is to play in the diagram. If Black had just moved, he must have played ...c7–c6 or h7/6–h5. The former blocks the path of the BB to f8, while the latter prevents the WR reaching d1. White's last move must immediately give Black a spare move, or he will still be forced to take back one of the pawn moves. Thus White must have just played Ra1xb1. The uncaptured piece can be a knight or a queen, but not a bishop (how could a BB reach b1?) or a rook (which does not provide a spare move).

165

The retraction could run 1 Ra1xNb1 Nc3–b1 2 Ra8–a1 3 Rh8–a8 (while Black passes with his knight) 4 Rh6–h8 5 Rg6–h6 6 Rg4–g6 7 Rh4–g4 8 Rh1–h4 9 Rd1–h1 Ba5–d2 10 Rd2–d1+ Bd8–a5 11 d3–d4 Be7–d8 12 a2xRb3 Bf8–e7 13 Kf5–e5 e7–e6+ etc. Returning to the question asked by the composer, the answer is that the WRb1 must have occupied a1, a8, h8, h6, h1, d1 and d2. In particular, it has visited all four corners of the board.

Diagram 228 features another unusual condition. It is easy to imagine a situation in which removing a man makes an illegal position legal, but apart from the trivial situation in which the removal exposes one of the kings to an impossible check, it is hard to see how removing a man can make a legal position illegal.

For the final position in this section we take an extraordinary twin in which a slight change in the position has profound consequences for the retro-analysis.

218 M. Zigman, Prize, The Problemist, 1977/8

May White castle?   a) Diagram   b) b3→f6

Taking the diagram position first, Black's pawns have made four captures, balancing the number of missing White men. These captures took place on the b-, d- and e-files. The first step is to note that White's g-pawn is not on the board. The only other possibility is that the pawn at h6 is really the g-pawn, but then Black must have captured the genuine h-pawn on the e-file (or further left). This requires four pawn captures by White, one to take the g-pawn to h6, one at a3 and two to allow the h-pawn to promote at f8. As only two Black men have been taken, this is impossible. By the same argument, White's g-pawn cannot have crossed to the e-file, since this needs three pawn captures in all. It follows that the g-pawn has made one capture on the f-file and then promoted at f8. All the missing Black men are now accounted for, so in particular White's f-pawn has never captured. Since it is another of the missing White men, it too must have promoted at f8.

166

What could Black have played last? Not ...c4xb3 because this leaves the pawn at c7 stranded on the wrong side of Black's c-pawn. One of the c-pawns would have had to make another capture to reach its present position, but we have already accounted for every capture so no more are allowed. Also not ...f7xe6, since this must have been played long ago to allow the two White pawns to promote at f8, while ...e7–e6 is obviously impossible as the f8 bishop is already at a7. It doesn't matter whose turn it is to move in the diagram, since if White has just played he can only retract an irrelevant move like Bc3–b4 or h5–h6 (not b2xa3, as WBc1 is on b4) which doesn't alter the situation. So we may assume that Black has just moved. We have shown no retractions are possible from b3 or e6, which only leaves a5 and b5 as candidates. If b5, Black must have just played ...Nc3/d4–b5 (Black can't uncapture as the BPs have made all the captures), but this leaves White with no previous move. So Black's last move was ...Nc4–a5 and we may immediately deduce that White's previous move was Ba5–b4+.

The next step is similar to the logic used in the last position. How is it possible to disentangle the top left corner (i.e. the arrangement of pieces on a2, a3, a4, a5, a6, a7, b3, b5, b6, b7, b8, c6, c7, c8, d5, d6, d7 and e6)? The b3 pawn cannot be retracted back on to the c-file until the c7 pawn has been pulled back at least as far as c4 and this can't be done until the c6 bishop is freed. The only way this corner can be unravelled is to retract ...f7xe6, freeing the BRd6 which moves to make room for ...d6–d5, the WBc6 moves, the c7 pawn and the WNb8 go back, in turn making way for the BBa7 and WQa6 to escape and the rest is easy. But ...f7xe6 can only be taken back after White has unpromoted his f- and g-pawns at f8. The only free White men which can go to f8 to be unpromoted are the two rooks, so the answer to part (a) is that White cannot castle, since both rooks are promoted pawns. Note the importance of proving that the WBb4 was immobilised at a5. Without this link in the chain of logic we would never be able to prove that the bishop wasn't one of the two men created by the f8 promotions.

Now move the b3 pawn to f6. There are only two ways the pawns on e6 and f6 could have arrived at their present positions: either (1) Black played ...e7xf6 and ...f7xe6, or (2) Black played ...e6 and ...f6.

Assume to begin with that case (1) occurred. Then all four missing White men are accounted for by Black's pawn captures at b6, e6, f6 and on the d-file. As in the first part of the problem Black must have taken White's g-pawn, so the g-pawn must have been transferred to the f-file by a pawn capture. Together with the capture at a3, this accounts for the two missing Black men. We claim that White must have promoted a pawn at f8. If the WPg2 promoted, it must have been at f8. If it didn't promote, Black must have taken it at f6. Black has also taken White's f-pawn. Since only one capture ever took place on the f-file and the captured piece was the g-pawn, it follows that for the f-pawn to have been taken it must have promoted at f8 first. So either the f-pawn or the g-pawn promoted at f8.

Once again, we have to find Black's last move. Black is still unable to retract ...e7—e6 because of the BBa7 and for the same reason ...e7xf6 is impossible. ...f7xe6 can be ruled out since we know White has promoted at f8, so this capture must have taken place long ago. As in part (*a*), we are reduced to a5 and b5.

This time, however, we cannot retract ...Nc4—a5. The reason is that after White's forced retraction Ba5—b4+, we find ourselves with the same problem of disentangling the top left corner. As before the only way to free the position is to retract ...f7xe6 and this means that White must unpromote a piece at f8. Because of the BPf6, the BPs form an impenetrable barrier and prevent either WR retracting to f8 to be unpromoted. Thus the position cannot be freed and is illegal.

By a process of elimination Black's last move was by the Nb5. This unveils an awkward check from the WBc6, which can only arise if White's previous move was a discovery from b5. White has two moves to bring a suitable piece to bear on b5 and the only candidate is the WRa1 (the other R takes three moves). It follows that White has just moved and played either Rb1—a1 or B moves to b4. The retraction runs 1 Rb1—a1 something 2 B moves to b4 Nd4/c3—b5 3 Rb5—b1+. This wasn't possible in part (*a*) of the problem since the pawn at b3 obstructed the rook's path to b5. The difficulty is the something. Black has no retrotempi to spare because he cannot, as yet, make a retraction with the e6 or f6 pawns. We have finally proved that case (*1*) is impossible.

We know now that Black played ...e6 and ...f6. Hence the BRh8 was permanently imprisoned by the d—h pawns and the BBc8, which has never moved. Thus the piece taken at a3 was the queen. Three of White's kingside pawns are missing and yet Black has made two pawn captures on the queenside. A count shows that Black must have taken a kingside pawn with one of these captures. White could not play exd to allow Black a capture at d5, since Black's rook could not have reached d5. It follows that one of White's kingside pawns took Black's rook at e7 or f7 and promoted. The logic now proceeds in exactly the same way as our analysis of case (*1*), until we reach the point where we derived a contradiction before. This time the sequence 1 Rb1—a1 something 2 Bc3—b4 Nb5—d4 3 Rb5—b1+ is possible, because Black has the reserve retrotempo ...f7—f6 which can be substituted for something. Incidentally, this proves that White's f-pawn took the BRh8 at e7 and then promoted at e8.

Our work is not yet finished, since the top left corner is still hard to disentangle. It isn't difficult to see that the only hope is to retract b2xQa3, which makes b4 accessible to Black's king in the sequence ...Kb4—a4 Rc5—b5+. This frees the WBc6 which, as we have seen, suffices to release the whole position. However, a pawn at b2 imprisons White's queen bishop, so this piece has to be retracted to c1 before White can uncapture the queen. With the bishop at c1 and pawn at b2, the WRa1 could not have escaped, so this piece must also go back. The rook at b5 can't move, so it must be the h1 rook which goes to a1 to be buried when b2xQa3 is

retracted. The rest is easy; one method is (with Ra1 and Bc1) to retract
1 b2xQa3 Kb4—a4 2 Rc5—b5+, free WBc6 and WQa6, play WNb8 to e8,
retract e7—e8=N and f6xRe7, retract BRe7 to h8 and BBa7 to f8, leaving
the 2 WNs to be uncaptured by Black's pawns.

The conclusion is that White cannot castle, this time because the rook
on a1 is the king's rook and the rook on h1 is the queen's rook.

The final section of this chapter and, indeed, of the whole book, covers
some miscellaneous conditions which don't fall into any other category.

After the complexities of Zigman's problem the next position should
come as a little light relief.

219 R. Smullyan, Manchester Guardian, 1957

Where is White's king?

Here we must assume that, in the course of play, White's king was
accidently knocked off the board. We are asked to replace the king on the
correct square. As in the last section, we cannot assume that White is to
play in the diagram. In fact, if it were White to move, his king would have
to be on b3, or else Black's king would be in check, but in this case Black
has no previous move, since he cannot lift both checks with a single
retraction.

So it is Black to move. What has White just played? Since the bishop
could not have moved to a4, it must have been Kb3—somewhere or
Kb3xsomething. At this point it is well to recall that the only way to give
double check without moving one of the checking pieces is by means of an
en passant capture. The awkward position of the king at b3 can be
explained only if Black played b4xc3 *en passant* in reply to c2—c4 by
White. Hence the last move was Kb3xPc3 and the king stands at c3 in the
diagram.

The next position is a strange mixture of forward and backward play.
Although problems of this sort are sometimes frowned upon as being
neither one thing nor another, the possibilities inherent in the interaction
of retro- and ordinary conditions are fascinating and as yet little explored.

Add one man so that White to play can mate in two

In this case we are given that White is to move in the diagram. At first sight there must be something wrong, since White already has a mate in two by 1 Ne8 and 2 Nc7, so the addition of a further piece would seem to be unnecessary.

To resolve this paradox, we have to start the retro-analysis. White has made at least five pawn captures on the kingside. On the queenside, if the WPb6 has already made a capture, it must have come from the a- or c-files, which already have WPs, so in this case White must have made two pawn captures on the queenside. Together with the five on the kingside this makes seven, but only six Black men are missing. It follows that the WPb6 has never made a capture.

Therefore the BPb4 has made a capture and by the same logic this implies two Black pawn captures on the queenside. There are already four on the kingside and the total of six exactly balances the missing White men. The immediate consequence is that the piece which has been knocked off the board must be Black. So there are really only five missing Black men and this balances the WP captures. All captures have now been taken into account. Where did the White captures take place? The h6-pawn (really White's d-pawn) took pieces at e3, f4, g5 and h6. The h3 pawn must have arrived via the capture ...g4xh3, so the history of moves in the bottom right corner must have been either ...g4xh3, then g2–g4 and h2xg3, or ...g4xh3, then h2xg3, g3–g4 and g2–g3. In either case, White's capture took place at g3. Thus all White's captures took place on black squares, so White cannot have taken Black's queen's bishop. This was the piece knocked off the board.

Where can the bishop be without disturbing White's mate in two by 1 Ne8? There are just three candidate squares, namely a2, e8 and h5. e8 can be rejected at once because Black has no previous move, but eliminating h5 requires a more subtle argument. Add the bishop at h5. White is to move, so what could Black have just played? It could not have been a

170

move by one of the pieces at h5, h8, h7, g6, f7, e7, h3 (...h4–h3 is impossible as the pawn arrived at h3 from g4), a8 (...Kb8–a8 leaves White without a prior move), c5 (...d6xc5 leaves Black making too many pawn captures) or a6, so it must have been ...b5–b4 or ...a5xb4. For Black's a- and b-pawns to have reached their present positions (remember White hasn't made a pawn capture on the queenside), the following sequence must have occurred: WPb2 advanced to b5 or b6, Black's a-pawn captured to go behind the b6 pawn, WPa2 advanced to a7 and finally Black played ...b7xa6. So the last move could not have been ...a5xb4, since this happened before the WP advanced to a7. It must, therefore, have been ...b5–b4, but in this case the two Black queenside pawn captures took place at b5 and a6. These squares, like e6, f5, g4 and h3, are white squares, so Black could not have captured White's queen's bishop. This contradiction proves that a black bishop was knocked off the board from a2.

Diagram 229 is another mixed problem, this time in helpmate form.

The conventions on castling and *en passant* captures given at the beginning of the chapter may have appeared clear-cut and unambiguous, but the next position provides an exception.

221 L. Ceriani, Europe Echecs, 1960

≠2

As there is a standard condition under the diagram, we may assume that White is to move.

The convention is that castling is assumed legal unless it can be proved illegal. So assume that Black can castle. In this case his last move could not have been with king or rook, so must have been with the BPb5. There are just two White men missing and one, the Bc1, never left its home square. Thus Black could not have just played ...c6xb5, which requires too many pawn captures. Nor could he have played ...b6–b5, as there is no way White could have given check. So he must have played ...b7–b5, with White's previous move being Rc6–a6+. White can mate in two by 1 c5xb6+ and 2 Qf8.

White's king and rook are also in the right position for castling, so why not apply the castling convention to White instead? Thus White has never moved his king. As the BNa1 must have arrived before White played a2xb3, the WRa1 could never have escaped from the first rank. Hence the WRa6 is a promoted pawn. We claim that Black cannot castle. If the promotion took place on f8, g8 or h8, the rook must have checked and displaced Black's king on its way out from the top right corner to a6. The same argument applies to promotion on d8, or by d7xc8 (WPd7 checked BK). Otherwise, the least number of pawn captures White could have made is nine (a2xb3, e3xd4xc5, f5xe6 and g2xf3xe4xd5xc6xb7), but there are just eight Black men missing.

So, to summarise, if White can castle, then Black cannot, and White mates in 2 by 1 0–0 (not 1 Rf1? Nxc2+). On the other hand, if Black can castle, then the last move was 1...b7–b5, and White mates in 2 by 1 c5xb6+. In fact, the solution depends on which player gains the benefit of the castling convention first. However, in each case there is a unique solution, so this problem is perfectly legitimate.

The final position in this chapter has a large dash of humour mixed in with the retro-analysis.

222 R. Kofman, Shakhmaty Bulletin, 1958 (version)

White retracts his last move and then mates in 3

The condition states that White has just moved. We have to take back his move and play so as to force mate in three. One certainly shouldn't take back moves in a game, but it is allowed in problems! White could mate in two from the diagram by 1 d2xc3, were Black unable to castle. White's retraction will therefore be designed not so much to arrange a mate as to prove that Black cannot castle. The positions of White's king and rook look suspicious, so let's try taking back 0–0–0. Then White's king has never moved, since he is still able to castle. As in the last problem, this means that the WRd3 is a promoted pawn. If the pawn promoted at g8 White must have made seven pawn captures, which is too many. The

172

promotion must have taken place at f8 (displacing the king), or at a8, b8, c8 or d8, when the rook must have emerged via d8, again nudging the king aside. Thus ...0–0 is illegal.

We still have the task of mating in three, so it is essential to prevent ...gxf2+. Thus White must play the very move he took back, 1 0–0–0! (threat 2 dxc3), which does indeed force mate.

Problems for Solving

223 P. O'Shea, 3rd Pr.
The Problemist, 1976

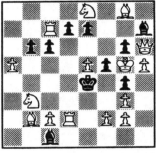

‡2

224 B. Barnes, 2nd Pr.
Problem TT, 1964

a) Diagram   b) Add BPg7   ‡2

225 H. Aloni, 1st Pr.
Israel RT, 1962

a) Diagram   b) b5→a3   h‡3

226 L. Lindner, 3rd Pr.
Magyar Sakkvilag, 1943

h‡2

173

227 J. Haas, 3rd Pr.
Die Schwalbe, 1975

Who mates in 1?

228 J. Haas, 1st Pr.
The Problemist, 1973

Remove a man (other than a king)
to make the position illegal

229 E. Fasher, 2nd Pr.
Israel RT, 1956

Black retracts his last move,
then h≠1

230 J. Haas, 1st Pr.
Problem TT, 1972

White retracts his last move and
then mates in 2

231 N. Plaksin, 1st Sp. Pr. Georgian 50th Anniv. Tny, 1971

Draw

174

Solutions to problems for solving

CHAPTER 1

16 (Mansfield, Massman and Loshinsky) Checking the set play reveals that Black is already in zugzwang: 1...B (orN)xe6 2 Bf3, 1...Be7/Bf7/Nd7 2 Nc7, 1...gxh5 2 Bf3, 1...Bd6 2 Qf3, 1...Bxd4 2 e4 and 1...Q moves is met by 2 Nc7 or 2 Qe5 according to the square Black moves to. So White needs a waiting move. The White king has no less than eight legal moves and all of these look like good candidates for a waiting move. But White must take care with his choice, since all except one of these run into pins, for example 1 Kf1/f2/f3? Qf7!, 1 Kh3? Bxe6!, 1 Kh2/g3? Bd6! and 1 Kg1? Bxd4!. The key is the one safe spot for the king, **1 Kh1!**.

17 (Shinkman) The mates 1...e4 2 Qxe4, 1...f6 2 Ndc7/ f4 and 1...f5 2 Qe7/g8 are set for all Black's moves apart from 1...d6. It is tempting to try to mate by Qc8 after 1...d6, but 1 Qg8/h8 allows 1...Kf5 and 1 Qc2 allows 1...f6/f5 so this cannot be arranged. The key is **1 Ba4!**, introducing the extra variations 1...Kxd5 2 Bb3 and 1...d6 2 Nbc7. Moreover, the ambiguity after 1...f6 and 1...f5 is removed so that the unique replies are 2 Ndc7 and 2 Qg8 respectively.

18 (Ellerman) The limited Black piece mobility suggests that zugzwang may be possible, even though a number of Black moves aren't provided with set mates. In this case 1...g4 will be a problem as the only mate which might be permitted by this move, 2 Qxh4, is covered by the f3 knight. So 1...g4 must be prevented indicating **1 Qg4** as a potential key. The variations 1...Nf5/g6 2 Qxg2, 1...Nf3 at random 2 Qh3, 1...Nh2 2 Nfg3, 1...Ng1 2 Neg3, 1...Rxf2 2 Qg1 and 1...Rxg4 2 Rh2 prove that this guess is correct.

19 (O'Bernard) The lines 1...d5 2 Bd3, 1...e6/5 2 Nxd6 and 1...Kf5 2 e4 prove that Black is already in zugzwang. It isn't easy for White to make a waiting move since a king move allows ...a2, the queen has to guard e3, d4 and g6 and the h4 rook has no reasonable moves. 1 Be6? d5 and 1 Bf7/ g8? e6 don't work so we are left with the e1 rook. A move of this would give up the mate by 2 e4 after 1...Kf5, but in fact this can be replaced by another mate provided White starts **1 Ra1!**. This clears the path for the queen to mate by 2 Qb1 after 1...Kf5.

20 (Mansfield) One of the most famous cross-check problems ever composed. The key, **1 Be4**, not only allows the bishop + knight battery to fire at White's king, but also gives a flight at e5. The threat is 2 Nxc4 and this is also the answer to 1...Ke5 and 1...Nc4 at random +. There are three star variations, two self-pins by 1...Nxd6+ 2 Bd3 and 1...Nxe3+ 2 Nb5 (2 Nc4 leaves e4 unguarded) and a self-block after 1...Ne5+ 2 Rd3. The key forms a third battery to add to the two already aimed at Black's king, but this extra battery can only fire if Black's knight pins itself by capturing one of the two front battery pieces.

21 (Mansfield) There are some interesting mates already set, for example 1...Qxd2+ 2 Nxd2 and 1...Ne2 2 d3, but there is as yet no reply to 1...Nxd5, which frees b5 and d3 for Black's king. It is likely that this will be met by a mate on the a6—f1 diagonal, which can only be arranged if the key moves the White queen to attack a6, e2 or f1. However, d5 must be kept under guard, for White cannot possibly mate after 1...Kxd5. This leaves f7 or f5 as possible destinations. 1 Qf7 has no threat, so the solution must be **1 Qf5** (threat 2 Rd4), with the main variations 1...Qd3 2 Nd4 and 1...Nb5 2 Nc5 showing self-block by Black allowing White interferences, combined with exploitation of the c1—c4 half-pin. Other variations: 1...Qxd2+ 2 Nxd2, 1...Nxd5 2 Qxf1, 1...Ne2 2 d3, 1...Qxb3 2 Bxb3 and 1...Ne4 moves 2 Rc5.

22 (Mansfield) The third of a remarkable trio of problems by British composer Comins Mansfield, whose achievements extended over more than half a century. In the diagram Black has an obvious defence 1...Rdxc5 giving a flight at d4. If the rook + bishop battery could fire, the rook at h4 would cover d4, but Black has two pieces (a6 and b2) ready to interpose at e2. In order to cope with 1...Rdxc5, the key must either threaten mate along the h8—d4 diagonal or the key must be by the Bc5 itself. The White queen must guard e6, which rules out Qg7 or Qxh8 as a threat, so the bishop must move, not along the a7—g1 diagonal, for this creates no threat, but to e7 or f8. 1 Bf8? Rd7 admits no mate, so **1 Be7** looks likely to be the key even though it gives two flights, both with check. The variations are 1...Kxe6+ 2 Bg5, 1...Kd4+ 2 Bf5, 1...Rxe6 2 Bf6, 1...Bxb7 2 Bc2 and 1...Qxb7 2 Bd3.

23 (Knuppert) White must make a strong threat to deal with Black's ...bxa3 and ...Qxd7. If we guess that the theme involves the unpin of Black's queen, we might try 1 Qh7 (threat 2 Qh3) so that 1...Qc5 is met by 2 Re1 and 1...Qxe5 by 2 Rxe5, but 1...Qd4! leaves White with no reply. The correct way to unpin the queen is by **1 Bd4!** (threat 2 Re3). 1...Qxd4 and 1...Qxe5 allow simple recaptures, but 1...Qxe4 2 Qb5 is neat while the star variation 1...Qxb3+ 2 Bb2 features a self-pin by the queen and a switchback by the bishop.

24 (Anderson) At the moment White's rook + bishop battery is effectively controlled by Black's bishop, since 1 Bc2 allows the king to move to c4. White would like to induce ...Rd3 or ...Rg6 to interfere with the h7 bishop and bring the battery to life, but at present there is no reason why the rook should move to these squares. The key **1 Kd6!** (threat 2 Qb7) provides an excellent reason and the checks are met by battery mates: 1...Rg6+ 2 Be6 and 1...Rd3+ 2 Bd5. The key also gives two flights, again leading to mates by discovery after 1...Kb6 2 Bc2 and 1...Kb4 2 Kxc6. There is a rather crude try 1 Ra4? (threats 2 Qb4 and 2 Bc2) which succeeds after every move except 1...Rg4!, but this try is an accident rather than part of the problem's theme.

25 (Ellerman) Once again, White needs a strong threat to cope with the obvious defence 1...dxe6 giving a flight at d5. Black's check 1...Rc4+ is already provided with the set mate 2 Nxc4, so White need not worry about it. The only reasonable way to give d5 extra protection is to move the e4 knight, even though White's king is thereby exposed to checks from the queen + knight battery. These checks can be met by Bc4, provided the h6 rook has been shut off by **1 Nf6!**. There are three knight checks which cannot be met by 2 Bc4 and these give rise to two interferences and a self-pin: 1...Nc6+ 2 Nc4, 1...Nf5+ 2 Qe4 and 1...Nxe6+ 2 d4. A number of side variations complete the picture: 1...Rc5 2 Nxd7, 1...Be4 2 Qxe4, 1...Qxh2 2 Qxh2 and 1...Qg3 2 Bxg3.

26 (Rinder) White's entire force is poised to take the pawn on f5, setting up a battery against Black's king, but which of the four available captures is correct? 1 Ndxf5? (threats 2 Rf4 and 2 Qg4) succeeds after 1...Kxf3 2 Qg4 and 1...Ne6/h5 2 Nd4, but fails to 1...Nxe3!. 1 R3xf5? (threat 2 Rfe5) leads to 1...Kxe3 2 Rf3, 1...Ng7 moves 2 Rf3 and 1...Rxd4 2 Rde5 but no mate is possible after 1...Nxf5!. 1 Nexf5? (threat 2 Re5) produces yet more mates after 1...Kxd5 2 Qc6 and 1...Ng7 moves 2 Ne3, but is refuted by 1...Rxd4!. The key is **1 Rdxf5!** (threat 2 Qg4), with the variations 1...Kxd4 2 Rd5, 1...Ng7 moves 2 Rd5 and 1...Nxe3 2 R3f4. Each of the four moves gives a different flight and in each case moves of the g7 knight result in a switchback of the key-piece to its original square. A slight defect is that one of tries has a double threat.

27 (Sammelius) There are interesting set mates by 1...Kxd5 2 Bc6 and 1...exd5 2 Bxd3, but White must make a threat. If the e5 knight moves, Re5 mate will be threatened, but where should the knight go? 1 Nf3/c6/xg6 are ruled out because they fail to provide for 1...Kxd5 and 1 Nf7 allows 1...Kf3, so there are three reasonable moves. 1 Nc4? introduces new mates after the two main defences by 1...Kxd5 2 Qa8 and 1...exd5 2 Nd2, but 1...d2! exploits the interference of the b5 bishop which no longer covers the potential escape route via d3. 1 Nxd3? produces more changes after 1...Kxd5 2 Nf6 and 1...exd5 2 Qf4, but 1...axb5! gives White's rook too many duties. The key is **1 Ng4!**, once again changing the replies to the captures at d5: 1...Kxd5 2 Ngf6 and 1...exd5 2 f3. A remarkable variety of mates in the set play, after the tries and following the key.

28 (Cheylan) Black has two flights, at e6 and f4. The mate 1...Kxe6 2 Qe7 is set, but no mate is provided for 1...Kf4. The try 1 Rd4? (threat 2 Rxe4) arranges to pin the knight after 1...Kf4 2 Qd6 and the flight granted at d4 leads to mate after 1...Kxd4 2 Nf3, but although 1...N at random allows 2 Qd6 the move 1...Nc5! blocks the queen's path to d6 and leaves White without a mate. The key is the even more generous **1 Rxe3** (threat 2 Qd6), not only granting the d4 flight, but also self-pinning the rook. 1...Kd4 is still met by 2 Nf3, but the best variation is 1...Kf4 2 Rxe4, exploiting a novel unpin of White's rook by the enemy king.

29 (Bwee) In order to overcome the possibility that the solver may overlook the try which the composer has carefully incorporated into his problem, some composers have experimented with twin positions as an alternative. Instead of a try and a key there are now two positions with different solutions. In this way the solver is obliged to find both moves to solve the problem completely. In Bwee's problem most of the action takes place on the b1–h7 diagonal. In each half a White rook + knight battery is controlled by two pieces at opposite ends of the diagonal. Each piece in turn loses control in order to defend against the threat and the battery fires in such a way as to shut off the other. This happens twice, once with each of the two batteries.

a) The key is **1 Rc3** (threat 2 Qb7) with two thematic lines 1...Rg6 2 Nd3 and 1...Qxb6 2 Ng6 together with two side lines 1...d6 2 Qc6 and 1...Bxc5 2 Qxc5.

b) Here the key is **1 Rf6** (threat 2 Rd6), with thematic lines 1...Qxb6 2 Nf5 and 1...Rg6 2 Nc2. There is only one side line, 1...Bxc5 2 Qb7. It is of interest to see why the key in one part fails in the other. In part *a*, 1 Rf6? is met by 1...Ne6! blocking the path to d6, while in *b*, 1 Rc3? is defeated by 1...Rg8! pinning the queen. The symmetrical keys and variations are elegant, but so far twin problems are still rather uncommon.

CHAPTER 2

42 (Mattison) White has a rook's pawn + wrong bishop combination, so he must prevent Black from sacrificing his rook for White's e-pawn. Thus 1 e7? Re1+ fails immediately. White must also prevent Black's rook reaching the back rank, for example 1 Kf5? Re1 2 Be5 Rc1 and ...Rc8, or 1 Bd2/g3? Rh1 and ...Rh8.

1 Be3+	Kb7

Relatively best. Black hopes for ...Rxa3 and ...Ra8, so he mustn't block the a-file with his king.

	2 e7	Rxa3

Not 2...Re1 3 Ke4, but now White must deal with the two threats ...Rxe3+ and ...Ra8.

	3 Ba7!	Ra1

Black fights on. 3...Kxa7 4 Kf4 (or 4 Kd4) Ra4+ 5 Kf5 Ra5+ 6 Kf6 Ra6+ 7 Kf7 wins, while 3...Ra2 4 Kf4 Re2 5 Be3 puts up less resistance than the main line.

	4 Kf4!	

The only move to meet the threat of ...Re1. 4 Ke4? Kxa7 and 4 Bf2? Ra8 are bad.

	4 ...	Rf1+

4...Re1 5 Be3 Rf1+ 6 Ke4 and 4...Ra4+ 5 Kf5 are worse. Where can White's king go after 4...Rf1+? 5 Ke3 Re1+ and 5 Ke4 Kxa7 are clearly no good.

	5 Bf2!	Rxf2+
	6 Ke3	Rf1
	7 Ke2	

and the pawn finally promotes. Mattison was a strong player in addition to being a fine study composer and it is unfortunate that he is remembered mainly for losing a famous rook ending to Rubinstein.

43 (Pogosjants) Black's king has a flight square at h3 so there is no point to 1 Nd6, for example, as Black can simply reply 1...g2.

	1 Bf1	Bb5!

Black must do something special or White will consolidate his material advantage, which is more than enough to win.

	2 Bg2	

Not 2 Nxg3 Kxg3 draw.

	2 ...	Bf1!
	3 Bxf1	g2

The point of Black's play. If White takes the pawn it is stalemate. Faced with the threats of ...gxf1=Q and ...g1=Q, it is hard to believe that there is anything better.

	4 Ng3!	g1=Q

Or 4...Kxg3 5 Bxg2.

	5 Nf5 mate.	

This study might well have come from the Golden Age since it has the characteristic feature of a single clear-cut line of play with a sharp finale, but in fact it is less than twenty-five years old.

44 (Benko) This study shows how a clever composer can find fresh ideas based on earlier work, in this case a position published by Steinitz in 1862. Here the colours are reversed, so White is trying to prevent the Steinitz combination.

1 Rd4!

1 Kg1? (1 Rd6/d7? Bh5 2 Re6/7+ Kf2 and White cannot force stalemate) h2+ 2 Kg2 (2 Kh1 Bg6 3 Rd4 Ke3 and 4...Be4+ wins for Black) Bh5 3 Rh8 (3 Rf8 loses to 3...Bf3+! 4 Rxf3 h1=Q+ 5 Kxh1 Kxf3 6 Kg1 g2) loses to Steinitz's discovery: 3...h1=Q+! 4 Kxh1 Kf2 5 Rf8+ Bf3+ 6 Rxf3+ Kxf3 7 Kg1 g2 and the pawn promotes.

1 ...   Bh5

A position with White's rook on the h-file and his king on g1 is completely drawn since ...h2+ can always be met by Rxh2. Thus 1...Be8 2 Rh4 Kf2 3 Rf4+ Ke3 4 Rh4 is a draw because Black must play ...Kf2 again to prevent Kg1 by White. 1...Bg6 2 Rh4 Kf2 3 Rf4+ is analogous.

2 Rh4

Unfortunately 2 Re4+ works just as well. If this were the main line of a problem such an alternative, called a dual, would effectively demolish the composition. The rules for studies are less strict and minor duals are permitted, although they still lessen the value of the study. Benko decided to publish this study in spite of the flaw and quite rightly so, for it is an interesting contribution to endgame theory.

2 ...   Kf2

2...Kf1 is met by 3 Rf4+, but now Rf4+ loses to ...Bf3+.

3 Rg4!

and Black is in zugzwang! 3...Bxg4, 3...g2+ 4 Kh2 Bxg4 and 3...h2 4 Rxg3 Kxg3 are all stalemate, while 3...Be8 4 Rf4+ Ke3 5 Rh4 and 3...Kf3 4 Rh4 lead to draws by repetition. If it were White to move then he would lose, so this is a position of mutual zugzwang.

45 (Adamson) This pawn ending is much trickier than it appears from the diagram.

1 Kf7

1 Ke7? (if White touches his b-pawn, then ...Kg6 also draws) Kg6 2 Kd6 Kf5 3 Kc6 Ke4 4 Kb6 Kd4 5 Kxa6 Kc4 and Black wins the b-pawn.

1 ...   Kh6

The only move, for 1...Kh8 2 b4 followed by Ke6 wins, while 1...a5 2 Ke6 allows White to save his b-pawn by playing b4 at the end of the line given in the last note.

2 Kf6!

2 Ke6? (2 b4? Kg5 draw) Kg5 3 Ke5 (once Black's king is allowed to the g-file the position is a draw) Kg4! 4 Ke4 Kg3! (not 4...Kg5? 5 b4, nor 4...a5? 5 Kd4 with a win for White in both cases) 5 Ke3 (5 b3, 5 b4 and 5 Kd4 are all met by ...Kf2) Kg2! (Black must defend accurately, for example 5...Kg4? 6 b3! wins for White, as we shall see in the main line of the study) 6 Ke2 (or else ...Kf1) Kg3 (6...Kg1 also draws) 7 b4 Kf4 8 Kd3 Ke5 9 Kc4 Kd6 draw. The reason why this is a draw, while the main line (with the two kings one square to the right) is a win, lies in the fact that b5 is inaccessible to White's king, so that after 9...Kd6 White is stuck. With the kings one square further right White can move to c5.

| 2 | ... | Kh5 |

2...Kh7 loses to 3 b4.

3 Kf5

3 Ke5? and 3 b4? draw after 3...Kg4, as in the note to White's second move.

| 3 | ... | Kh4 |

3...Kh6 4 b4 Kg7 5 Ke6 Kf8 6 Kd7 wins.

4 Kf4

4 Ke4? Kg3 5 Ke3 Kg2! draws as usual.

| 4 | ... | Kh3 |
| 5 | Kf3 | |

5 b4? Kg2 6 Ke3 Kf1 draw.

| 5 | ... | Kh2 |

5...Kh4 6 b4 Kg5 7 Ke4 Kf6 8 Kd5 Ke7 9 Kc6 Kd8 10 Kb7 wins.

6 Kf2

White must still follow Black's king as 6 b3/b4? Kg1 is a draw.

| 6 | ... | Kh3 |

6...Kh1 7 b4 and 6...a5 7 Ke3 are easy wins.

7 b3!!

The trap is 7 b4? Kg4! 8 Ke3 Kf5 9 Kd4 Ke6 10 Kc5 a5! (10...Kd7? loses to 11 Kb6 a5 12 Kxa5) 11 bxa5 Kd7 with a draw.

| 7 | ... | Kg4 |

7...Kh2 8 b4 wins, as does 7...a5 8 Ke3.

8 Ke3	**Kf5**

9 Kd4 Ke6 (9...Kf4 10 b4 wins) **10 Kc5 Ke5** (10...a5 11 Kb5 a4 12 Kxa4)
11 b4! (11 Kb6? Kd4 draw) **Ke4 12 Kb6** and wins.

46 (Kaminer) After 1 h7 Black cannot prevent promotion, but he can
work up dangerous counterplay against White's king.

1 h7	**Bh5**

Now the obvious continuation is 2 h8=Q (2 h8=N+? Kf6 drops a piece)
Bxg6+ 3 Ka1 but after 3...Be7! Black has dangerous threats. The only way
to avoid immediate loss of the queen is by 4 Nf3 Bf6+ 5 Ne5+ but 5...Ke7
leaves White without a move. He must lose his queen and probably the
game too. The solution is to use the g6 knight as a desperado.

2 Nf4!!	**gxf4**

Black must accept, for example 2...Bg4 3 h8=Q Bf5+ 4 Ka1 gxf4 (or else
Nh5) 5 Nf3 wins. However, the significance of the White's sacrifice isn't
clear, for Black's pawn appears no worse placed on f4 than on g5.

3 h8=Q	**Bg6+**
4 Ka1	**Be7**

4...Bf8 5 Nf3 Bg7+ 6 Ne5+ Kf6 7 Qg8 wins.

5 Nf3	**Bf6+**
6 Ne5+	**Ke7**

All as before, but now White reveals the point of his second move.

7 Qh4!!	

The pinner pinned! Black must take or Qxf4 wins.

7 ...	**Bxh4**
8 Nxg6+	

and **9 Nxh4** leaves White a piece to the good with an easy win.

47 (Nadareishvili) Two pieces down White must make his passed pawns
count quickly.

1 g6	**Kf6**

1...e5 2 g7 Bb3 3 h6 Nf3 4 h7 Ng5 5 g8=Q or 4...Nh4 5 g8=Q Ng6+ 6 Kg7
wins.

2 g7	**Bh7!**

A surprising sacrifice. If White accepts he can only draw, e.g. 3 Kxh7 Nf3
4 g8=Q (4 e4 attempting to transpose to the main line fails to 4...Ng5+ 5

182

Kg8 e5! and now 6 Kh8 Nf7+ 7 Kh7 Ng5+ or 6 h6 Kg6 7 Kf8 Nh7+ 8 Ke7 Nf6 and Black is at least drawing) Ng5+ 5 Qxg5+ (White must give up his queen to prevent perpetual check) Kxg5 6 h6 c4 7 Kg7 c3 8 h7 c2 9 h8=Q c1=Q 10 Qh6+ Kg4 and Black is saved by the pawn on c7. As originally published there was no pawn at c7, because at that time the ending of Q+P v Q was considered to be a draw. Later this view was revised, so the above line became a win for White after 11 Qxe6+. Fortunately the cure was simple in this instance, but there have been cases where studies were rendered unsound by changes in theoretical verdicts, without any possible remedy. Sometimes composers need to be gifted with precognition!

3 e4!

Threatening e5+ followed by Kxh7, so Black must arrange to take the irritating pawn with his knight.

3 ...   Nf3

3...e5 4 Kxh7 is more or less the same as the main line.

4 e5+!

4 Kxh7 transposes to the note to Black's second move.

4 ...   Nxe5

White has completed his foreplan, the sole purpose of which was to jettison the e3 pawn.

5 Kxh7   Nf3

Once again Black aims for perpetual check, but the h6–c1 diagonal lies ominously open.

6 g8=Q

6 h6? Ng5+ and ...Kg6.

6 ...   Ng5+
7 Qxg5+   Kxg5

8 h6 c4 (8...Kf6 9 Kg8 promotes with check) 9 Kg7 c3 10 h7 c2 11 h8=Q c1=Q 12 Qh6+ and wins, thanks to the selfless e3 pawn.

48 (Troitsky)
1 Rc2+   Kb3

1...Kb1 loses without a fight after 2 Ne2 a1=Q 3 Nc3+ Qxc3+ 4 Kxc3 a2 5 Rb2+ Ka1 6 Rh2 followed by mate.

2 Rc1

This looks decisive as 2...Kb2 3 Kd2! a1=Q 4 Nd3+ Ka2 5 Nb4+ Kb2 6 Rxa1 Kxa1 7 Kc1 a2 8 Nc2 is mate, and an unwary solver might be deluded into believing this to be the main line.

2	...	**a1=Q!**

Studies differ from problems in that Black's moves can often be harder to find than White's! This applies especially to many modern compositions which aim to blend active play by both sides.

3	**Rxa1**	**Kb2**

3...a2 4 Rf1! transposes.

4	**Rf1!**

Not 4 Ra2+? Kxa2 5 Kc2 Ka1 and White's knight is too far away from b3. Likewise 4 N moves Kxa1 5 Kc2 a2. The choice of f1 as opposed to e1, g1 or h1 is motivated by the final position.

4	...	**a2**

Now 5 Kd2? a1=Q 6 Nd3+ Ka2 7 Nb4+ Kb2 only draws.

5	**Kc4!**	**a1=Q**
6	**Nd3+**	**Ka2**
7	**Nb4+**	**Kb2**
8	**Rf2+**	**Kb1**

8...Kc1 (8...Ka3 9 Nc2+) 9 Na2+ Kb1 10 Kb3 wins, but if White had played 4 Re1? his rook would be on e2 and this allows 8...Kc1 9 Na2+ Kd1!.

9	**Kb3!**

and Rf1 mate cannot be stopped. If White had played 4 Rg1/h1? Black would now save himself by 9...Qa7/a8!.

49 (Pachman) White's material advantage of rook for bishop is enough to win, but Black has immediate threats of ...Bxc5 and ...f1=Q+. White must also take care to preserve his last pawn.

1	**Ne4+**

Not 1 Ne6+? Kf5 2 Ng7+ Kg6 and White loses his knight.

1	...	**Kf4**

Black aims to meet Nxf2 by ...Kg3. The alternative 1...Kg4 is simply answered by 2 Ke2.

2	**Rh4+**

Not 2 Ke2? Nd4+ and 3...Kxe4 nor 2 Nxf2? Kg3 3 Rh5 Nc3+.

2	...	**Ke3**

If Black's king retreats White can take the f2 pawn in safety.

3	**Nxf2!**

184

3 Ng3? is surprisingly answered by 3...Kd3! threatening mate in two by 4...Nc3+ 5 Kc1 Ba3, and after 4 Rxb4 (4 Kc1 Ba3+ 5 Kb1 Nc3+ 6 Ka1 Kc2 wins for Black) Nc3+ 5 Kc1 Na2+ Black even has the advantage.

3 ...   **Nc3+**

3...Be7 (3...Kxf2 4 Rxb4 Nc3+ 5 Kd2 Nd5 6 Rd4 Ne7 7 g4 wins) 4 Ng4+ Kf4 5 Nf6+! Kg5 (5...Ke3 6 Nd5+) 6 Rh5+ and 7 Rxb5 wins for White; other moves allow White to preserve his material plus.

4 Ke1!

4 Kc2? Kxf2 5 Rxb4 allows Black to win the g-pawn by 5...Nd5 followed by ...Ne3+ and ...Nxg2.

4 ...   **Ne4+**

Because the bishop is attacked Black doesn't have a really dangerous discovered check. 4...Nd5+, 4...Na2+ and 4...Ba5 are all met by 5 Kf1.

5 Kf1   **Ng3+**

5...Nxf2 6 Rxb4 and 5...Nd2+ 6 Kg1 are hopeless.

6 Kg1   **Ne2+**

6...Be1 (6...Be7 7 Rh3 Bd6 8 Nh1 wins) 7 Ng4+ Kf4 (7...Ke2 8 Rh8 and 9 Re8+) 8 Nh6+ Kg5 9 Rh3 Kf4 10 Nf7 Ke3 11 Rh6 wins, but Black can set a few traps by 6...Bc5. If then 7 Ng4+? Kf4+ 8 Kh2 Nf5 White loses material, while after 7 Rh3 Kf4 White is so tangled up that he must repeat moves by 8 Rh4+. The correct line is 7 Rc4 Ne2+ (7...Bd4 8 Kh2 Nf1+ 9 Kh3 wins) 8 Kf1 Ng3+ 9 Ke1 Bd4 (to stop Rc3+) 10 Rc8 followed by Re8+ and White disentangles his pieces.

7 Kh1

Not 7 Kh2? Bd6+ and ...Kxf2.

7 ...   **Be1**

Further checks let White out by 7...Ng3+ 8 Kh2 Nf1+ 9 Kg1. After 7...Be1 White is in danger of losing a piece, for example 8 Ng4+? Kf4 9 Nf2+ Kg5 (Black need not repeat) 10 Rg4+ (10 Re4 Ng3+) Kf5 or 8 Nd1+? Kd2.

8 Rh3+!   **Kxf2**
9 Rf3 mate.

After Black's efforts to harass White's king the sudden turn around comes out of the blue.

50 (Réti, corrected by Rinck) White can stop Black's pawns after either bishop check, but only one leads to a win.

1 Bf5+

1 Bc6+? Kd6 2 Rd4+ Ke5 3 Re4+ Kd6 4 Rxe3 e1=Q 5 Rxe1 only leads to stalemate.

1	...	Kd6 (or d8)
2	Rd4+	Ke7

2...Ke5 3 Re4+ and 4 Rxe3 wins without trouble.

3	Re4+	Kd8

It seems incredible that White has a better move than 4 Rxe3, which draws after 4...e1=Q 5 Rxe1 stalemate.

4	Bd7!!	e1=Q
5	Bb5	

and Re8 mate cannot be prevented. The position of the bishop at b5 defends White's king from queen checks at b1 and b4.

51 (Pogosjants) White can't push his pawn immediately as 1 d6? allows 1...Nf5+ and 2...Nxd6.

1	Kf6	Kh6
2	d6	Ne8+!

A difficult move to see, but the only one to continue the fight since 2...e3 3 d7 e2 4 Bxe2 Ne8+ 5 Ke7! and 2...Nh5+ 3 Ke5 win easily.

3	Bxe8	e3
4	d7	

Not 4 Bb5? e2 5 Bxe2 stalemate.

4	...	e2

So that after 5 d8=Q e1=Q White has no check and Black draws easily.

5	d8=N!	e1=N!

5...e1=Q 6 Nf7+ Kh5 7 Ne5+ either mates by 7...Kh6 8 Ng4 or wins the queen after 7...Kh4 8 Nf3+.

6	Nc6!	

Black's knight can arrive in time to prevent mates at f5 or g4 so White must head for g8, which is too far away. White arrives one tempo ahead of Black's knight check, which would free his king from the mating net.

6	...	any
7	Ne7	any
8	Ng8 mate.	

52 (Moravec) It is astonishing that this fine study only gained tenth prize, since it contains a wealth of interesting play.

1 Kh7!

Black's king is badly placed, trapped on the edge of the board, so 1 Ra4? g5 is ridiculous. But why not 1 Kxg7? The point is revealed in the note to Black's fourth move.

	1 ...	h4

There is a second interesting line which echoes White's refusal to take a pawn at move one: 1...g5 2 Kg6 g4 (2...h4 3 Kxg5 h3 4 Kg4 h2 5 Kg3 h1=N+ 6 Kf3 wins) 3 Kg5! (not 3 Kxh5? g3 4 Kg4 g2 5 Kg3/h3 Kh1! 6 Rxg2 stalemate) g3 4 Kh4 g2 5 Kh3! (5 Kg3? h4+ 6 Kh3 Kh1 draw) and wins.

2	Kg6	h3
3	Kg5	h2
4	Kg4	g5!

After 4...h1=Q 5 Kg3 Black immediately loses his new queen, but if White had played 1 Kxg7? Black would be able to cover a1 by ...Qh8. 4...h1=N also loses quickly after 5 Kf3 g5 6 Rd2! g4+ 7 Kxg4 Nf2+ 8 Kf3 Nh3 (8...Nh1 9 Ra2) 9 Kg3.

5	Kg3	h1=N+
6	Kf3	g4+
7	Kxg4	Nf2+
8	Kf3	Nd3

8...Nh3+ 9 Kg3, 8...Nd1 9 Ra1 and 8...Nh1 9 Rb2 lose at once.

9 Ra5!

and now:

1) **9...Ne1+ 10 Ke2 Ng2** (10...Nc2 11 Ra4) **11 Ra1+ Kh2 12 Kf3 Nh4+ 13 Kg4 Ng2** (13...Ng6 14 Re1 threatens Re8 and leads to two similar variations after 14...Nh8 15 Re2+ Kg1 16 Kg3 Kf1 17 Re6 or 14...Nf8 15 Re2+ Kg1 16 Kg3 Kf1 17 Rf2+) **14 Rc1!** and we have transposed to the position after 12 Rh3 in the note to Black's second move of Diagram 41, with the board turned by 90 degrees.

2) **9...Kh2/h1 10 Rd5 Nb4** (or the knight is lost at once) **11 Rd6** and Black has no knight moves, while king moves are eliminated by the lines 11...Kh1 12 Kf2, 11...Kg1 12 Ke2 Kg2 13 Kd2 Kf3 14 Kc3 Na2+ 15 Kb2 Nb4 16 Kb3 and 11...Kh2 12 Rd2+ Kh3 (12...Kg1 13 Rd1+) 13 Rd1 Kh2 14 Rd6 and the king must now move to g1.

3) **9...Nb4 10 Rg5+ Kh2** (10...Kh1 11 Kg3) **11 Rg2+ Kh3** (11...Kh1 12 Kg3) **12 Rg6 Kh2 13 Rd6** transposes to line 2.

CHAPTER 3

69 (Stuart-Green) If it were Black to move, White would be able to mate immediately, for example 1...B moves 2 Qh2, 1...N moves 2 Qe5 or 1...f2

2 Ne2. Thus if White had a waiting move he would be able to mate in two moves. Naturally there are no waiting moves and White is obliged to spin the solution out to three moves. Problems of this type are called **pseudo-two-movers**. The solution is best found by a process of elimination. 1 Q moves b2+ 2 Qxb2 provides Black with the move 2...b3 which saves the day, 1 e5 Nc5 blocks the e5 square and frees the Black knight, while the brutal moves 1 Nexf3 gxf3 and 1 Ngxf3 gxf3 2 Rfg1+ Kf2 don't lead to mate. Thus the solver is led to consider **1 Nh3**, placing Black in zugzwang. The variations **1...Kxh4 2 Nf4+ Kg3** (2...Kg5 3 Rxh5) **3 Nxh5, 1...f2 2 Nxf2 B moves 3 Rfg1, 1...gxh3 2 Rhg1+** and **3 Nxf3, 1...Nf6** (or anywhere else) **2 Nf4 f2** (2...N moves 3 Nxh5) **3 Ne2** and **1...B moves 2 Qf2 mate** verify that it is the correct key. Although White was unable to maintain the initial zugzwang position, he could abandon it to set up different zugzwangs at the second move, an interesting type of changed play.

70 (Shinkman) Black is stalemated so White must free his king on the first move. It is much easier to mate Black if he is forced to approach White's king, so it is very unlikely that Black will be allowed to move to the b-file. Assuming that White's king remains at e4 throughout, Black can be mated at c6, d6 or e6, but not at c7, d7 or e7. The mate with BKc6 and WQd5 looks especially promising, so suppose that the bishop stays at a5. Then White must play 1 Qb something, forcing 1...Kd7. White cannot mate a king at d6, e6, e7 or e8, so these squares must be covered by the queen at move 2. Thus e5 is the logical spot for the queen, so **1 Qb2 Kd7 2 Qe5** looks best and indeed mates after **2...Kc8 3 Qc7** or **2...Kc6 3 Qd5**. Bohemian problems often require this sort of inspired guesswork, spotting an attractive mate and working out how it might be forced.

71 (Havel) Black's king can escape to e4 or e6 and mates are not prepared for either flight. The e4 square is particularly menacing, since if Black's king can reach d3 there is not the slightest hope of delivering mate. Since the problem won a first prize, it is unlikely that the key will take away the e4 flight, so we have to find a way to prevent the king slipping away further to d3. 1 Rd7 is possible, but this takes away e6 so we should only look at it as a last resort. Meeting 1...Ke4 by 2 Qg6/h7+ is no help — 2...Kd5 and 2...f5 are both adequate answers. It seems that 1...Ke4 must be answered by 2 Nf2+, which implies that the bishop makes the key. If it moves to c5, b6 or a7, the line 1...Ke4 2 Nf2+ Kd5 (or else Qg4 mates) 3 Rxf6 (or 3 Rc7 in the case of 1 Bc5) finishes Black. 1...Ke6 also needs a reply, which eliminates 1 Ba7. 1 Bb6 Ke6 2 Rxf6+ Kd7/e7 3 Qe6 and 1 Bc5 Ke6 2 Ne3 any 3 Qe8 prove that the remaining moves cope with both king flights, but which is correct? It turns out that 1 Bb6 meets with the subtle refutation 1...Ne4, and if 2 Ne3+ then 2...Ke6. The key is therefore **1 Bc5** (threat 2 Rxf6+ Ke4 3 Nf2) and apart from 1...Ke4/e6, the other lines are **1...Ne4 2 Nh6/e3+ Ke6 3 Qe8, 1...Nd3 2 Rxf6+ Ke4 3 Qa8** and **1...Kf4 2 Nxf6** (threat 3 Qg4) **e4 3 Nd7**.

72 (Würzburg) An over-the-board player's eye would surely be drawn to the possibility of Qxb7+, which leads to mate after ...Raxb7 by Rxa6. At the moment there is no answer to ...Rbxb7, but this can be remedied by an appropriate key. 1 Rd6 threatens 2 Qxb7+ (and 2 Rd8), but 1...Ne6 defends. The rook must move beyond the range of Black's knight by **1 Rc6!**. The threat is 2 Qxb7+ Kxb7 (or else Rxa6/Rc8) 3 Rxc5. After **1...bxc6 2 Qxc6+** there are similar mates at a6 and c8 by the queen, **1...Rb8 moves** allow the back-rank mate **2 Qc8+** and finally **1...b6+** (or ...b5) allows **2 Rxb6+**. A beautiful problem with a classically simple setting.

73 (Loyd) Two batteries point at Black's king, but while both e4 and d4 remain unguarded they are ineffective. This is one of those problems which can only be solved by a flash of inspiration, so there is no point in attempting to give a logical argument leading to the key. Some solve it immediately, while others puzzle for hours without finding the key. The astonishing solution runs **1 Ke2!!** (threats 2 R along the f-file+ Kxe4 3 d3/ Bd3, and 2 Ke3) **f1=Q+** (the other lines are 1...f1=N+ 2 Rf2+, 1...Bf4 2 Rf7/f8+, 1...Nxb4 2 Bd3+ Kd4 3 dxc3 and 1...Kxe4 2 Bd3+ Kd4 3 Rf4) **2 Ke3** and although Black has ten different checks he cannot avoid mate next move.

74 (Cumpe) Black's king has four possible moves, but the only mate prepared is 1...Kxd4 2 Re1 Kc4 3 Re4. The most difficult move to deal with is 1...Kf6, heading for open spaces. Against this, White's best chance appears to be 2 Qh8+, so that if the king moves to the seventh rank White can mate with his rook. This requires the key to be a king move or a rook move along the first rank. On closer examination, the variation 1...Kf6 2 Qh8+ Kg5 causes difficulties due to White's lack of control of f4, which prevents a rook mate. Even after 1 Rf1 there is no mate. 1 Rg1 prevents ...Kg5 completely, but 1 Rg1 Kf6 2 Qh8+ Kf7 3 Rg7 isn't mate. The only remaining possibility is **1 Rh1**, so that **1...Kf6 2 Qh8+ Kg5** allows **3 Qh4**. We have already seen **1...Kxd4 2 Re1**, while the other lines run **1...Ke4 2 Qg3 Kxd4 3 Rh4** and **1...Kf4 2 Kd5 Kg5 3 Qh4**. The key is as surprising as in Loyd's problem, although not in such a spectacular and violent manner.

75 (Kipping) It doesn't take long to realise that White cannot force mate without the participation of his king. 1 Kb5 is the natural try, threatening both 2 Ne7+ Ka7 3 Nc8 and 2 Kb6 followed by Nc7 or a move of the c6 knight. Black's only defences to the first threat are 1...Rg5, 1...Rg6 and 1...Rg8, but the first two fail against 2 Kb6. However, 1 Kb5 Rg8 2 Kb6 is met by 2...Rc8! and Black avoids mate. In this line White is handicapped by the position of his king, which prevents a mate by 2 Nd4+ Ka7 3 Nb5. Could **1 Ka5** be the key? It looks outrageous to allow Black to promote with check, but after **1...e1=Q+** (forced, as 1...Rg6 2 Kb6 and 1...Rg8 2 Nd4+ mate) **2 Kb6** the new queen isn't much help to Black. However he chooses to prevent 3 Nc7, White can always mate with the bishop + knight battery, the knight moving to a5, b4, d4, e5 or e7 as appropriate. It is impossible to imagine how a problem such as this might be improved.

76 (Grasemann) The bishop + king battery is all set to fire at Black's king, but at the moment Black controls all the White king's flights. The key is most easily found by a process of elimination. White's queen cannot move without allowing ...f5+, or if 1 Qxf7 then 1...Ng5+ and the bishop goes with check. The knight and pawn control c5 and b5 respectively. If Black's king could reach one of these squares then the flights at b4 and c4 would make mate impossible. Other moves, such as 1 Bh1 and 1 Re8, create no threat. That leaves the b8 bishop as a potential key-piece. If it moves b8 is freed for the knight, but 1 Be5, for example, carries no threat, since 2 Nb8+ Kc5 leads to nothing. Therefore **1 Bd6** must be considered. Although this creates a short threat of 2 Nb8, in other respects it is an excellent key, giving Black's king a flight and unpinning the knight. **1...Kxd6 2 Ne5+ Kc5/c7 3 Qe7** disposes of the flight, but what about the knight checks? **1...Nc5+** interferes with the rook to allow **2 Kf5+** (Black mustn't be allowed to take f3 with check) **Ne4+** (2...Nxf3 3 Nb8) **3 Be5**, while **1...Ng5+** interferes with the bishop, permitting **2 Ke3+ Ne4+ 3 Bf4**.

77 (Kraemer) Black is stalemated and the only way this can be lifted is by a rook move along the b-file, allowing Black's king access to g7. The problem is to choose the right square on the b-file. 1 R at random Kg7 gives Black's king considerable freedom, but White can restrict it by 2 Qb7+. Then 2...Kf8 and 2...Kh6 are met by 3 h8=Q, while provided the first move wasn't to b8, White can mate after 2...Kf6 by 3 Rb6. Thus the only tricky move is 2...Kh8. In this case the unfortunate aspect of White's second move is revealed, since the queen blocks the rook's path to b8. However, White can compensate for this by opening a path to b2 with **1 Rb1! Kg7 2 Qb7+ Kh8 3 Qb2**.

78 (Kraemer) Various ingredients have to go into the pot before Black is well and truly in the stew. White cannot readily unpin the a4 knight as this gives Black a check at c5 and the immediate 1 Qa1 (threat 2 Qh1) is foiled by 1...Nd1. If White could bring his bishop to the g1–a7 diagonal Ra7 mate would ensue, but 1 Bd6 is met by 1...Bd4. Suppose White plays a waiting move, such as 1 Bf6. Then 1...Bd2/e1 allows 2 Bd4 and if Black plays to d4 or e5 White plays 2 BxB, forcing the b2 knight to move allowing 3 Qg2. Unfortunately there is no reply to 1...Bxf6. f6 is not the only square on the long diagonal and White's first move could just as well have been to d4, g7 or h8. In each case 1...BxB is the only worrying reply, but after **1 Bh8! Bxh8 2 Qa1 Nd1** White mates by **3 Qxh8**. In different lines White's queen moves to a1, h1 and h8, giving a pleasant impression that the whole board is being utilised in the problem.

190

79 (Scheel) In 77 and 78 the key was an integral part of the problem's theme, but here the key serves merely to introduce the play. There are two pointers to the key; first, Black has an unprovided flight at g3, and secondly White's queen is underemployed at a2. It makes sense to look at queen moves first and we can at once reject moves like 1 Qe6? (threat 2 Qh3), which don't provide a mate in response to 1...Kg3. 1 Qd5 doesn't suffer from this criticism as 1...Kg3 2 Qg5+ mates, but there is a triple threat of 2 Be5+, 2 Qe5+ and 2 Qd6+ so it comes as no surprise to find that 1...Ng6! is an adequate defence. The only remaining square on the a2–g8 diagonal which looks plausible is b3 and, indeed, after 1 Qb3 Kg3 White can choose between 2 Bf6+ Kf4/g4 (2...Kh2 3 Qh3/g4) 3 Qf3 and 2 Bd2+ Kg4/h4/h2 3 Qh3. Moreover, there is a threat of 2 Bd2 when Black cannot meet 3 Bf4 and 3 Qh3. Black can only exploit the position of the queen at b3 by 1...c4! when 2 Bd2 fails because Black takes the queen with check. Thus we are led to **1 Qa3**, with the same threat. **1...c4 2 Qd6+** and **1...Ng6 2 Be1** are the less interesting defences, although the latter involves an interference down the g-file preventing 2...Rg8 as a defence to 3 Bg3. The main lines are 1...Re8, 1...Rf8 and 1...Rg8 in each case preparing to move to the third rank should White play 2 Bd2. White's strategy is the same in all three lines. He moves the bishop to threaten Qh3 and when the d7 knight moves to stop this he mates by 3 g4. The choice of square for the bishop is determined by the need to cut off Black's rook, e.g. **1...Re8 2 Be5+ Nxe5 3 g4**, **1...Rf8 2 Bf6** or **1...Rg8 2 Bg7**. Unfortunately 1...Rg8 can also be met by 2 Be5+, a weakness in an otherwise excellent problem. Note that the analogous 2 Bd4 is not a threat since it can be taken with check.

80 (Burger and Matthews) White would like to threaten Rf7 mate by 1 K moves, but at the moment this exposes White's king to checks. However, if White forms a battery by taking on e5 at move 1, Black's checks can be met by battery mates. 1 Nxe5? doesn't work because of 1...Rd1 2 K moves R checks and when the knight moves Black can interpose his queen at e5. So the key must be **1 Rxe5**. When White unpins the e5 rook by a king move he must be careful to force Black to check with his queen since, as we saw above, a rook check leaves the queen free to move to e5. Thus the threat is 2 Kf7 Qa2/b3+ (or else 3 Re4/f5) 3 Rd5/e6. Black's main defences are 1...Rc1/d1/e1/a3 (1...Ra6/a7/a8 2 Kh6 and 1...Rh1 2 Kf8/g8 are less important). All these prevent 2 Kf7 by threatening to capture a vital White piece. **1...Rc1** forces White to make the accurate choice **2 Kf8!** so that **2...Qa3/b4+ 3 Rc5** shuts off the rook and queen at the same time. Similarly **1...Rd1 2 Kg8 Qa2/b3+ 3 Rd5** mates with the cutting point being at d5. The other two defences are rather different. **1...Re1 2 Kxg6** is possible now that Black's rook can't move to the third rank and leads to a necessary double check after **2...Qb1/c2+ 3 Re4/f5**, and lastly **1...Ra3 2 Kh6** exploits the lack of a rook move to the h-file. Six different squares for the king at move 2 is a fine achievement with relatively light force.

81 (Anderson) If the c6 rook moves White threatens Qb5 mate, but Black has two possible defences, 1...Bd3 and 1...Bf5. White can prevent one defence by moving the rook to c4 or e6, but Black only needs one to stop the mate. However, we might guess that Black will be induced to invalidate one of the two bishop moves with his first move, allowing White to mate by an accurate choice of rook destination at move 2. The knight at f4 is a likely candidate for getting in the way of the bishop, since moves to e6 and d3 block one or other of Black's defences. The next question is to ask what White's threat might be, that 1...Nd3 and 1...Ne6 stop it? Both moves cover c5, so the threat could be 2 Nc5+. This doesn't work yet because of ...Ka5, but **1 Rb1!** supports the b-pawn to threaten 2 Nc5+ Ka5 3 b4. A trial and error approach wouldn't come up with a move like Rb1 since the rook looks far more likely to be useful at a1 than at any other square. After 1 Rb1 Black has four defences, which fall naturally into two pairs. The first pair is **1...Nd3 2 Re6** and **1...Ne6 2 Rc4**, as expected, but the second pair is rather surprising: **1...Bxb1 2 Rc2** and **1...Be7 2 Rg6**. In these lines Black suffers because his bishop is on one side of both critical squares and can be shut off from them with a single move. If the bishop were between the critical squares this couldn't happen. Finally **1...bxc6 2 Kb8** mates by **3 Qc8** or **3 c8=Q** as appropriate.

82 (Rehm) The line-up along the fifth rank looks likely to be the focus of the problem, but at the moment the a5 rook wouldn't mate even if the intervening pieces were removed since f6 would be undefended. Suppose for the moment that the key defends f6. If Black played 1...Nxd5 White could shut off both Black bishops to mate by 2 d4+ Ne3/f4 (2...Kh5 3 Bg4) 3 Bd3, while after 1...Nxf5 White achieves the same end by different means after 2 d3+ Ne3 3 Nc3. These elegant symmetrical variations are too good to be anything but the main point of the problem, so we now have to find the key. It must be 1 R on f6 moves, or 1 Qe6/f7/e7. The rook moves create no threat and by a process of elimination (1 Qe7? Re8! and 1 Qe6? Be5!) we arrive at **1 Qf7!** (threat 2 Rxg6+). Apart from the two main lines given above there are three side variations: **1...gxf5 2 Qxg8+, 1...Bxf6 2 Qxf6+** and **1...Kh5 2 Rxg6**.

CHAPTER 4

94 (von Gottschall) The threat is brutal but the variations subtle, a combination making for hard solving. After **1 Qc1** (threat 2 Qe3) there are two variations:
1) **1...Kb6 2 Na4+ Kb7** (2...bxa4 3 Ba6! and mates by 3...Kxa6 4 Qxc6 or 3...c5 4 Qh6) **3 Qxc6+! Kxc6** (3...Kb8 3 Qc8) **4 Be4**.
2) **1...Kd4 2 Bh7!** (threat 3 Qe3+ Kc4 4 Bg8) **Kxe5** (2...Kc4 3 Bg8+ and 4 Qe3) **3 Qe3+ Kf6** (3...Kd6 4 Qe7) **4 Qe7**, explaining the choice of square for White's second move.

95 **(Breuer)** Stalemate looms in many lines, for example after 1 Qxh8. If only White's queen were a rook there would be a mate in two by 1 Rxh8 Kf6 2 Rf8. Such apparently irrelevant thoughts often lead to the solution, although whether this is logic or lateral thinking is hard to say. **1 Qh1!** (1 Qb8 Rg8 2 a8=R Rd8+! and White cannot mate in four) **Rxh1** (anywhere else on the h-file, White just takes the rook, while if 1...Rd8+ 2 Kxd8 followed by Qh6–g7 mates in four) **2 a8=R! Rh8** (or else Rf8) **3 Rxh8 Kf6 4 Rf8.**

96 **(Kraemer)** This is a very enjoyable problem to solve since the position forces the solver to find each finesse in turn. Moves like 1 Qh4? can be quickly rejected as Black's rook becomes too active after 1...Rh1, so the idea must be to play the knight to c7. White might consider 1 Nd8/d4 intending 2 Ne6, or 1 Nb4/e7 intending 2 Nd5, four possibilities in all. In every case 1...b1=Q and 1...Rxe1 don't help Black, so the only defence is 1...c2 (1...Rd1 2 Qxd1 and 3 Qd5), threatening a fatal check at c1. White's only move is 2 Qc1!, blocking the pawn's progress. With the c-file sealed Black's threats are nullified and it is hard to see how Black can continue the fight. So at first sight there are four possible keys. The next finesse is 1 N moves c2 2 Qc1! b1=B!!, aiming for stalemate. The significance of White's first move now becomes clear, for if the knight is on d4, d8 or e7, there is no effective way for White to lift the stalemate.

After **1 Nb4! c2 2 Qc1! b1=B!**, on the other hand, White can play **3 Nd3! exd3 4 Qh1.**

97 **(Siers)** White has ample force to mate, but his pieces are obstructed by an army of White pawns. Nevertheless, it seems easy to mate in five. White's first move must be a move by the Be4, but then he can play Rg5–g2 confining the Black king to the first rank and then Rh8–h1 mating. The flaw in this argument is that Black can play 1 Bb7 (say) Kb1 2 Rg5 Kc2 3 Rg2+ Kd3, leaving White unable to lift the stalemate at move 4 yet mate at move 5. White's bishop could have gone to any square on the long diagonal at move one, so it might be that White can perform an Indian-style self-interference at g2, for example 1 Bh1 Kb1 2 Rg8 (the other rook is left at c5 to cover f5 when Black's king is at e4) Kc2 3 Rg2+ Kd3 4 pass Ke4 5 Rd2. However, Black can improve by 3...Kd1! because the h1 bishop prevents White bringing the other rook to the first rank. White had a spare tempo in the above line, so he can afford to wait to see which way Black's king is going before deciding whether to play to g2. The rook must still come to the second rank, or Black's king doesn't have to decide, so it must play firstly to h2. The solution runs **1 Bh1! Kb1 2 Rh8! Kc2 3 Rh2+ Kd3** (3...Kd1 4 Rg5 and 5 Rg1) **4 Rg2 Ke4 5 Rd2.** It is strange that the solution involves chasing the king out from the corner, where it is most vulnerable, to the centre of the board, where mate is most difficult to deliver.

98 (Schneider) Black can only move his pawn, for example 1...Be3/d4/c5/b6 2 Bb8+ Ka8 3 Bf4/e5/d6/c7+ Ka7 4 BxB mate, or 1...Bxh2 2 Bf2 or 1...Rxh2 2 Bb8+ Ka8 3 Bxh2+ Ka7 4 Bxg1. Nevertheless ...d2 and ...d1=Q+ is a major threat, so White must arrange to take the pawn with his king at d2. This involves playing Kc3xd2, but without allowing Black to give a bishop check (followed by ...g1=Q). Each time White intends moving his king, he must position his bishop to act as a shield: **1 Bb8+ Ka8 2 Be5+ Ka7 3 Kc3 d2 4 Bb8+ Ka8 5 Bf4+ Ka7 6 Kxd2** and mates in three more.

99 (Vukčević) White would like to play 1 Ne6 (threat 2 Ng7) with the variations 1...Be5 2 Ng7+ Bxg7 3 g4 and 1...Kg4 2 Nf4/g7, but Black has an irritating check 1...Bf2+. If White replies with a king move Black's own king escapes via g4 and g3. Black has few constructive moves, so why not move the king first, by 1 Kb8 say, threatening 2 Ne6? The answer is that 1...Rxc3 attacks the bishop and disrupts the mating net, for example 2 Bd7 Rc4! 3 Ne6 Be5 and the rook covers f4 and g4, while the bishop defends g7. Other king moves are no better. If White could nullify the ...Rxc3 defence he could mate in four by a suitable king move and this is the aim of White's foreplan. The solution runs **1 Ne6 Bf2+ 2 Nc5!** (threat 3 g4 and if 3...Bxc5+ 4 Ka8 and the bishop cannot return to g3) **Bg3 3 Nd7** (threat 4 Nf6, which is not prevented by 3...Kg4 or 3...Be5, so Black has to check again) **Bf2+ 4 Nb6!** (White must always avoid a king move on pain of ...Kg4) **Bg3 5 c4!** (threatening 6 Nxd5, when Black cannot cope with both Nf6 and Nf4) **Bxc4** (the only way to cover d5, but now the c-file is blocked so White can go into reverse gear) **6 Nd7 Bf2+ 7 Nc5 Bg3 8 Ne6 Bf2+ 9 Nd4 Bg3** (now White can afford a king move since his knight isn't attacked) **10 Kb8!** (10 Ka8/b7? Bb5! delays the mate) and mates in three more.

100 (Fargette)   **1 Be1+**

Not 1 Kc5? Ne6+.

1 ...   b4
2 Bf2

Black's main defence is perpetual check from the knight, aided by the fact that White cannot take the knight without stalemating Black, for example 2 Bg3? (2 Bd2? and 2 Bh4? are met the same way) Ne6! followed by ...Nd4—e6+.

2 ...   Nd5

2...Na8 3 Bg1 mates next move. White's aim is to return to this position with Black to move. His bishop is very well placed attacking b6 and having the option to attack from different directions by Be1—b4 or Bh4—d8, but it must go on a lengthy tour before returning to f2.

194

3 Bd4!

Or *1*) 3 Ba7? (3 Bc5? Ne7+) Ne7+ 4 Kc5 Nc8 5 Bb8 Nb6 (threatens perpetual check on d7 and e5) 6 Kc6 Nd5 and now 7 Bg3 Nf4! transposes to line 2, while on 7 Be5/d6/h2 Black plays 7...Ne7+ 8 Kc5 Nd5 9 Be5/d6 (White cannot win unless he can attack b4) Nb6 10 Kc6 Nd5 and White cannot escape from the threatened perpetual checks.

2) 3 Bg3? Nf4! 4 Bh2/h4 Ne6 with perpetual check at d8 and e6.

3) 3 Bh4? Nc7! followed by ...Ne6 as before.

4) 3 Bg1? Ne7+! 4 Kc5 Nd5 5 Bh2 (5 Bf2/d4 Nb6 6 Kc6 Nd7 leads to checks on d7 and e5) Nf4! and ...Ne6 draws.

| 3 | ... | Ne7+ |
| 4 | Kc5 | Nd5 |

4...Nc6/f5/c8/g6 5 Bf6 Nb6 (5...Ne7 6 Bh4 Nc6 7 Be1) 6 Kc6 and 7 Bd8+ mates, or 4...Ng8 5 Be5 and 6 Bc7.

5	Be5	Nb6
6	Kc6	Nd5
7	Bb8!	

Not 7 Bd6? (after 7 Kc5? Nb6 White must return, while 7 Bg3? Nf4 and 7 Bh2? Ne7+ will transpose to the note to White's third move) Ne7+ 8 Kc5 Nd5 9 Bb8/e5 (9 Bg3 Nf4) Nb6 10 Kc6 Nd5 drawing.

| 7 | ... | Nb6 |

7...Ne7+ 8 Kc5 Nd5 9 Ba7 and mates next move.

8 Bg3!

Not 8 Bf4? (8 Ba7? Nd7! followed by perpetual on e5 and d7) Nd5! 9 Bg5 (9 Bg3 Nf4! or 9 Be5/d6 Ne7+!) Nc7! 10 Be3 (or else ...Ne6) Nd5 11 Bf2 which does lead to mate, but is two moves too slow. 8 Bh2? Nd5 is similar to lines we have already seen after 9 Bg3 Nf4 or 9 Be5/d6 Ne7+ 10 Kc5 Nd5.

| 8 | ... | Nd5 |
| 9 | Bf2 | Ne7+ |

9...Ne3 10 Bh4 and mate in 12.

| 10 | Kc5 | Nd5 |

10...Nc6 11 Be1 also mates in 12.

11 Be1

Not 11 Bh4? Nc7! 12 Kc6 Ne6 drawing.

| 11 | ... | Nc3 |
| 12 | Bh4 | Ne4+ |

12...Na4+ 13 Kc6 Nb6 14 Be7 is mate in 16.

| 13 | Kc6 | Nf6 |

13...Ng5 14 Bf2.

| 14 | Bg5 |

and **15 Bd8+**, mating in 16 moves as required. This problem is astonishingly intricate for such slight material and is worth close study.

101 (Jahn) If it were Black to move, then White could mate in two. Surprisingly the main line does not involve White returning to this position having lost a tempo, but there are plenty of other zugzwang positions. It is very easy to become confused while tackling this problem and repeat positions, as certain strong players at the Toluca Interzonal (1982) can testify! **1 Qa8+** (White must not allow the king to escape to a6 or b6, e.g. 1 Qc8? Rh6) **Ra6 2 Qb8** (2 Qb7? Ra8! leaves White in zugzwang) **Ra8** (2...Ka4 3 Qc7 leads to mate in 7 and 2...Rh6 3 Qa7+ Ra6 4 Qc7+ transposes to the main line) **3 Qb7 Ra6 4 Qc7+ Ka4** (4...Rb6 5 Qd8 is the initial position with Black to move, so White mates in 7) **5 Qd8 Ra7** (5...Ra5 6 Qb8 Ra6 7 Qc7 is the same) **6 Qb8 Ra6** (6...Ra5 7 Qb7 mates in 8) **7 Qc7 Ra8 8 Qb6 Ra5 9 Qb7** and mate next move.

102 (Fargette) White's knight does battle with Black's bishop, occasionally assisted by the king. White can try to reach f6 with his knight, but Black's bishop is able to frustrate this naïve plan. However, White has other methods of attack, since he can play Kf6 and try to reach e7 instead. Even more alarming for Black is the possibility that White might play Ke6, waiting for Black to commit himself before deciding whether to play Kf6 or Ke7. The first step is to compile a list of corresponding squares.

1) WKe7:	*WN*	*BB*	*2) WKf6:*	*WN*	*BB*
	b6	c6/e6		b6	b7/e6
	e3	f3/e6		e3	e4/e6
	d6	g6/c6		d6	d7/f5

The only entry that needs an explanation is the entry for WKf6, WNd6, since it seems that Black's bishop can be anywhere on the c8–h3 diagonal. However, Black must be prepared to play ...Bg6 or ...Bc6 in reply to Ke7 by White, so the only viable squares are d7 and f5. The same argument allows us to cross out all references to the e6 square in the above table. For example, if White has Ke7, Nb6 and Black plays ...Be6, White replies Kf6 and Black is in zugzwang. The squares b6, e3 and d6 are all accessible from c4, so we must now consider the position with WNc4. With WKe7, Black must be prepared to go to c6, f3 and g6 according to White's knight move, so BB must be on e4, or on a square attacking c4. Similarly with WKf6 and WNc4, BB must be on c6 or a square attacking c4. So far we haven't found any way for White to break the correspondence, but now consider WNd6 and WKe6, and suppose Black is to move. The threats are Ne8/e4, so Black must either play ...Bc6/g6 or he must check. In the first case White plays Ke7, so we need only consider the second case. If the check is on the a2–f7 diagonal White wins by 1 Kf6 Be6 (to stop Nc8/f5) 2 Ke7 and BB cannot reach c6/g6. If the check is on the c8–h3 diagonal it must be on d7 or f5, or Black cannot meet 1 Ke7. So suppose ...Bd7+; then 1 Kf6 Bf5 (forced from the table) 2 Nc4 wins as BB cannot play to c6. In fact we need not consider ...Bf5+ since this cannot arise from the given original position, but White wins in this case too, by 1 Ke7 Bg6 2 Kf6 Bf5 3 Nc4, as before. This proves that White can win from almost any initial position (except WNa1, BBd1 and similar accidents) and the only question is whether White can mate in eight moves by this method. He can, e.g. **1 Nd6 Bc6 2 Ke6 Bd7+** (2...Bd5+ 3 Kf6 Be6 4 Ke7 mates in 6) **3 Kf6 Bf5 4 Nc4 Bc8** (4...Be4/e6 5 Ne3) **5 Ne3 Be6 6 Ke7** and mates in two more moves.

CHAPTER 5

118 (Rusinek) White is a rook down, but he has a dangerous pawn at b7 and chances to harass Black's king.

1 Nf2+

The immediate 1 Bd6? fails to 1...Rxd6 2 b8=Q (2 Nf2+ Kg1 3 Nh3+ Kf1! 4 b8=Q Be5+ followed by ...R checks wins as the pawn at d2 prevents stalemate) Be5+ 3 Kh4 Rd4+ and 4...Bxb8.

1	...	Kg1
2	Nh3+	

Move order is important. After 2 d4? Bxd4 Black covers f2 and wins by 3 Nh3+ Kh1 4 Bd6 Rxd6 5 b8=Q Be5+ and 6...R checks.

2	...	Kf1
3	d4!	

Not 3 Kxh2? Be5+ 4 Kh1 Rh8, but now White genuinely threatens to take the knight, which cannot escape by itself. Thus Black must capture the d-pawn, increasing the danger of stalemate.

3	...	Bxd4
4	Bd6!	Rxd6
5	b8=Q	Be5+
6	Nf4	Rg6+

6...Rd3+ 7 Kh4 attacks Black's rook.

7 Kh3

Not 7 Kh4? Rg4+ when Black can safely take the queen.

7	...	Rh6+
8	Kg3	Bxb8

and Black has saved his rook, only to deliver stalemate. It is usually difficult to arrange a stalemate with pin, but Rusinek succeeds admirably.

119 (Pachman) This study looks more like a middle-game and the play is correspondingly violent. There are brutal threats of mate by 1...Qc3+, 1...Qe5+ and 1...Kb3+. Many moves fail immediately, for example 1 Kb1? Qb4+ 2 Kc2 Qb2+ 3 Kd3 Ne5+, 1 Ka2? Kb5+! 2 Kb1 Qb4+ etc., 1 Qd3? Kb5+!, 1 Qc2+? Kb4+ 2 Kb1 Na3+ and 1 Rd3? Qe5+. The most tempting try is 1 Qg3?, answered by 1...Nxe2! 2 Qb8 (2 Qd3 Kb5+) Qc3+ 3 Ka2 (3 Kb1 Na3+ 4 Ka2 Qc2+ 5 Qb2 Nc3+) Qc2+ 6 Ka1 Qxd1+ 7 Qb1 Qd4+ mating. White's first move follows by the principle of elimination.

1 Rd2!	Kb3+

Other moves aren't dangerous, for example 1...Qc3+ 2 Ka2 Qb3+ 3 Ka1 (3...Qa3+?? 4 Ra2), 1...Kb4+ 2 Ra2 Qe5+ 3 Kb1 or 1...Kb5+ 2 Kb1 Qb4+ 3 Kc1 Qc3+ 4 Kb1. This position provides a striking demonstration of the defensive power of a rook on the second rank operating in front of an attacked king, a potential well known to players.

2 Kb1	Na3+
3 Kc1	Qc3+

3...Qc5/c7+ are simply answered by 4 Kd1, but now White is deprived of both 4 Kd1 Qa1+ and 4 Rc2 Qe1 mate.

4 Qc2+!	Nxc2
5 Rd3	Nxe2+
6 Kd1	Qxd3+
7 Nd2+	

A frustrating position for Black! If he moves his king White is stalemated, while if Black captures he is left with just his knights. Another elegant pin-stalemate.

120 (Kubbel) This study is an exercise in choosing the right move-order.

1 Bf2+

Not 1 h7? c2+ 2 Kh4 (2 Kg4 Nf6+ wins the h-pawn and 2 Kf4 allows Black to promote with check) Ne7! 3 Bd2 (or else Black promotes first and gets the first check) Rxa2 followed by ...Ra8 winning on material.

1 ...	Kh1

Of course 1...Kf1 allows mate in one.

2 h7

Again White must take care. If he sacrifices on d5 prematurely, he loses by 2 Bd5+? (2 Bc5? Rxa2 3 h7 Rh2! with a g-file skewer) cxd5 3 h7 c2+ 4 Be3 (4 Kh4 still loses to 4...Ne7) Rxe3+ 5 Kf2 Rf3+! (opens the c1–h6 diagonal) 6 Kxf3 Nh6 7 h8=Q c1=Q and White has no checks. Next move Black can check, free his king and win with the extra piece and pawn.

| 2 | ... | c2+ |
| 3 | Be3! | |

3 Kg4? Nf6+, 3 Kf4? c1=Q+ and 3 Kh4? Ne7 are just as bad as before.

| 3 | ... | Rxe3+ |
| 4 | Kf2 | |

4 Kf4 is still met by 4...c1=Q setting up a deadly discovered check.

| 4 | ... | Rh3 |

4...Rf3+ doesn't work now as White still has his bishop.

| 5 | Bd5+! | |

The final trap — 5 hxg8=Q? Rh2+ 6 Kf3 c1=Q wins on material.

5	...	cxd5
6	hxg8=Q	Rh2+
7	Kf3	c1=Q
8	Qg2+!	Rxg2

with a fantastic mid-board stalemate.

121 (Kubbel and Herbstmann) Everybody knows that K+2N v K is a draw, but what about K+3N v K+N? In general, it is possible for the superior side to avoid a piece exchange, when the king and three knights form too strong an attacking force to be resisted. The defending king is easily driven to the corner and mated. So unless the K+N can force an exchange immediately, or draw quickly some other way, they will lose.

| 1 | Ng1! | |

Not 1 Ng5? Ke3 2 Nf3 Nf4+ winning the knight.

| 1 | ... | Ne3+ |

Black can't promote to a knight at once since f1 is undefended. If 1...Nf4+ 2 Kh1 e1=N (2...Ng3+ 3 Kh2 and Black must repeat) White forces stalemate by 3 Nf3+! Nxf3.

| 2 | Kh3 | |

Not 2 Kh1? e1=Q nor 2 Kh2? e1=N! with a Black win in both cases.

| 2 | ... | Nf4+ |

2...e1=N 3 Nf3+ Nxf3 is another stalemate.

| 3 | Kh2 | Ng4+ |

3...Nf1+ (3...e1=N 4 Nf3+ Nxf3 5 Kg3 forks the knights) 4 Kh1 e1=N 5 Nf3+ Nxf3 is stalemate number 1 again.

4 Kh1	**Nf2+**

Poor Black! He still can't promote because 4...e1=Q/R stalemate at once, 4...e1=N 5 Nf3+ Nxf3 stalemates too and 4...e1=B 5 Nf3+ and 6 Nxe1 draws.

5 Kh2	**e1=N**

The only remaining try, or Black has to repeat the position.

6 Nf3+!	**Nxf3+**
7 Kg3	

Never before has a king forked three knights simultaneously!

7 ...	**Ke3**

The only way to defend the knights, but now White is stalemated.

122 (Yakimchik)   1 Ne4!

The only move since 1 Nf5 (1 Nf6+? Kg6) Kg4 2 Nf6+ Kh3 3 Ng3 (3 Ne4 Nd1+ and 4...h1=Q wins) Kxg3 4 Ne4+ Kg2 5 Nf2 Nd1+ wins for Black.

1 ...	**Kh4**

1...Kg4 (1...Nd1+ 2 Kf4 followed by Ng3 is safe enough) 2 Nf2+ Kg3 3 Nh1+ Kg2 4 Ng5 Kxh1 5 Nf3 eliminates the pawn.

2 Nhg5!

After 2 Nf2? Nd1+ 3 Nxd1 h1=Q Black wins. Although Q v 2N is sometimes a draw, in this position the knights are too scattered and the queen rapidly picks one up, for example 4 Nf2 (4 Nc3 Qh3+ and 5...Qd7+ or 4 Kd2 Qe4 or 4 Nb2 Qb7) Qb7 followed by ...Qe7+.

2 ...	**Nd1+**

Not 2...h1=Q (2...Nc4+ 3 Kf4 only makes matters worse) 3 Nf3+ and White picks up the queen by a knight fork next move.

3 Kf4!	**h1=Q**
4 Nf3+	**Kh3**

Now 5 Neg5+ Kg2 is a Black win, but White can force the queen to g2, blocking a vital flight square.

5 Ng3!	**Qg2**
6 Ng5+	

followed by **7 Nf3+** with a draw by perpetual check.

123 (Gurevich) If White can keep both pawns he stands to win, for Black's king is too far offside to obstruct the advance of the b4 pawn effectively. Moreover, Black's bishop would have to emerge via b1, costing yet more time. So Black must play to win the b3 pawn.

1 Kd5

1 Ke5? just loses the pawn after 1...Ng5.

<table>
<tr><td>1</td><td>...</td><td>Nd2</td></tr>
</table>

After 1...Nf6+ 2 Kc4 Black can no longer hope to capture b3.

<table>
<tr><td>2 Kd4!</td><td>Nxb3+</td></tr>
</table>

We must continually bear in mind the positional draw of Diagram 108, but at the moment 2...Bxb3 3 Kc3 Ba4 4 Kxd2 Bb5 5 Ke3 wins for White, since Black's king is too far away to prevent White's monarch escaping from the b5–f1 prison. If Black refuses to take the pawn at all, White wins by 3 Kc3.

3 Kc3

Black must lose a piece, but White must take care not to rush the capture, e.g. 3...Na1 4 Nc6! (not 4 Kb2? Bc4 5 Kxa1 Bb5 6 Kb2 Kf6 7 Kc3 Ke5 and Black arrives in time to make a draw) B moves (4...Nb3 5 Kb2) 5 Nd4 and 6 Kb2 wins the trapped knight and the game.

<table>
<tr><td>3</td><td>...</td><td>Nc1</td></tr>
</table>

A more difficult defence, for 4 Kb2? only draws after 4...Nd3+.

<table>
<tr><td>4 Kd2</td><td>Nb3+</td></tr>
</table>

4...Bc4 5 Kxc1 Bb5 still loses after 6 Kd2 Kf6 7 Ke3 Ke5 8 Bc5 Kd5 9 Kf4 (threatening Kf5–f6–e7–d8–c7–b6) Ke6 10 Ke4 followed by Kd4, Bf8 and Kc5.

5 Kc2

White gradually edges closer to the corner. 6 Kb2 is threatened.

<table>
<tr><td>5</td><td>...</td><td>Na1+</td></tr>
</table>

Now what? 6 Kb2 Bc4 transposes to the draw in the note to White's third move.

6 Kc1!

White's patience will earn its just reward in the end. 7 Bd4+ is the threat, for example 6...Bc4 7 Bd4+ Kg6 8 Bxa1 Bb5 9 Kd2 Kf5 10 Ke3 or if 7...Kf7 in this line then 8 Bxa1 Bb5 9 Kd2 Ke6 10 Ke3 as in the note to Black's 4th.

<table>
<tr><td>6</td><td>...</td><td>Kf7</td></tr>
</table>

6...Kg6 leads to the same conclusion. After 6...Kh6/h7/f7/f8 7 Kb2 Bc4 8 Kxa1 Bb5 9 Kb2 Black's king is too far away and White reaches d4.

7	**Kb2!**	**Bc4**
8	**Nc6!**	

Exploiting the bad position of the king at f7/g6, White prevents the knight escaping by 8...Nb3 on account of 9 Ne5+.

8	**...**	**Bb5/d5**
9	**Nd4** and wins.	

124 (Korolkov) Black's knight covers c8 whereas there is no obvious way White can prevent, or even delay, the promotion of Black's pawn.

1 Ra8!

The only move. White intends to capture both pawn and knight with check, but even this doesn't guarantee the draw for Black's queen threatens to mate at g3.

1	**...**	**e1=Q**

Or 1...Nc8 (1...Nxa8 2 c8=Q e1=Q 3 Qxa6+ draws) 2 Rxa6+ Kb1 (2...Kb2 3 Nf4) 3 Nd4 e1=Q 4 Ra1+ Kxa1 5 Nc2+ winning the queen.

2	**Rxa6+**	**Na4!**

After 2...Kb3 3 Rxb6+ Ka4 4 Ra6+ Kb5 (4...Kb4 5 Rb6+ Ka5 6 Ra6+) 5 Nd4+ Black's king has no satisfactory move.

3	**Rxa4+**	**Kb2**

After 3...Kb3 White continues as after Black's 5th move in the main line.

4	**Rb4+**	**Ka3**

4...Qxb4 removes the mating threat and allows White to promote in safety.

5 Rb3+!

Not 5 Ra4+ Kxa4 and Black really does win. The purpose of this sacrifice is to give White's knight a check at d4.

5	**...**	**Kxb3**

Forced or White promotes.

6	**Nd4+**	**K moves**
7	**Ne2!**	

An amazing position. The knight prevents the mate at g3 and blocks all paths by which Black's queen can stop the impending promotion. The best chance is 7...Qxe2 8 c8=Q Qh2+ 9 Kg4 Qg3+ but 10 Kh5 draws easily enough.

125 (Pachman) If both sides lose their knights then the ending is a draw, so White must play to win Black's knight while retaining his own.

	1 Nf5+	**Kg6**

1...Kf6 loses to 2 Nd6+ Nf3+ 3 Rxf3+ Qxf3 4 Rf2.

	2 Nh4+	**Kg5/h5**
	3 Rc5+	

3 Rf5+? Kh6 leads nowhere.

	3 ...	**Kg4**

Not 3...Kxh4 4 Rf4+ and mate next move.

	4 Rc4+	

Better than 4 Rxe1 Kxh4, when the queen stops the check at e4.

	4 ...	**Kh3**

Black's knight is doomed so he must hope for counterplay based on the active position of his king.

	5 Rxe1	**Qa7+!**

White has too many threats (such as Rce4) for slower methods.

	6 Kh1	

Not 6 Kf1? Qf7+ and the loose rook at c4 drops off.

	6 ...	**Qf2**

Hoping for 7 Rc3+? Kxh4 drawing.

	7 Re3+!!	**Qxe3**
	8 Ng2	

Black has no checks and must therefore cover the mate at h4. After 8...Qf2/g5/e7 White wins by 9 Nf4+ K moves 10 Nd3/e6/d5+ respectively.

	8 ...	**Qh6**

The only square safe from White's knight. Now 9 Nf4+ achieves nothing so White must take time out to prevent ...Qc1+.

	9 Rf4!	

Curiously both sides moves are absolutely forced and it seems almost a coincidence that the result is a win for White.

	9 ...	**Qh5**

9...Qg5 10 Rf3+ Kg4 11 Rg3+ is no better.

	10 Rd4	

White meets the threat of ...Qd1+ and at the same time threatens Nf4+ himself.

10	...	Qh6
11	Rc4	

White once again covers the first rank and finally puts Black in a fatal zugzwang. 11...Qf6/g5/h5 all lose to 12 Nf4+.

126 (Bron) Four minor pieces normally beat a queen, but only if they are initially well co-ordinated. Here the pieces are scattered so if one of the pawns can safely promote, White will have to be satisfied with a draw.

1 Na5+

There is no point in giving aimless checks, for example 1 Nd8+? Kc8 2 Nb6+ Kxd8 3 Bg5+ Kc7 4 Nd5+ Kb7 and Black will win.

1	...	Ka6

1...Kxa8 2 Bf3+ Ka7 4 Be3+ and 5 Kc2 wins, as does 1...Kc8 2 Nb6+ with mate to follow.

2 Nc7+

Not 2 Be2+? Kxa5 3 Bd2+ (3 Bc7+ Kb4 4 Bd6+ Kb3 is also bad) Ka4 4 Nb6+ Kb3 5 Bc4+ Ka3 and once again Black stands to win.

2	...	Kxa5
3	Bd2+	Ka4

3...Kb6 4 Be3+ and 5 Kc2.

4 Be8+ Kb3

Or 4...Ka3 5 Nb5+ Ka2 6 Nc3+ Kb3 (6...Ka3 and 6...Ka1 are both met by 7 Be3) 7 Bf7+ followed by Nb1+ and Be3 stops the pawns.

5 Bf7+ Ka4

5...Ka3 6 Nb5+ Ka4 7 Nc3+ wins.

6 Kc2!

White has gone as far as possible by checking and must now play a quiet move to complete the net around Black's king. The threat is 7 Bb3+ Ka3 8 Nb5 mate, so Black's next two moves are forced.

6	...	b1=Q+
7	Kxb1	g1=Q+
8	Ka2!	

After 8 Kc2? (8 Kb2? Qg7+ and ...Qxf7) Qc5+ 9 Kb2 Qb6+ 10 Ka2 Black can force stalemate by 8...Qb2+!.

8	...	Qg8!

204

An ingenious defence to the threats of Be8 mate and Bb3 mate.

9 Bd5!

Not 9 Be6? Qf7! with an unusual fork of c7 and e6.

9	...	Qf7

White had no direct threat, for example 10 Ne6 Qc8 11 Nd4 would have allowed 11...Qc4+!, but Black was in zugzwang. The queen had to stay on the g8–b3 diagonal to maintain the pin and 9...Qe6 can be taken by the knight.

10 Ne6

Threat 11 Bc6 mate. Black is curiously powerless to cover this square, e.g. 10...Qd7 11 Nc5+ or 10...Qe8 11 Bb3+ Kb5 12 Nc7+.

10	...	Kb5
11	Nd4+	Ka4

Forced, but now White is defending b3 with his knight.

12 Bb3+

winning the queen.

127 (Gunst) Of course Q v RP on the seventh is in general a draw, but what happens if a bishop is added? Normally the win would be easy, but here there is a special situation. After 1 exd8=Q Kg1 White has the choice between shedding his bishop to prevent an immediate promotion (2 Qd4+ Kxf1 3 Qe4 Kg1 4 Qg4+ Kf2 5 Qh3 Kg1 6 Qg3+ Kh1 etc.), or of entering a Q+B v Q ending. This can be done in several ways, but all are drawn, for example 2 Qd1 h1=Q 3 Bc4+ Kh2 4 Qd6+ Kg1 5 Qd4+ Kh2 6 Qf4+ Kg1 and White cannot make progress. White would like to bring his bishop to the long diagonal in this type of ending, but at the moment this allows a Black queen check, as after 6 Qe5+ Kg1 7 Bd5 Qh4+! in the above line.

1 e8=Q!

Preserving the bishop so that 1...Kg1 2 Qe3+ Kxf1 3 Qh3+ Kg1 4 Qg3+ Kh1 5 Qf2 is not stalemate, but mate after 5...Bb6 6 Qf1+ Bg1 7 Qf3 instead. 1...Ba5+ 2 Kb5! leaves this line unaffected.

1	...	Be7+!
2	Qxe7!	

2 Kc4? Kg1 3 Bg2 Kxg2 4 Qa8+ Kg1 5 Qa1+ Kg2 6 Qb2+ Kg1 7 Qd4+ Kg2 8 Qg4+ Kf2! (8...Kf1? and 8...Kh1? lose as in the last note) 9 Qh3 Bd6! (9...Kg1? 10 Qg3+ wins) 10 Kd3 Kg1 (Black avoids defeat despite the proximity of White's king because White cannot check at g3) 11 Qg4+ Kf2 12 Qe2+ Kg1 13 Ke3 Bc5+! with a draw. Compared with the last note

White only draws here because his queen starts from a bad position hidden behind Black's bishop, so he can never give a check at f3 or g3.

2 ...   Kg1

Why is White's queen better at e7 than d8? The answer is that Black's potential queen checks at b7, e4 and h4 are all dealt with, so White can utilise his spare move to bring the bishop to the long diagonal.

3 Ba6!   h1=Q
4 Bb7

with complete domination of the queen. 4...Qh5/6/8 5 Qe1+ Kh2 6 Qh1+ wins while 4...Qh3 5 Qe1+ Qf1 6 Qg3+ leads to mate.

128 (Evreinov)   1 c6

It is important to immobilise Black's bishop. After 1 b4? (1 Kh4? Bf1 amounts to the same) Bf1 2 Kh4 Kg1 3 Kg3 c6 4 Rd2 Bg2 5 Rd1+ Bf1 White cannot make progress.

1 ...   h2

1...bxc6 2 Rxa6 h2 3 b4 Kg2 4 Ra2+ Kg3 5 Ra1 Kg2 6 Kf6 h1=Q 7 Rxh1 Kxh1 leaves White with a won king and pawn ending.

2 b4   Kg1

Black threatens 3...h1=Q 4 Ra1+ Bf1 so White has to give up his rook immediately. 3 b5? Bxb5! is fine for Black.

3 Rxh2   Kxh2
4 b5

Both sides have become immobilised on the queenside so everything depends on the manoeuvres of the two kings. Note that White cannot occupy d7 since Black can pin the c-pawn by ...Bxb5.

4 ...   Kg3
5 Kf6!

5 Kf5? Kf3 6 Ke5 (or 6 Ke6 Ke4) Ke3 7 Ke6 Ke4 8 Ke7 (White has to lose a tempo to reach d8 − 8 bxa6 is objectively best as both sides promote and the result is a draw) Kd5 9 Kd8 Kd6 10 Kc8 Bxb5! 11 cxb7 Ba6 and Black wins.

5 ...   Kf4
6 Ke7   Ke5

It turns out that e5 is a very bad square for Black's king, but 6...Ke4 7 Kd8! Kd5 8 Kxc7 Kc5 9 bxa6 wins for White in any case.

7 bxa6!

Not 7 Kd8? Kd6 and Black wins as above. White's liquidation succeeds for a surprising reason.

        7   ...   **bxa6**

8 Kd7 a5 9 Kxc7 a4 10 Kd7 a3 11 c7 a2 12 c8=Q a1=Q 13 Qh8+ and Black loses his queen. White's threatened king march to d8 was designed to lure Black on to the h8—a1 diagonal.

129 (Halberstadt) Clearly White must move the g8 bishop, but where should it go to? After 1 Bc4, for example, Black draws by 1...Kb1 2 Kb4 Kc2 3 Kc5 (the pawn at g7 and bishop at h8 are paralyzed) Kd2 4 Kd4 Ke1 5 Ke5 f1=Q 6 Bxf1 Kxf1 7 Kf6 (the bishop at h8 is irrelevant and a knight draws against any pawn on the seventh except a rook's pawn) Kf2 8 Kg6 Ng8 9 Kf7 Nh6+ 10 Kg6 Ng8 11 Kh7 Ne7 etc. Therefore White must stop ...Kb1.

        1 Bh7!   **Ng8!**

After 1...Ka2 White promotes with check.

        2 Bxg8

2 Bd3? Kb2 3 Kb4 Kc1 4 Kc3 Kd1 leads to the same draw as in the first note.

        2   ...   **f1=Q**
        3 Bc4!

With only one bishop in play White must choose the right square or Black can draw by perpetual check. 3 Bd5? Qe1+ 4 Ka6 Qe2+ is one such.

        3   ...   **Qxc4**

3...Qf5+ 4 Bb5 and 3...Qe1+ 4 Ka6! bring the checks to an instantaneous end.

        4 g8=B+!

It is only fitting that White's heroic bishop, which single-handedly neutralised Black's queen, should be reborn at g8. 4 g8=Q+ Kb1 draws easily after 5 Qg1+ Kc2, or gives stalemate after 5 Qxc4.

        4   ...   **Kb1**
        5 Bxc4

and wins.

130 (Bilek) If Black can give up his rook for White's pawn his passed queenside pawns will guarantee at least a draw. Thus ...Rh8 must be prevented. If White ever checks out of turn he lets Black off the hook, for example 1 Rg4+? Ka3 2 Rg8 Rc1 3 Rg5 (3 Rg3+ Ka4 4 Rg4+ b4 5 Kh5 Rc8 6 Rg8 Rc1 forces a draw by repetition) Rc8 4 Rxb5 a4 5 Rg5 Rh8 drawing even minus the b-pawn.

1	**Rg8**	**Rc1**

1...Rc6+ loses more quickly after 2 Kg5 Rc5+ 3 Kh4 Rc1 4 Rg4+ Kc5 (4...Ka3/b3 5 Rg3+ and 6 h8=Q) 5 Kh5 and the pawn promotes.

2	**Rg4+**

2 Rg5 Rc8 forces White to return to g8.

2	**...**	**Ka3**

2...Kc5 3 Rg5+ and 4 h8=Q is the idea of the study, which occurs time and time again on various ranks.

3	**Kh5**

3 Rg5? Rc8 draws as in the first note.

3	**...**	**Rc8**

Or 3...Rc5+ 4 Kh4 Rc8 (4...Rc1 5 Rg3+ and 6 h8=Q) 5 Rg8 Rc4+ 6 Kg3 Rc3+ 7 Kf2 Rc2+ (Black has to drive White's king closer since 7...Rh3 loses to 8 Rg3+) 8 Ke3 Rh2 9 h8=Q (White has gained three tempi with his king in this line, making the difference between a draw and a win) Rxh8 10 Rxh8 Kb2 11 Kd2 b4 (11...a4 12 Rb8 a3 13 Rxb5+ Ka1 14 Kc3 a2 15 Rh5 wins) 12 Ra8 b3 13 Rxa5 Kb1 14 Kc3 b2 15 Kb3 Kc1 16 Rc5+ Kb1 17 Rh5 Ka1 18 Ra5+ Kb1 19 Ra2 and White wins.

4	**Rg8**	**Rc1**

After 4...Rc5+ White wins as in the last note.

5	**Rg3+**

The same manoeuvre gradually forces Black's king down the board. 5 Kg4? Rh1 6 h8=Q Rxh8 7 Rxh8 is two tempi worse than the above line so Black draws by 7...b4 8 Kf3 b3 9 Ke2 b2 10 Rb8 Ka2.

5	**...**	**Ka2**

Not 5...Ka4/b4 6 Rg4+ and 7 h8=Q, nor 5...Kb2 6 h8=Q+.

6	**Kh4**	**Rc8**

6...Rc4+ 7 Kh3 Rc8 8 Rg8 Rc3+ 9 Kh2 wins more quickly.

7	**Rg8**	**Rc1**
8	**Rg2+**	**Kb1**
9	**Kh3**	**Rc8**

9...Rc3+ 10 Kh2 Rc8 11 Rg8 Rc2+ 12 Kh1 is the same.

10	**Rg8**	**Rc1**
11	**Kh2**	**Re2+**
12	**Kh1**	

and the pawn promotes. There is some similarity between this study and the famous Lasker manoeuvre. In both cases a repeated sequence of moves causes both kings to move down the board until finally Black suffers from lack of space.

131 (Afek) This is another rook and pawn ending, in which White must be careful how he goes about winning Black's rook in return for the f-pawn. At the moment Black threatens 1...Rxf7+ 2 Kxf7 Kg4 with a clear draw, so White's first move is more or less forced.

1 Rg8

Not 1 Rb8? Kg3 2 Kg8 Rxf7 3 Kxf7 h4 drawing comfortably. After 1 Rg8, Black is in zugzwang, astonishing though this appears. It may seem to make little difference whether Black pins the pawn from a7 or b7 but in fact 1...Rb7 loses quickly. To see why, let us suppose that it is White to move. He might play 2 Kf6 Ra6+ (giving up the rook for the pawn is always hopeless when Black's king is trapped in front of the pawns on the h-file) 3 Ke5 Ra5+ 4 Kd4 Ra4+ 5 Kc3 Ra3+ 6 Kb4 (now Black must give up his rook, but he has forced the White king to the other side of the board) Rf3 7 f8=Q Rxf8 8 Rxf8 Kg3 9 Kc3 h4 10 Kd2 h3 11 Ke2 and now 11...h2 draws. But White could win if circumstances were slightly different, for example if he could gain a tempo somehow, then it would be White to play in the position after 11 Ke2 and he wins easily by Rg8+. Alternatively, if Black's h7 pawn were absent then 11 Ke2 h2 wouldn't save Black after 12 Rg8+ Kh3 13 Kf2 h1=N+ 14 Kf3 Kh2 15 Rg7 winning the knight. Now we can see why 1...Rb7 (or any other square on the same rank) loses. After 2 Kf6 Rb6+ 3 Ke5 Rb5+ 4 Kd4 Rb4+ 5 Kc3 Rf4 6 f8=Q etc., White has indeed gained a tempo since his king stands on the c-file instead of the b-file, so he wins. 1...Kg3/4/5 2 Kh8+ and 1...Kh3 2 Kf6 Ra6+ 3 Kg5 Ra5+ 4 Kh6 Rf5 (4...Ra6+ 5 Kxh5) 5 f8=Q Rxf8 6 Rxf8 h4 7 Kh5 Kg3 8 Rg8+ Kh3 9 Rg4 are hopeless, so Black has just one move.

1 ...   h6

Black uses his only pass move. If White could lose a tempo and return to this position with Black to move, the above analysis proves that Black would be in a fatal zugzwang. How can White do this? 2 Kg6 Ra6+ 3 Kh7? (White should repeat the position by 3 Kg7) is tempting because White achieves his aim after 3...Ra7? 4 Kg7, but Black can play 3...Rf6! 4 Kg7 (4 Rg7 threatens Kg8 and f8=Q to win the rook while keeping Black's king on the h-file, but Black can pre-empt this plan by 4...Rxf7! 5 Rxf7 Kg3 with a draw) Kg5! 5 Ra8 Rxf7+ 6 Kxf7 h4 drawing. If White moves his rook from g8 Black can safely continue ...Kg3, so it isn't easy to make progress. If White could reach the position after 2 Kg6 Ra6+ 3 Kh7 Rf6 with the rook already on g7, then Kg8 wins, and the key idea is to transfer the rook from g8 to g7 with gain of tempo. The only way to execute this plan is to play the king to h2 and interpose by Rg2. Black will have to return to a8 with his rook to prevent promotion, when White can occupy g7 without wasting time.

2	Kf6	Ra6+
3	Ke5	Ra5+
4	Ke4	Ra4+
5	Kf3	Ra3+
6	Kg2	Ra2+

Stalemate traps start to appear, but none of them work, for example 6...Rg3+ 7 Kf2!.

7	Kh1	Ra1+

7...Rh2+ 8 Kg1 wins.

8	Kh2

Not 8 Rg1 Ra8 9 Rg7?, when Black can inch his h-pawn forward by 9...Kh3 and 10...h4, gaining a vital tempo. White should repeat moves by 9 Rg8.

8	...	Ra2+
9	Rg2	Ra8
10	Rg7!	

Next White must march his king to g6. It doesn't matter whether Black checks or not since he will have to return to a8 sooner or later.

10	...	Ra2+

The lines 10...Rg8 11 Rg4+! Rxg4 12 f8=Q and 10...Rf8 11 Kg2 (11 Kg1? Kh3) Rg8 12 Kf3 Rxg7 13 f8=Q are similar. In both cases the bad position of Black's king leads to the loss of the h-pawns within a few moves.

11	Kg1	Ra1+

11...Ra8 12 Kg2 Ra2+ 13 Kf3 etc. amounts to the same thing.

12	Kf2	Ra2+
13	Kf3	Ra3+
14	Kf4	Ra4+

If Black tries to move his king by 14...Ra8 15 Kf5 Kh3 he leaves the h5 pawn undefended and White wins as after 1...Kh3 in the note to White's first move.

15	Kf5	Ra5+

15...Ra1 16 Kg6 transposes to later analysis after 16...Ra8 or 16...Ra6+. The alternative 16...Rf1 (16...Rg1+ 17 Kh7 Rf1 18 Kg8 and 19 f8=Q wins) 17 Rg8! Kh3 (17...Kg4 18 Kxh6+ Kh4 19 f8=Q and 17...Rg1+ 18 Kxh6 are hopeless, while 17...Rf2 18 f8=Q transposes) 18 f8=Q Rxf8 19 Rxf8 Kg4 (19...h4 20 Kh5 Kg3 21 Rg8+) 20 Ra8 h4 21 Ra4+ Kg3 22 Kh5 h3 23 Ra3+ Kg2 24 Kh4 h2 25 Ra2+ Kg1 26 Kg3 h1=N+ 27 Kf3 h5 28 Rg2+ Kf1 29 Rh2 Kg1 30 Rxh5 Nf2 31 Rd5 Nh3 (or 31...Kf1 32 Rd2) 32 Ra5 Kh2 33 Rh5, although lengthy, offers Black no chances.

16 Kg6 Ra8

16...Ra6+ 17 Kh7 Ra8 (17...Rf6 18 Kg8) 18 Rg8! Ra7 19 Kg7 returns to the position after 1...h6, but with Black to move.

17 Kh7!

After 17 Kxh6 Rf8! (the only move) a position arises in which Black to play loses, but with White to move he can only draw. For example, if Black is to play then 18...Ra8 19 Rg8 Ra6+ 20 Kg7 Ra7 21 Kf6 and 18...Rh8+ 19 Kg6 Ra8 20 Rg8 transpose to the main line, while with White to play 18 Kg6 (18 Kh7 Rxf7! 19 Rxf7 Kg4 draws) Kg4 19 Rg8 (19 Kf6+ Kf4) Rxf7 20 Kxf7+ Kf3 21 Rh8 Kg4 22 Kf6 h4 23 Ke5 h3 24 Ke4 Kg3 25 Ke3 Kg2! (25...h2? 26 Rg8+ Kh3 27 Kf2 wins) 26 Rg8+ (or 26 Ke2 h2 27 Rg8+ Kh1!) Kf1! (26...Kh1? loses this time: 27 Kf3 h2 28 Ra8 mates) and there is nothing better than to force ...Kg2 again by Rh8.

17 ... Rf8

Black was in zugzwang (again!) as the following lines prove: 17...Rb8 18 Rg8 Rb7 19 Kg6 Rb6+ 20 Kf5 etc., as in the analysis of 1...Rb7, or 17...Kh3 18 Rg8 Ra7 19 Kg6 Ra6+ 20 Kxh5 capturing Black's pawns.

18	Kxh6	Rh8+
19	Kg6	Ra8
20	Rg8	

This is essentially the position after White's first move, but without Black's rear h-pawn. As explained in that distant note, White can win by marching his king to the b-file.

20	...	Ra6+
21	Kf5	Ra5+

22 Ke4 Ra4+ 23 Kd3 Ra3+ 24 Kc2 Ra2+ 25 Kb3 Rf2 26 f8=Q Rxf8 27 Rxf8 Kg3 28 Kc2 h4 29 Kd2 h3 30 Ke2 h2 31 Rg8+ Kh3 32 Kf2 h1=N+ 33 Kf3 Kh2 34 Rg7 and finally wins!

132 (Puhakka) Probably the most difficult solving exercise in the whole book. The first observation to make is that if Black can play ...h5 he will draw unless White can take it with his bishop. The reason is that the reply gxh5 leaves White with a useless RP + wrong bishop combination, while if he replies g5 Black can bring his king over to the passed g-pawn and draw by deflecting White's bishop with his h-pawn. The only exception to this ...h5 rule occurs when White's king is very near the kingside (g3, for example). Apart from this rather trivial observation, it isn't easy to see how to solve the position. White's aims aren't clear and it is extremely hard to decide what the first move should be! 1 Kb2, 1 Bh5, 1 Be8 and even 1 Kb1 are candidates, and at the moment there is no reason to prefer one rather than another.

In this situation it is sometimes helpful to work back from the end of the study. It is quite easy to establish the results of positions near the end and these provide a basis for working further backwards; the procedure is repeated until one is near the initial position. At each stage there are clear target positions (the ones which have already been proved to be wins) and this breaks down a horribly complex piece of analysis into manageable chunks. This is in fact precisely the way computers construct chess databases, but thanks to the intervention of human discrimination the manual method usually only requires a dozen or so intermediate positions, whereas the machine would probably look at tens or hundreds of thousands.

It seems to me that this technique is the only practical way to solve Diagram 132, but it still isn't easy. The hardest step in this method is to choose the 'right' end positions. White's bishop must stay on the e8–h5 diagonal to stop ...h5 and if Black's king is going to be floating around the e4–f4 area, the bishop may as well stay on h5. At any stage Black may play ...d3, which alters the character of the position by changing the squares accessible to the two kings. We can't hope to understand positions with the pawn on d4 unless we already know when Black can successfully push ...d3, so first let's assume the pawn has already advanced to d3. Keeping these factors fixed we can explore various positions for the two kings.

Position 1: WKd2 v BKe4, BPd3   Black to play loses.
The most obvious zugzwang position. Black's only move is 1...Kd4, but then 2 Bg6 Kc4 (or White takes the pawn with his king) 3 Bxd3+ Kc4 4 Bg6 wins. However, White to play only draws (where we state only that Black to play loses this will be taken for granted), for example 1 Ke1 Ke3 2 Kd1 Kd4 or 1 Kc3 Ke3 2 Kb2 Kf2 (not 2...d2? 3 Kc2 Ke2 4 g5+ winning) 3 Kc3 (3 Kc1 Ke1) Ke3 and White cannot make progress.

Position 2: WKe1 v BKe3, BPd3   Black to play loses.
There are two lines:
A) 1...Kf4 (1...Ke4 2 Kd2 – 1) 2 Kf2 Ke4 3 Kg3 (White's king is now close enough for the bishop to abandon its post at h5) d2 4 Bg6+ Ke5 5 Bc2 h5 (5...Kf6 6 Kh4) 6 g5 followed by Kh4 and wins.
B) 1...Kd4 (1...d2+ 2 Kd1 Kd3 3 Be8 Ke3 4 Bf7 Kf4/d3 5 Bh5 Ke3 6 Kc2 or 5...Kc3 6 Bg6) 2 Kf2 Ke4 (2...d2 3 Ke2 Kc3 4 Kd1) 3 Kg3 as in A.

Position 3: WKe1 v BKe5, BPd3   Black to play loses.
If Black plays to the fourth rank the lines are as in Position 2, while 1...Kd5 2 Kf2 Kd4 (2...Ke4 3 Kg3 is also 2) 3 Be8 wins. White to play cannot win, for example 1 Kd1 (1 Kf2 Kf4 or 1 Kf1 Ke4) Kf4 2 Kd2 Ke4 as in 1.

Position 4: WKd1 v BKf4, BPd3   Black to play loses.
1...Ke3 2 Ke1 – 2, 1...Ke4 2 Kd2 – 1 and 1...Ke5 2 Ke1 – 3 complete the analysis.

Position 5: WKd1 v BKd4, BPd3 Draw, whoever moves first.
If White moves first 1 Kd2 Ke4, 1 Kc1/e1 Ke3 and 1 Bg6 Ke3 2 Be8 (2 Ke1 Kf4 3 Bh5 and now either ...Ke3 or ...Ke5) Kf3! (not 2...Kf4? 3 Bh5 − 4, nor 2...Kd4? 3 Kd2 Ke4 4 Bh5 − 1) 3 Bh5 Kf4 4 Kd2 (4 Ke1 Ke3/5) Ke4 all lead to earlier draws. If Black moves first he has only one move to draw, namely 1...Kd5!. Then 2 Bg6 (2 Ke1 Ke5, 2 Kd2 Ke4 and 2 Be8 Ke4 are also drawn) Ke5! 3 Be8 (3 Kd2 Kf4 4 Bh5 Ke4) Ke4 3 Ke1 Kf4 4 Bh5 Ke3/5 leads to a familiar draw.

It isn't possible to use the technique of corresponding squares in this ending, although White's bishop plays a minor role, because in some positions White can win by bringing the bishop into action.

Position 6: WKc1 v BKd5, BPd3 White to play wins; Black to play draws.
1 Bg6! Ke5 (1...Kd4 2 Kd2 − 1; 1...Kc4 2 Kd2 Kd4 3 Be8 Ke4 4 Bh5 − 1) 2 Kd1 (in position 5 Black took care to arrive at this position with White to move) Kd5 (2...Kf4 3 Bh5 − 4; 2...Kf6 3 Bh5 Ke5 4 Ke1 − 3) 3 Ke1 Ke5 (3...Kd4 4 Kd2) 4 Bh5 is Position 3. Black draws by 1...Ke5. We can now consider positions with Black's pawn on d4.

Position 7: WKe2 v BKf4, BPd4 White wins, whoever moves first.
If Black moves first 1...Ke4 (1...Ke5 2 Kf3 followed by Kg3 and Be8−a4) 2 Kf2 Kf4 (2...d3 − 2) 3 Kg2! d3 (or else Kg3 and Be8−a4) 4 Kf2 is Position 2. To show that White wins with the move is more difficult and we defer this until one more position has been investigated. For the moment, therefore, we can only assume that Position 7 is a win with Black to move.

Position 8: WKe1 v BKe4, BPd4 White wins, whoever moves first.
With White to play 1 Kf2 reaches 7. If Black moves first we have 1...Ke3 (1...Kf4 2 Ke2 is 7 with Black to move, 1...d3 2 Kd2 is 1, 1...Kd3 2 Kf2 and 3 Kg3 wins, 1...Ke5 2 Kf2 Kf4 3 Kg2 is 7 again and 1...Kd5 2 Kf2 d3 3 Ke3 Kc4 4 Kd2 is 1) 2 Kf1 Kf4 (2...d3 3 Ke1 is 2, 2...Ke4 3 Kf2 is 7 and 1...Kd2/d3 loses to 2 Kf2 and 3 Be8) 3 Kg2 transposes to 7.

Now we are ready to prove the other half of Position 7. White to play wins by 1 Ke1! and now 1...d3 2 Kf2 is 2, 1...Ke3 2 Kf1 is 8, 1...Ke4 2 Kf2 is 7, 1...Ke5 2 Kf2 is 8 and 1...Kg3 2 Kd2 Kf4 3 Ke2 is 7 with Black to move. Finally 1...Kg5 2 Kf2 Kf4 (or else Kg3) 3 Kg2 is 7.

Position 9: WKd3 wins against any Black K position, whoever is to move.
This is in sharp contrast to Position 5. We may as well assume that White is to move. After 1 Ke2 Black has the choice between 1...Kf4 − 7, 1...Ke4 2 Ke1 − 8 and 1...Kc4 (or anywhere else) 2 Kf3 and wins. The power of our method of analysis stands out clearly here, since the manoeuvre Kd3−e2−e1, which would otherwise be very hard to see, is found automatically.

It has become apparent that White is much better off when the pawn is still on d4, but he doesn't always win.

Position 10: WKd1 v BKe3, BPd4 Black to play loses.
1...Kd3 (1...Kf4 2 Ke2 − 7 or 1...d3 2 Ke1 − 2 or 1...Ke4 2 Ke1 − 8) 2 Ke1 Ke3 3 Kf1 transposes to 8. But White to play only draws, for example 1 Kc2 (1 Ke1/c1 d3) Ke4! (not 1...d3+ 2 Kc3 winning after 2...d2 3 Kc2

213

or 2...Ke4 3 Kd2) 2 Kc1 (2 Kd2 d3) Kd3! (2...Ke3? 3 Kd1 is 10 and 2...K anywhere else 3 Kd2 Ke4 4 Ke1 is 8) 3 Bg6+ (3 Kd1 and 3 Kb2 are both met by 3...Ke3) Ke2! and White has nothing better than to return to h5.

Position 11: WKc2 v BKe4, BPd4   Black to play loses.

When White is to play the position may be found in the analysis of 1 Kc2 just above. Black to play loses after 1...d3+ 2 Kd2 — 1, 1...Ke3 2 Kd1 — 10 or 1...K anywhere else 2 Kd3 — 9.

Position 12: WKc1 v BKf4, BPd4   Black loses, whoever moves first.

1 Kd2 Ke4 2 Ke1 wins whoever is to play, while 1...Ke3 2 Kd1 — 10, 1...d3 2 Kd1 — 4, 1...Ke4 2 Kc2 — 11 and 1...Ke5 2 Kd2 Ke4 3 Ke1 — 8 wraps it up when Black is to move.

Position 13: WKb2 v BKe5, BPd4   Black to play loses.

We are rapidly converging towards the initial position. When Black is to move 1...Kd5 (1...d3 2 Kc3 Ke4 3 Kd2 — 1, 1...Ke4 2 Kc2 — 11, 1...Kf4 2 Kc1 — 12) 2 Kc1 Ke4 (2...d3 3 Bg6! — 6, 2...Ke5 3 Kd2 Ke4 4 Ke1 — 8, 2...Kc4 3 Kd2 wins) 3 Kc2 is Position 11. When White is to move 1 Kc2 Ke4 is 11, 1 Kb3 Kf4 leaves White with nothing better than transposition by 2 Kc2 Ke4, while finally 1 Kb1/c1 allows 1...d3 followed by 2 Kc1/d1 Kd4 or 2 Kd2 Ke4 as appropriate.

Using the above library of positions we can go back to the initial diagram and work out the solution.

White's four possibilities are as follows:

1) 1 Be8? Ke5 2 Kb2 draws after 2...Kf4 3 Bh5 d3 (or even 3...Ke5 — 13) 4 Kc1 (4 Kc3 Ke3 5 Kb2 Kf2) Ke3 5 Kd1 Kd4 — 5.

2) 1 Bh5? Kd5! 2 Kb1 (2 Kb2 Ke5 — 13) d3! 3 Kc1 (3 Kb2 Ke4 4 Kc3 Ke3 — 1) Ke5 4 Kd1 Kd4 — 5.

3) 1 Kb1? d3! and now:

3a) 2 Bxd3 Kf6 followed by ...Kg5 and ...h5 draws.

3b) 2 Bh5 Kd5 transposes to 1 Bh5?.

3c) 2 Be8 Ke5 followed by ...Kd4 draws, as in 5.

3d) 2 Kc1 Kf6 3 Be8 (3 Bh5 Ke5) Ke5 4 Kd1 (4 Bh5 Kd4 will lead to 5 and 4 Kd2 Kf4 5 Bh5 Ke4 is 1) Ke4 and we have transposed to the analysis of 5.

3e) 2 Kb2 Ke5 followed by ...Kf4 and ...Ke3 draws.

4) 1 Kb2! (the only move to win) and now 1...Ke5 2 Bh5 — 13 or 1...Kf6 (1...Kd5 2 Kc2 reaches d3 and wins according to 9) 2 Be8! (not 2 Bh5? Ke5 draw) Kg5 3 Bh5 Kf4 4 Kc1! — 12.

The winning line might run 1 Kb2! Kf6 2 Be8! Ke5 3 Bh5 Kf4 4 Kc1! Ke4 5 Kc2! Ke3 6 Kd1 Ke4 7 Ke1! Kf4 8 Ke2! Ke4 9 Kf2 Kf4 10 Kg2! d3 11 Kf2 Ke4 12 Kg3 — an astonishing duel between the two kings.

CHAPTER 6

147 (Zilahi) This is a problem in which logic is no help — either you see the idea or you don't. The answer runs **1 Qxd6+ Kb5 2 Kd5 Nc3.** It is astonishing that Black has to take White's queen with check in order to arrange a mate, but this is the only solution.

148 (Eberle) 1 Kg1 Ka1 2 Qg7 Qd4. Each first move replaces one pin by another and Black's second move changes an effective pin of the White queen into an ineffective one; ineffective because the pinning piece is itself pinned. This is the only way a pinned piece can deliver mate.

149 (Feather) A barrier of Black men separates his king from the main White force, which is trained on the c4 and c5 squares. In fact Black's king must be deflected on to the c-file to be mated, but two White pieces are attacking each square. Black's queen must obstruct one piece while the other sacrifices itself. The mating lines run 1 Q moves Bxc4+ 2 Kxc4 Qxc5 and 1 Q moves Nxc5+ 2 Kxc5 Rxc4. In the first case Black's queen move must be along the d4—h4 line or Kxc4 won't be possible, but Black must not give check, so the queen has to take the rook. In the second case the same logic proves that the queen must capture at g1. All the moves in the solutions are captures.

150 (Schneider) e7 is hard to control, except by a mate down the e-file. This suggests the conversion of the pin into a battery by playing the White knight to the e-file, allowing a Black bishop move. At present the knight move would deliver check and if Black attempts to answer this by Bd5 we run into a problem after 1 Ra8 (for instance) Ne3+ 2 Bd5 because the knight must cover d6 and block the first rank simultaneously. Taking the bishop at move 1 is a better way to deal with the irritating check. There are two possible captures corresponding to the two solutions. Try 1 R1xa2. There are two rooks to shut off, one by the Black bishop and one by the White knight. The bishop must go to c2 (not d3 as it could interpose at e2 or e4), leaving the knight to deal with the lines c2—e4 and a3—e3 by moving to d3. It follows that White must choose e5 at move 1 to give the solution **1 R1xa2 Ne5 2 Bc2 Nd3**. In the same way we can find the second line **1 R3xa2 Ne3 2 Bb1 Nc2**.

151 (Kricheli) This superb problem is also difficult to solve. There are two batteries pointing at f2 and h4, the Black king's flight squares. White would like to mate by Ne4 or Nxh5, but this needs a self-block at g4 and the only Black pieces available for this duty, queen and bishop, leave the mating squares covered. The solution is to play the Black king to the flight squares before delivering mate. The rear battery pieces have to be neutralised first or the king will be unable to move, so the two symmetrical variations run **1 Qxe7 Ne4+ 2 Kh4 Rf4** and **1 Bxf7 Nd5 2 Kf2 Bh4**.

152 (Kricheli) b6 is unguarded, suggesting that the bishop and knight battery will deliver the fatal blow, probably by Nc4 or Nf5 in order to cover d6.

Each of these moves runs into a White interference; Nc4 interrupts the queen's guard of b5, while Nf5 frees d5. There are two potential ways to deal with each interference. Either Black can carry out a self-block on the square in question, or the White queen can be unpinned to cover the square directly.

Suppose, first, that Nc4 is the mating move. In this case Black can either play Be2—b5 blocking, or the queen can be unpinned by Bd1 to play over the critical square to a6, so that she maintains her guard of b5 even after the knight has moved to c4. The first possibility 1 Be2 pass 2 Bb5 Nc4 turns out to fail through lack of a White waiting move, so the second holds. The only difficulty is that Black has trouble finding a waiting move after 1 Bd1 Qa6. 2 Qxd5 is the only one, when White must take care to play 2 Nc4 rather than 2 Nf5, which would unpin the queen.

Now suppose that White mates by Nf5. This interferes with the Rg5 and if White plays Re5 to cross the critical f5 square, he frees the h6 bishop to interpose at e3. Black can't block the h6—e3 diagonal in two moves without opening a different line to e3. Thus we are left with the direct guard by 1 Bd1 Qd3 2 pass Nf5, which fails through lack of a Black pass move, or a self-block. Since White intends Nf5 the queen is no good, so the only chance is to use the bishop. 1 Bf3 pass 2 Bd5 Nf5 looks very promising, but now it is White who has trouble with a waiting move. There is just one, namely d6+.

An astonishing problem, with perfect symmetry between the strategy of the two solutions.

153 (Gandew) The criss-crossing lines h1—d1, h5—d1, d8—d1, a4—g4 and a3—g3 are all likely elements of the two solutions; the solver's task is to find the right way to combine them. Assuming that the h5 bishop will deliver mate, there are five Black men ready to interpose on the h5—d1 line needing to be nullified.

Taking the diagram position first, White's e-pawn could shut off the queen and one of the Black rooks by advancing. The other rook could be obstructed by a Black piece on the d-file, which could not itself interpose on the h5—d1 diagonal on account of a pin by the Rd8. The Rh1 will pin the fifth piece. White's two moves must be a move by the d-pawn, which Black then captures, and a move by the e-pawn to mate. This leaves the f3 pawn to be removed by a Black capture, as follows: **1 Nxf3 d4 2 Nfxd4+ e3**.

In b) Black can't take the f3 pawn because the queen could interpose at f3. If f4 is the mating move, the pawn neutralises the queen and the a4 rook, but first it must be unpinned by Bd3. This bishop move has to be a capture of the d-pawn or the bishop will be free to interpose at e2, so the solution runs **1 Bxe2 d3 2 Bxd3 f4**.

154 (Benko) Black's king is badly placed in the corner and if he can be deprived of the flights at a2 and b2, White's battery will mate. The set play **1...Kd3 2 Nc3 Kc2 3 Na2 Nb3** puts this plan into action. Black has no waiting move and the actual solution is completely unexpected in that Black's king moves out from its vulnerable corner square to be mated in the middle of the board: **1 Kb2 Rd5 2 Kc3 Rc5+ 3 Kd4 Nb3**.

155 (Takács) Congratulations to anyone who solved this one! The mating positions differ drastically from the diagram position and even guessing the theme (different promotions by the b6 pawn on different squares) doesn't help much. The set play is **1...Bxa8 2 Ba7** (not Bc7 interfering with the future queen) **b7 3 Kc6 b8=Q**. With Black to play, there are various tempting lines which barely fail, for example 1 Ba7 Bxa8 2 pass b7 3 Kc6 b8=Q is impossible as there is no waiting move and 1 Bc7 Bxa8 2 Bd8 b7 3 Kc6 b8=Q checks White's king! The solution is **1 Qa6 Ba8 2 Qc8 b7 3 Kc6 bxc8=N**.

156 (Loyd) Critical play in the helpmate presented with utmost simplicity! **1 Kf6 Ra8 2 Kg7 Bb8 3 Kh8 Be5**. A classic setting.

157 (Páros) What could be simpler than to arrange a back rank mate by Kxb7? Black could play, for example, Rf4–f7 and Bg7, the only problem being that White has no waiting moves after 1 Rf4. Black can play Bg7 first, however, allowing the pawn to promote. Making a queen or a rook is a bad idea, since this forces the king to move, but a bishop or a knight looks harmless enough. Alas these pieces don't provide a suitable waiting move, for example 1 Bg7 h8=B 2 Rf4 or 1 Bg7 h8=N 2 Rf4, and now what? The next idea is to make use of the newly created piece at h8. A bishop at h8 means Black doesn't have to block g7, so he can move his own bishop elsewhere, freeing White's to make a pass move. Unfortunately there isn't a good square, since e5 gives check and d4 or f6 blocks the path of the rook to f7. This explains the c3 pawn, for without it 1 Bb2 h8=B 2 Rf4 Bd4 3 Rf7 Kxb7 would be a cook. If White makes a knight, there is a potential solution by 1 Bg7 h8=N 2 Ra4 (for example) pass 3 Q moves Kxb7, but once again Black cannot provide White with a reasonable waiting move. Having explored these finesses we can now go full circle back to the very first plan of Bg7 and Rf4–f7, since White can provide a waiting move by **1 Bg7 h8=N 2 Rf4 Nf7! 3 Rxf7 Kxb7**, an idea which is peculiarly hard to visualise.

158 (Masanek) If you solved this in less than half an hour then give yourself a well-deserved pat on the back! Several tempting lines fail because of the White king's position, for example 1 Re8 fxe8=Q+ 2 Kh6 Bc4 3 Kh7 Qh5 would work but for Black's check. In the actual solution White plays f8=Q and mates the enemy king on h7 with his bishop. The BBb1 has to be captured, so White must play Ba2 and Bxb1. Black's rooks cannot be allowed to interpose, so they have to flee to the a-file: **1 Ra8 f8=Q 2 Rga7 Ba2 3 Kh7 Bxb1**.

159 (Kardos) White's pawn must promote to have a chance of giving mate. The first move is e3, so it takes six moves to promote the pawn, and even this modest objective can only be achieved if White can play exf4 at move 2. The solution must start 1 f1=R (to avoid checking the White king) e3 2 Rf4 exf4. If White promotes to a queen, Black has to waste time moving his king and as we have already played one rook promotion we might guess that the theme of the problem involves rook promotions. If White plays 6...f8=R he has to decide between 7...Ra8 and 7...Rf3 for the mating move. The former needs a self-block at b3, but a rook would give check while anything else can interpose on the a-file. Thus the final move is 7 Rf3 and the block at a2 has to be a rook. The solution runs **1 f1=R e3 2 Rf4 exf4 3 e3 f5 4 e2 f6 5 e1=R f7 6 Ra1 f8=R 7 Ra2 Rf3**.

CHAPTER 7

169 (Ivanov) The main feature of this problem is that three White pieces are converging on g2. If any two of these were eliminated the third could sacrifice itself to force ...Qxg2 mate. Black has three legal moves, 1...cxd2, 1...e4 and 1...Bxg7, each nullifying one of the attacks on g2. This suggests that the key should be a move reducing the number of attacks to two. The Rd2 cannot move away, but it can be eclipsed by 1 Be2. However, Black chooses his reply so as to eliminate the piece which has already been dealt with, in this case by 1...cxd2!. The same argument applies to 1 Ng6? Bxg7! and to 1 Nc6? e4!. The queen differs from the other two pieces in that she can simply move off the a8–g2 diagonal, which has the same effect as the white interference. Black's reply will be 1...e4 in any case, but if White chooses **1 Qb8!**, then 1...e4 can be met by 2 Qxh2+ Qxh2 mate, so this is the solution.

170 (Seider) If the knight on b5 were absent, Black's only legal move would be ...g2 mate. Thus White's aim is to capture the knight or to immobilise it by pinning. After 1...Na7 2 Rxa7, 1...Nc7 2 dxc7, 1...Nxa3 2 Rxa3 or 1...N elsewhere 2 NxN, this is accomplished, so White only needs a waiting move to solve the problem. Alas, the queen can't move without giving the king a flight and other plausible tries fail, for example 1 d7? Nc7, 1 d3? Nc3 or 1 Ra8? Nxd4. This leads us to consider changed play. The formation in the bottom right corner is rather suspicious, because if it's only function is to arrange ...g2 mate, the Bg1 has no purpose at all. This clue indicates that Black will mate by ...Nxg3, when the Bg1 is needed to cover f2. The key is **1 Nxg3**, placing Black in zugzwang. The defences 1...Nxa3, 1...Nc3, 1...Nc7 and 1...Na7 are met in the same way as in the set play, but 1...Nxd4 and 1...Nxd6 need new replies now that the knight has departed. Because the new mate covers e2, White can afford to move his queen, so the changed play is **1...Nxd6 2 Qe7** and **1...Nxd4 2 Qe4** (not 2 Qg4 covering g3).

171 (Bettmann) The mating move must be ...Rxa6, but at the moment Black threatens to play ...bxa6, destroying the mating net, so the key must prevent this. The only genuine possibility is **1 a8=B!** (not 1 a8=Q? Rxa6+). Then White must eliminate the newly created piece at g1 in order to force ...Rxa6.

Suppose Black plays 1...fxg1=Q. A quick check shows that all the Black queen's squares are adequately guarded with the exception of c5 and f1, the latter because the recapture by the Qh3 leaves d7 free for Black's king (and the queen covers a6, but that is incidental). If we suppose for the moment that c5 is covered by White's second move then 2...Qxf1 can be met by 3 b5+ Qxb5. It might appear that in this case 2...Qxc5 can be dealt with by 3 bxc5, but then b4 is freed for White's king. 2 f8=B removes this problem, since 2...Qxc5 3 Bxc5 really does force mate, but Black can reply 2...Qg8!. The alternative is to meet 2...Qxc5 by 3 b5+ as well, but then d6 must be covered as well as c5. This suggests 2 f8=Q and it is easy to check that it works.

Now consider 1...fxg1=R. Here 2...Rxf1 is a threat, since neither 3 b5+ nor 3 Qxf1 is a satisfactory reply. Thus White must cover f1 with another piece. 2 Rf2? Rh1 and 2 Rh1? Rxh1 fail, so the only move is 2 f8=R!. By now you should have guessed the theme of the problem! 1...fxg1=B threatens 2...Bxc5, but although 2 f8=Q doesn't work, we can revert to the 2 f8=B! idea which failed before but succeeds here since there is no need to cover g8. Finally 1...fxg1=N attacks the White queen and threatens 2...Nf3 since 3 Qxf3 would free d7. If the Qh3 could be relieved of its guard duty, then the knight could be captured next move, so 2 f8=N is correct.

The task of meeting four Black promotions with the corresponding White ones is called the Babson-task and although achieved many years ago in the selfmate field, it is only very recently that a directmate Babson-task has been composed.

172 (Prokop) This is hard to solve because there is no clear indication as to the mating position. One possibility is WKc1, BKc3, BPc2 with Black's only legal move being ...Bb2. White needs a piece, probably the rook, covering the fourth rank to force this, but that is a minor problem. For example, if the White knight were transparent White could play 1 Ra4 Kc3 2 Qc7+ Kb2 3 Qh2+ Kc3 4 Qc2+ bxc2+ 5 Kc1 Bb2. The real problem here is bringing the queen to c2. This leads to the idea of 1 Bb1 Kxb1 2 Qg6+ Kb2 3 Ra4 Kc3 4 Qc2+ bxc2+ 5 Kc1 Bb2, based on the fact that the White bishop was irrelevant at the end of the first line. However, at the moment we have found no reason why the bishop shouldn't move to h7, c4, b5, e2 or f1 on the first move. The reason must lie in the variation 1...Kc3. After 1 Bb1 Kc3, for example, White faces immediate problems because the king threatens to escape at b4 or c4 and since we don't want to allow ...b2, which would make a mate virtually impossible, the reply to ...Kc3 is sure to be a check. If the bishop travels on the f1—a6 diagonal then c4 is defended and 1 B moves Kc3 2 Ne4+ forces the king back to b2, giving White a free move since Black is already constrained to go to b1 next. If we try e2 first, on the grounds that it blocks a White king flight, we need to find a selfmate in three after **1 Be2 Kc3 2 Ne4+ Kb2**. Even this isn't easy, because it involves a new mating position, but the problem has been reduced in length by two moves, so it shouldn't take too long to find **3 Qd2+ Kb1 4 Nc3+ Bxc3 5 Qc2+ bxc2 mate**.

173 (Ivanovsky & Harichev) Black's limited force greatly restricts the possible mating positions and since the king and pawn must remain confined in the bottom right corner, only the bishop is available. In fact the White king must be on a8, with blocking bishops at a7 and b8, one of these being provided by the underpromotion of the d-pawn. In this case White could play, for example 1 Qe4+ Bg2 2 Qf3 Bxf3 mate. In order to have enough time to advance the d-pawn, White needs a man-oeuvre to gain a tempo, which can be repeated once for each step forward by the pawn. With the queen at d1 and Black to play, White can continue 1...Kg2 2 Qg4+ Kh1 3 Qf3+ Bg2 4 Qd1+ Bf1 5 free move Kg2 etc, gaining a tempo once every four moves. Note that this only works with the White king on a7, for once it has moved to a8 this manoeuvre self-pins the queen. Therefore White must promote the d-pawn and play the bishop from d8 to b8, leaving the moves Ka8 and Ba7 until the very last moment. The solution runs **1 Qd1 Kg2 2 Qg4+ Kh1 3 Qf3+ Bg2 4 Qd1+ Bf1 5 Be3** (making way for the pawn without losing control of g1 when the pawn advances to d4) **Kg2 6 Qg4+ Kh1 7 Qf3+ Bg2 8 Qd1+ Bf1 9 d4 Kg2 10 Qg4+ Kh1 11 Qf3+ Bg2 12 Qd1+ Bf1 13 d5 Kg2 14 Qg4+ Kh1 15 Qf3+ Bg2 16 Qd1+ Bf1 17 d6 Kg2 18 Qg4+ Kh1 19 Qf3+ Bg2 20 Qd1+ Bf1 21 d7 Kg2 22 Qg4+ Kh1 23 Qf3+ Bg2 24 Qd1+ Bf1 25 d8=B Kg2 26 Qg4+ Kh1 27 Qf3+ Bg2 28 Qd1+ Bf1 29 Bc7 Kg2 30 Qg4+ Kh1 31 Qf3+ Bg2 32 Qd1+ Bf1 33 Bb8 Kg2 34 Qg4+ Kh1 35 Qf3+ Bg2 36 Qd1+ Bf1 37 Ka8** (at last) **Kg2 38 Qg4+ Kh1 39 Qf3+ Bg2 40 Bea7 Bxf3 mate**.

174 (Anderson) There is a great deal of set play in this position, so it is worthwhile discovering which Black moves lack a set reply. The main idea involves shutting off the Rf6's guard of f1, so as to force the reply ...Ne2. The variations run 1 ...Be7 2 Re6 Ne2, 1...Bg7 2 any Ne2, 1...Nf7 2 Nf4 Ne2, 1...Nxg6 2 Rxg6 Ne2, 1...Qg2 2 c3 Qb2, 1...Qf3 2 g4 Qd1, 1...Qxe4 2 Ref3 Qe1, 1...Ne2+ 2 Rf1 Qxf1, 1...Nf3+ 2 Re1 Qxe1, 1...Nh3+ 2 Bd1 Qxd1, 1...Bxd6 2 Rxd6 Ne2 and finally 1...Kxd7 2 Re6 Ne2. This leaves just two moves without a set answer, namely 1...Bh6 and 1...c3. White must arrange to meet these without disturbing the set mates which already exist. There are several plausible tries which fail because White can be forced to give mate himself, for example 1 Rf5? (threat 2 Rg5 Ne2) Nf7! forces 2 Nf6, 1 Bg4? (threat 2 Nf4) c3 2 Rxf8 and 1 Nc5? leads to a mate by the White queen. Finally 1 Rc3? (threat 2 Nc5 Nf3) fails to 1...Kxd7.

The key is **1 Kb1!**, putting Black in zugzwang. The two added variations are **1...c3 2 Kc1 Ne2** and **1...Bh6 2 Kc1 Nf3.**

CHAPTER 8

181 (Rice) Black need only transfer the rook from g2 to c8 and White can mate by Nd7. In order to shield the White king from the Bh1, Black must also play ...g2. If a Black piece could temporarily interpose at f3 this could be accomplished straight away, but the only suitable piece is the Rb7, which is itself immobilised. To free the Rb7, Black must play his king to c6, so the solution starts with a move by the Bc7. It runs **1 Bd8 2 Kc7 3 Kc6 4 Rf7 5 Rf3 6 Rc2** (it takes fewer moves to play the Rg2 to c8 and the Rf3 to b7 than the other way round because the Rg2 can't reach b7 in two moves) **7 g2** (now Black can go into reverse) **8 Rf7 9 Rb7 10 Kc7 11 Kb8 12 Rc8 13 Bc7 Nd7.**

182 (Rehm and Helledie) The diagram position is exceptional in that it contains a promoted Black piece. However, the play was sufficiently noteworthy for the judge not only to ignore this infringement of the conventions, but even to award the problem a first prize! If only the Ba1 were at b2 instead of the rook, then White could mate by Nd2. The rook must be transferred to c3 to shield the White king from check. The problem is to free the Rb2, since the queens are unable to provide a shield. The only possibility is to play the Black king to c3, using the queens at c2 and d2 to shield Black's king from the rook and bishop. So the solution is **1 Qc6 2 Qc2 3 Kc4!** (3 Qa4 4 Qc6 5 Qg2 6 Qd2 7 Kc3 is one move slower) **4 Qd3 5 Qd2 6 Kc3 7 Rb3** (heading for c3) **8 Kb2** (the Black king makes way for the rook without exposing the White king to check) **9 Rc3 10 Qa4** (the most economical method; the queen returns to a4 in one move) **11 Kb3 12 Qb2 13 Qba3 14 Bb2 Nd2.** Both Black queens and the Black king complete closed tours to return to their original squares. The use of the White king to ensure that the paths of the Black queens are unique is particularly interesting.

183 (Ugren) This problem reminds me of those sliding block puzzles where you have to try to reverse the position of two pieces! The only feasible final position has BKa2, BNb3, BBb1, BRb2 and mate by Rxa4. The knight has to be provided by the promotion of the a3 pawn, while by a process of elimination we can deduce that the Black queen must end up at a1. The first task is to arrange the promotion of the a-pawn. It's quite easy to play a few moves and then get stuck, for example 1 Bb3 2 a2 and now 3 Qa3 is the only move, but it doesn't help because the next one has to be 4 Qb2! Since 1 Qb3 leads nowhere, 1 Bb3 must be right, so the mistake must have been at move two. Thus **1 Bb3 2 Ra2** (not 2 Qa2?) **3 Qa1** (not 3 Ka1? – initially we can proceed by a process of elimination) **4 Rab2 5 Ba2** (not 5 a2?) **6 Rb3 7 Qb2 8 Ka1 9 Bb1** (the bishop has arrived at its final destination) **10 a2 11 Qa3** (11 Ra3 12 Qb3 13 Kb2 14 a1=N takes too long) **12 Kb2 13 a1=N 14 Qa2** (14 Ka2 15 Qb2 16 Ka3 17 Qa2 etc. takes two moves longer) **15 Ka3 16 Rb2 17 Nb3 18 Qa1 19 Ka2 Rxa4.**

184 (Lindgren) The mating move cannot be e2—e4, since the e3 pawn cannot be removed, so it must be c5xd6. With the Black king on e7, we need further pieces on d6, e6, f6, f7, f8, e8 and d8. Since the Rb7 and Ba8 cannot move, this means that all the Black pawns promote, using up eighteen moves. The Pe2 must therefore be taken, and the only sensible method is to play g1=N and Nxe2. The knight then needs two more moves to reach its destination, which must be e6 since no other square on the above list can be reached in two moves. These knight moves, and the two moves by the Black king, bring the total so far to twenty-three moves, leaving ten for the pieces at a1, e1, g4, h1, h1 and h1. The piece ending at d8 must be a bishop.

Suppose for the moment that this bishop comes from e1. Then the absolute minimum number of moves required is 1 for a1, 2 for e1, 1 for g4 and 2 each for the h1's, making 10, which leaves none to spare. But the only square which can be reached from a1 in one move is f6, and the same holds for g4, so one of these pieces will have to consume an extra move, taking us over the limit.

Thus the d8 bishop comes from a1. So we need two moves for a1 and two for the h1's, leaving one each for e1 and g4. So we have e1=R and Re8 (Q would check WKc6), while the Ng4 moves just once, to f6. The three remaining pieces must reach f7, f8 and d6 in two moves each from h1. Because of the WPd3, which Black doesn't have time to take, a piece at h1 can only reach d6 in two moves if it is a queen (Rh6—d6 is impossible because Black's **last** move is to d6, and by this time there will be blocking men at e6 and f6), and then only via h2. Since the queen must stay at h2 until the very end, this must be the last of the three h-pawns. To avoid checking the White king from h1, there must be a shield. This has to be the Pg5 advancing to g2. However the g-pawn will eventually take at e2 to free the e-pawn to play to e8, so the e-file has to remain open until near the end. In particular, Ke6 must be delayed until after Nf6. Thus the f-file is blocked at all stages. This prevents h1=R and Rf1—f8, for example, and the reader may check that this forces all the h1 promotions to be queens. So the g-pawn must be freed before anything else can happen, and this determines the move-order completely.

The solution is **1 a1=B 2 Bf6 3 Bd8 4 Nf6 5 g4 6 g3 7 g2 8 h1=Q 9 Qh5 10 Qf7 11 h5 12 h4 13 h3 14 h2 15 h1=Q 16 Qh6 17 Qhf8 18 h5 19 h4 20 h3 21 h2 22 h1=Q 23 Qh2 24 g1=N 25 Nxe2 26 Nf4 27 e2 28 e1=R 29 Re8 30 Ke6 31 Ke7 32 Ne6 33 Qd6+ cxd6.**

185 (Morse) Sir Jeremy Morse's problem was the first ever to show seven promotions in a serieshelpmate. In the previous problems we have virtually proved that the solution is unique, but in casual solving this isn't necessary. The composer should have already verified that the solution is unique, so we can make plausible guesses about the solution, and if these guesses lead to the answer then we need not explore alternative sets of assumptions. The situation is different in solving competitions, since finding a cook usually earns bonus marks, so all possibilities have to be explored.

Here the Black king is mated at f5 by e2—e4. Seven blocking men are necessary, but the most obvious problem concerns the path of the king from a7 to f5. Since the WNb7 controls the only exit routes via a5 and d8, the knight must be captured. This requires yet another Black piece, so all the Black pawns except the Pc7 promote. After the Nb7 is taken, the king can emerge via c8 to f5. Since we know that the order of moves must be unique, there has to be a reason why we cannot play Kb8 at any time, and a reasonable guess is that the Nb7 will be taken by a rook which enters via b8. A premature Black king move would block the rook's path. Since h2 must be taken, we may also guess that f1=N, Nxh2 and Ng4 will be played.

Now we can start on the arithmetic. Promoting the pawns takes 23 moves, the BKa7 needs 6, the R which takes on b7 needs 3, and the Nf1 needs 2, totalling 34. Thus ten are left for the queen and five pawns remaining. Hence two of these take just one move. The h1 promotions need two each, but the queen can make do with one move if she plays to f6. The pieces at e5 and f4 must be bishops (f4 cannot be a knight as no promotion square is within two N moves of f4 except c1, and even this would require that one of vital e2, d3 pawns be taken). f1 and h1 are white squares, so the two bishop promotions take place at c1. One of these can reach f4 in one move, while the other can play to e5 via b2, freeing the Pb3 without loss of time. This accounts for all forty-four moves. The queenside moves are Qf6, c3, c2, c1=B; now Pd6 can't move until unpinned by Bb1—a2—e6, so the first bishop must take at b2 and play to e5. b3 promotes and plays to e6, freeing d6 to take at c5 and promote to the other black-squared bishop at f4. Unfortunately the very first move of this sequence, Qf6, blocks the path of Black's king to f5. Thus Black's king must be freed before any queenside moves can be played, so it is a rook from h1 which captures at b7. In fact this rook must arise from the third promotion at h1, since only when the h-file is clear can a rook reach b7 from h1 in just three moves. Thus all the kingside pawns promote before any queenside moves can be played.

This gives the sequence 1 f1=N 2 Nxh2 3 Ng4 4 h2 5 h1=R 6 Rh5 7 Rg5 (the only destination square which can be reached in two moves) 8 h5 9 h4 10 h3 11 h2 12 h1=R 13 Rh6 14 Rhg6 15 h5 16 h4 17 h3 18 h2 19 h1=R 20 Rh8 21 Rb8 22 Rxb7 23 Kb8 24 Kc8 25 Kd8 26 Ke7 27 Kf6 28 Kxf5 29 Qf6 30 c3 31 c2 32 c1=B 33 Bxb2 34 Be5 35 b2 36 b1=B 37 Ba2 38 Be6 39 dxc5 40 c4 41 c3 42 c2 43 c1=B 44 Bcf4 e4.

186 (Tomson) We need to guess the mating position before any further progress can be made. With e2, e1 and f1 blocked, White could sacrifice his queen at e3 or d4 to force BxQ mate. If the sacrifice is at e3, then something has to cover d5. Thus White needs to promote four pawns. There are three on the b-file, and the other can only be the f-pawn. To allow fxg5, a shield must be inserted at f3. This extra piece is one too many, so somehow two functions must be combined in one piece.

The solution is to sacrifice at d4 rather than e3. The queen can be guarded by a knight from f3, which also operates as a shield. Now there is no need to cover d5 and White saves a piece. The Pb6 must be unpinned at some stage, but if White plays b8=N, the knight can serve by playing to d4 on its way to f3. This suggests **1 b8=N 2 Nc6 3 Nd4 4 b7 5 b8=Q** (the Pb4 gives the clue here, for the only reason why White cannot play b5 earlier is if White needs b5 for a Qb8−b5−f1 manoeuvre) **6 Qb5 7 Qf1 8 b5 9 b6 10 b7 11 b8=R** (this must be a rook or a queen to reach e1 in two moves, but a queen would check as it passed over b1; note that Qb4−e1 isn't possible, since the knight must move to f3 before the queen plays to e1) **12 Rb1 13 Qb6** (the rook can't go to e1 until a shield arrives at e2, so the next step is to free the Nd4 to unpin the f-pawn, which will promote to a bishop and play to e2; White couldn't play Qb6 earlier since various pieces had to travel down the b-file) **14 Nf3 15 fxg5 16 g6 17 g7 18 g8=B 19 Bc4 20 Be2 21 Re1 22 Qd4+ Bxd4.**

CHAPTER 9

202 (Pruscha) The Black rook and bishop cover Ne8 mate and Nf5 mate respectively, so there is a potential Novotny at e6. The knight is already involved in the mates, so the only piece which can go to e6 is the queen. White needs to cover d7 and e7 to make this work, which suggests **1 Rh7** is the key. Without guessing the theme of the problem, it would be very hard to find this surprising rook move, which gives away a flight at e5. After 1...Ke5 2 Ne6+ Kd6 (or 2...Ke4 3 Nc5) 3 Qe7 or 1...Re7 2 Nf5+ and 3 Qxe7 White mates easily, so Black's only defence to the threat of 2 Qe6+ is to play his bishop across the critical square by **1...Bg4** (or h3). This ruins the Qe6+ Novotny, but now **2 Ne6!** works instead, followed by Qd7 or Qe7 mate as appropriate.

203 (Bron) White must take action to support his main asset, the pawn at g7.

1   c4

This threatens 2 Bd5, for example 1...Kh6 2 Bd5 Bxd5 3 cxd5 and 4 d7 wins.

1   ...   Bxc4
2   d7

Not 2 Bd5? Bxd5 3 d7 because of 3...Rg2+ 4 Kh3 Rg3+ with perpetual check.

	2 ...	**Rd3**

It's tempting to play 3 Bd5, but Black can't reply 3...Rd2+! 4 Kg1 (4 Kh3 loses to 4...Bxd5) Rxd5 5 g8=Q Rd1+ winning, so White must adopt a finesse.

	3 Bf3+!	**Kh6**

Or else the Pg7 promotes with check after 4 Bd5 etc.

	4 Bd5!	**Rd2+!**

Even now this is the best defence. 4...Rxd5 5 g8=Q Rd2+ 6 Qg2 forces the d-pawn home.

	5 Kg1	**Rxd5**
	6 g8=N+!	

This is the point of the check at move 3. 6 g8=Q still loses.

	6 ...	**Kg5**
	7 Bc1+	

Black is finally forced to a white square and White can pick up the rook with a knight fork.

	7 ...	**Kf5**
	8 Ne7+	**Ke6**
	9 Nxd5	**Kxd7**

Destroying the main enemy, but exposing himself to a final tactic.

10 Nxb6+ and **11 Nxc4** winning.

204 (Kazantsev) Black threatens ...Rd1+ mating and after 1 Be1? Rxg6 2 Bf2 Rxc6 White has lost too many pawns. Black can stop the rest by ...Rc8 and win on material.

	1 Nc2	**Bg7**

After 1...Rxg6 2 Bb6 Rd6 3 Bd4! Bg7 4 c7 White even wins.

	2 c7	

Threatening to promote with check. After 2 a7? a2 White cannot meet the threat of 3...a1=Q+ 4 Nxa1 Rd1+.

	2 ...	**Rc6**
	3 a7	**Rxc2**

Or 3...a2 4 Bc3! (Novotny) Bxc3 (4...Rxc3 5 a8=Q and Black has lost control of a1) 5 a8=Q a1=Q+ 6 Nxa1 and the rook cannot now mate at c1.

	4 Bd2	**a2**
	5 a8=Q	**a1=Q+**

6	Qxa1	Bxa1
7	c8=Q+!	

Not 7 Bxf4? Be5! 8 B moves (what else?) Rxc7 and wins.

7	...	Rxc8
8	Bc3!	

A striking Novotny. 8...Bxc3 9 g7! Bxg7 (9...Ba1 10 h8=Q+ is the same) 10 h8=Q+ forces stalemate, while 8...Rxc3 9 h8=Q+ Kg4 10 g7 is at least a draw for White.

8	...	Rb8
9	Bb2!	

Not 9 h8=Q+? Rxh8 10 Bxh8 f3 11 Bd4 Bxd4 12 g7 f2 and wins.

9	...	Rd8
10	Bd4!	Re8
11	Be5!	

with a draw by perpetual Novotny!

205 (Loshinsky) At the moment there isn't a Novotny in sight, since although various pieces can move to d5, neither the Rb5 nor the Bc4 is actually defending against a mate threat. These threats must be provided by the first move, but it appears particularly hard to arrange a mate threat on the c4—g8 diagonal. The only chance, however remote it might seem, lies in the move Ne6. At present the f7 pawn covers this square, which is also blocked by the rook. However, if the Re6 were to move, then Black would have a strong inducement to move his f-pawn, in order to give check. The key must carry a threat, so **1 Rg6** is the most promising move, intending 2 Nh3+ gxh3 3 Bg3. 1...Bf1 fails to 2 Ne6+ fxe6 3 Qf8, while otherwise Black must move his f-pawn. In each case the Rb5 defends against mate by e6 while the bishop prevents Ne6, but White must choose the right piece to play to d5.

First, **1...f6+** is met by **2 d5!** (2 Bd5? frees f5, while 2 Nd5+? Rxd5 avoids mate) followed by e6 or Ne6. After **1...f5+**, on the other hand, 2 d5? fails to 2...fxe4!, but with f5 blocked White can play **2 Bd5!** with impunity. 2 Nd5+? was still refuted by 2...Rxd5. After **1...fxg6+**, there cannot be a Novotny based on e6 and Ne6, since 2 d5? fails to 2...g3! now that the rook is not available to cover g4 after 3 Ne6. However, the opening of the f-file has introduced a new mating possibility, Qf8, which White can exploit by **2 Nd5+!**.

A perfect problem in every way.

206 (Karpov) Let's try to arrange a mate by the White king. White needs to defend the Bd2, but not by Kc3 because of the knight at d1. However, 1 b3 or 1 b4 is viable, followed by 2 K mates. Black's two moves must deal with the Bh7 and Rh6. A Grimshaw at g6 will cut off one of them, but this still leaves the piece at g6 to stop the mate. The solution is to use the pinned Black queen to interfere with the remaining piece by sliding along the pin-line. Suppose, for example, that Black plays Bg6 and Qe4. Of all the squares around White's king, only b3 is accessible, so White must take care not to block it with his b-pawn. The solution is **1 Bg6 b4 2 Qe4+ Kb3**. In the other solution, which involves Rg6 and Qe6, only b4 is free, so this one runs **1 Rg6 b3 2 Qe6+ Kb4**.

207 (Rukhlis) There is already a set Grimshaw at d4 by 1...Bd4 2 Qe4 and 1...Rd4 2 Nc3, but if this is to be the main idea, the point of the WRd1 is far from clear. The mates 1...Rc4 2 dxc4 and 1...Re4 2 Qxe4 work perfectly well without the rook. White can only make good use of it by **1 d4!** (not 1 Bd4? Nxg6, amongst others), threat 2 Nb6. The original mates arising if Black plays to d4 have been prevented by the opening of the b1–g6 and h3–a3 lines, but they have been replaced by the pin-mates 1...Rxd4 2 Nb4 and 1...Bxd4 2 Nf6. Black has two other defences based on playing to d3, which prevents White cutting off the other guard of d4 by Nb6. This causes a Black Grimshaw after which the set mates reappear: 1...Rd3 2 Qe4 and 1...Bd3 2 Nc3.

208 (Rehm) The White rook and knight battery generates mating ideas, for example 1 Nh6+ Ke5 2 Nxf7, prevented only by the Rb7, and 1 Ne3+ Ke5 2 Nc4, covered by the Rc8. Black's defensive lines intersect at c7, suggesting a Plachutta-type interference. White's problem is that he must keep making instant threats, or ...g5 disrupts the battery. After **1 Bc7!** White threatens 2 Bxd6+ in addition to 2 Ne3+/Nh6+, so Black is forced to take the bishop with one of the rooks. After **1...Rbxc7**, for example, White needs to deflect the Rc7 off the 7th rank in order to mate by Nh6+. 2 Bc6 would threaten 3 Ne3+ Ke5 4 Nc4, but Black doesn't have to take the bishop; instead, 2...g5! defends. White must invert his order of moves by **2 Ne3+ Ke5 3 Bc6!**, when Black really does have to take the bishop, allowing mate after **3...Rxc6 4 Ng4+ Kf4 5 Nh6+ Ke5 6 Nxf7**. After 1...Rcxc7 there is a symmetrical variation: **2 Nh6+ Ke5 3 Bd7! Rxd7 4 Ng4+ Kf4 5 Ne3+ Ke5 6 Nc4**.

209 (Kubbel) Congratulations if you solved this! Several Black men are already occupied defending against mate threats; the pieces at h7, g5 and e1 are preventing mates by Nfd3, Rd5 and Ne6 respectively. There are several ways these pieces could mutually interfere with each other, but at the moment no White pieces are able to play to one of the crucial squares. The key **1 Bg4!** threatens the Novotny interference 2 Bf5, followed by mate at d3 or d5. A quiet threat in a three-mover usually makes the solving process more difficult, and this problem is no exception. Black has a variety of defences featuring a wide range of interferences and obstructions:

1) The variations **1...Rge5 2 Ne6+ Rxe6 3 Rd5** and **1...Ree5 2 Rd5+ Rxd5 3 Ne6** form a type of Plachutta which doesn't involve the capture of a White piece at the critical square. This is called a **Wurzburg–Plachutta** and it stands in the same relationship to the Plachutta as the Grimshaw does to the Novotny.

2) After **1...Nh3** (to meet 2 Bf5 by Nxf4 covering d3 and d5) **2 Bf3!** (threat Rb5, so Black must play to e4 to free c6 for the king) there is a Grimshaw at e4 by **2...Re4 3 Nfd3** and **2...Be4 3 Ne6**.

3) Black can defend by playing the Bh7 across the critical square f5. After **1...Bc2**, the knight cannot occupy c2 so White plays **2 Bd2** (threat Bb4) **Rd5 3 Rxd5**. On the other hand, **1...Nc2** (so that if 2 Bf5? then 2...Nb4!) prevents the bishop occupying c2, which can be exploited by **2 Be6!** (threat 3 Na4) and if **2...Rxe6 3 Nxe6**, or **2...Rd5 3 Rxd5**. Notice that this is a case of mutual obstruction between bishop and knight; it is not an interference. The former involves denying access to a square, while the latter involves denying access to a line.

4) Finally **1...Bb1** avoids the obstruction at c2, but as it turns out c2 is a critical square, and by crossing it Black allows **2 Bd2 Nc2 3 Nfd3**.

210 (Whyatt) Another three-mover with a quiet threat, and again hard to solve. I gave the hint that there is a Black Grimshaw so the solver's eye should have been drawn to the square g6. At first sight there is no conceivable reason why Black should want to play ...Bg6 or ...Rg6, but one possible motivation would be to play his rook to the first rank. 1...Bxf5 fails to 2 Nxc4, so these are in fact the only two moves to free the rook. In turn, this suggests that the threat might be 2 Kc8/d8. This makes sense after **1 Bxc6!**, threat 2 Kd8 unpinning the bishop for 3 Bd7. Black's queen is tied to the mates at c5, d4 and d5, so cannot defend. Notice that White can also unpin the Bc6 by 2 Bc5 and 2 Rc5, but these aren't threats because of 2 Bc5 Bxf5! and 2 Rc5 Rxf6!, exploiting the White Grimshaw at c5. However, after the Grimshaw moves at g6, one of these defences is ruled out and White can choose his own move at c5: **1...Rg6 2 Bc5!** or **1...Bg6 2 Rc5!**. The similarity with Diagram 200 is striking.

211 (Vukčević)   **1 d4!**

White plunges straight in with a Plachutta at d4. The Ra4 must control g4, while the Rd5 holds d3. It might seem that this is immediately fatal, but fortunately for Black the White lines of action cross at f5, so Black can play a counter-Plachutta.

1	...	**f5!**
2	**Qxf5**	

This move and the next represent the heart of the problem. White needs to transfer his queen to d7 without loss of time in anticipation of the line d7–h7 being opened later.

228

2	...	Raxd4
3	Qd7!	

The threat is Bd3+, so the rook has to return along the fourth rank
(3...Rf4 4 Bxf4 gxf4 4 Qxg4+ and 3...Re4 4 Bxe4 f5 5 Qxf5 lead to mate
in seven).

3	...	Ra4

Or b4 or c4; it makes no difference.

4	d4!	f5!

Plachutta and counter-Plachutta again, but now the White queen gains
access to h7.

5	Bxf5	Rdxd4
6	Qh7!	

The point of White's play is that he can switch from a double line-up on
one diagonal to a double line-up on the other diagonal in just a single
move. Black is left with the wrong rook on d4 and lacks a tempo to set up
a defence with rooks on d4 and d5.

6	...	Re4

There is no satisfactory way to meet the threat of Bd3+.

7	Bxg4+	Rxg4
8	Qd3 mate.	

CHAPTER 10

223 (O'Shea) Black has made one pawn capture, from the h-file to the
g-file, and this balances the single missing White man. Since Black could
not have played ...hxg last move, Black hasn't just taken a piece. Moreover,
the last move wasn't a move/promotion at c1, nor a move by the BBh7.
Could it have been ...b7—b6? In this case BBc8 was taken on its original
square and BBh7 is a promoted pawn. The only missing Black pawn is the
a-pawn and as all Black captures have been accounted for, it must have
promoted at a1. This would produce a black-squared bishop, so the last
move wasn't ...b7—b6. A similar argument rules out ...g7—g6. In this case
BBc1 is a promoted pawn, but it could have been produced by a promotion
at a1, so we have to look a little deeper. The pawn at a5 must have made a
capture to allow Black's a-pawn to reach a1 and together with the BBf8
and the five White pawn captures implied by the kingside pawn structure,
this gives seven White captures, more than the number of missing Black
men. Finally Black could not have just moved his king, since moves from
d3, d4, d5 or f4 leave the king in illegal double checks, while moves from
e3 and f3 are impossible since the White pawns have no previous move.
Thus the last move was ...f7—f5 and the key **1 e5xf6** leaves Black in

zugzwang, as the variations 1...b5/bxa5 2 Nc5, 1...c5 2 Bd5, 1...d6/d5 2 Rxe7, 1...e6/e5 2 Nd6, 1...gxh5 2 Qxh7, 1...exf6+ 2 Nxf6, 1...Bxb2 2 Re2, 1...Bxd2+ 2 Nxd2 and 1...Bxg8 2 Qxg6 prove.

224 (Barnes) *a*) there is no reason why White shouldn't castle, so the key is **1 Ba3** (threat 2 Ke2), with the lines 1...Qxg2 2 Ne2, 1...Rxd2 2 Kxd2, 1...Rb4 2 0–0–0 and 1...Rxe4+ 2 Nxe4. Note that playing 1 Ke2? first fails to 1...Qxg2.

b) Suppose that White's king has never moved. A Black rook could not have reached h1 without checking the White king, so this rook must be a promoted pawn. Then Black's pawns must have made at least five captures (e.g. ...h4xg3xh2 and ...e5xf4xg3xh2), but only four White men are missing. Thus White's king has moved and he may not castle. The solution is **1 Ke2** (threat 2 Bb2/a3) leading to mate after 1...Qa8 2 Ba3, 1...Rxe4+ 2 Nxe4, 1...Rxd2+ 2 Bxd2, 1...Rb4 2 Bb2 or 1...Ra4 2 Ba3. The pawn at g7 prevents the defence ...Qxg2.

225 (Aloni) *a*) The first part doesn't involve any retro-analysis and has the solution **1 Qf7 Kb2 2 c3+ dxc3 3 Qb3+ cxb3.**

b) The solution of part (*a*) fails, but we can prove that White's last move was b2–b4. The only alternative is a king move, but Kb2–c3 leaves the a3 pawn with no move, while Kd4–c3 results in an illegal double check. Thus Black may begin **1 cxb3** and the rest of the solution runs **1...Kxd3** (not 1...Kc4 2 Qxd2 and White has no waiting move) **2 Qxd2+ Kc4 3 Qa5 cxb3.**

226 (Lindner) This problem contains a diabolical trap for the unwary solver. Many of you probably reasoned like this: White's last move wasn't with the rook or knight, since this would have left Black in check, while a king move from g3, g4, g5 or h5 gives rise to an illegal double check. All sixteen Black men are on the board, so the last move wasn't e3xd4. It must, therefore, have been d2–d4 and the solution is 1 exd3 Kxh3 (White's only waiting move) 2 d4 Na3. Unfortunately there is a serious flaw in the logic. White's last move **could** have been Kg3–h4 if the previous moves were 1...g4xf3+ 2 f2–f4. So one *en passant* capture proves that another isn't allowed. The solution is actually **1 Bxd4 Rxb3 2 Rc5 Nd2.**

227 (Haas) We have to work out which player is to move. Suppose Black has just moved. We can eliminate moves by the Bg8, Qh8 and Rd3 completely, together with the king moves ...Kd7/e7–e6, which leave an impossible double check. The only candidates are ...g6–g5, a promotion at g1 or h1 and ...Kd6–(or x)e6. The first is ruled out because the BBg8 is left with no entry. Pawn promotions require at least three Black pawn captures, one more than the number of missing White men, so the last move must have been 1...Kd6–(or x) e6. This leaves the king in double check from the Rd4 and Bh2, but we have already seen that this can be arranged with the aid of an *en passant* capture. The sequence of retractions can be extended to 1...Kd6xPe6 2 Pd5xPe6+ e7—e5, but what was White's move immediately prior to this? If 3 Kf4—e4+ then Black's last move must have been ...g6—g5+, when the position of the BBg8 is impossible, so it must have been 3 g3—g4+. Taking this move back leaves us with an even more difficult task. All the arguments which applied to the diagram position still operate, so we are once again left with only the Black king to provide the last move. Moves from c5, e6 and d7 are genuinely impossible and c7 scarcely looks more promising, so it seems that we have come to the end. One of the difficulties with retro-analytical problems is that the solver is not forced to uncover all the hidden points in the position to find the right answer. For example, many solvers would stop here faced with the 'obvious' illegality of Black's king moves, and they would correctly deduce that Black is to play in the diagram. They would have overlooked the retraction 3...Kc7—d6 4 b7xa8=N+. Retractions involving promotions and *en passant* captures are particularly easy to overlook and it is advisable to double-check an apparently illegal position to make sure that further retractions really are impossible. We have come to the end of the argument now, since replacing a Black piece at a8 leaves only five missing Black men, one of them the BBf8. So only four are available for White pawn captures, but five captures are necessary for the pawns to reach their present positions.

So White has just moved in the diagram and Black plays 1...Nf2 mate.

228 (**Haas**) I hope that you managed to borrow another rook to set up the position! The answer is to remove the BBh7. We must prove that this makes the position illegal.

The only missing Black pawn is the h-pawn, so this must have promoted to produce the third Black rook. It could not have promoted at g1 as the newly created rook would have been trapped in the corner. Therefore it must have made captures on the g-file, the f-file and at e1. Another pawn capture took place at b6 or b5 and the WRh1 was taken at g1 or h1. This accounts for all missing White men.

The next step is to try disentangling the top left corner. The first point is that White cannot retract a4—a5. The reason is that originally the bottom left corner had WBc1, WPb2 and BRe1. Black's knight buried itself on a1, White played b3 to free the bishop, but with the a-pawn at a4 the BRe1 could never have escaped. Thus a4—a5 occurred long ago to free the BRe1. Two Black men are missing. One was taken at e3, so we cannot retract b4xa5 since this implies two White queenside pawn captures. Thus no retractions are possible by the Pa5, Pb5, Qa6 and Rb6. If the White king plays to a8, he cannot retract Bb8—a7 as the BQ has no previous move. Can White uncapture a piece in the top left corner? Try Ka8xpiece b8. The piece cannot be a rook or queen as White would be in an illegal check, a bishop gives two black-squared bishops and a knight leaves BBc8 as the only missing Black piece. This is impossible as White's only pawn capture occurred at e3, a black square. Similar arguments eliminate Kb8xa8 and (with WKa8) Bb8xa7. White is equally unable to retract f2xe3, as this took place ages ago to allow Black's h-pawn to e1. The significance of proving that White can't uncapture a Black piece is that in order to retract Black's rooks away from their present positions at c7 and d7, they have to be played out via the 8th rank. This will give an illegal check to the White king unless there is a Black piece available to use as a shield. We have proved that White can't uncapture a piece, so the only possibility is to use the Black king as the shield.

The plan is to put the WK at a8 and BK at c8, then retract ...Rd8–d7, ...Re8–d8 and ...Rd7–c7. The first objection to this is that while Black's king is at c8, White is in retrostalemate, so before Black starts the above plan he must journey with his king to g1, via c5 and a3, to uncapture a White rook. This rook will provide White with an unlimited supply of retrotempi while his king is bottled up at a8. The second objection is more serious. With WKa8, BKc8, BRe8, BRd7, we seem to be home and dry, for Black may retract ...c7–c6 to free the BRb6 to be unpromoted at e1. But how did the WK get to a8? Via e6, d7 and c8, obviously! Unfortunately if White is to retract his king out via d7 and e6, Black's king must be removed first and this will expose the White king to an illegal check. The only way out of this dilemma is to use another Black piece as a shield on the eighth rank while Black's king moves out of the way. b8 and c8 are no good since the king's path to d7 is still blocked, so the shield must be at d8. There isn't very much room in Black's position and the poor rooks will have to be at d7 and e8 if d8 is blocked, but then White's king gets stuck when it reaches c8, since the d7 rook cannot be moved.

This completes the proof that the position without the BBh7 is illegal, but it is interesting to see how it can be disentangled when the Bh7 is present. The retractions run 14...Kf2xRg1, 26...Kd8–e8 27 Ka8 b8 Kc8–d8 28 R moves Rd8–d7 29 R moves Re8–d8 30 R moves Kd8–c8 31 R moves Bf5–h7 32 R moves Bc8–f5. Then retract BK out of the way, Rc7 goes back to d8, WK comes to c7, BBc8 moves to h5, BRs go to a8 and b8, WK to d7 and finally Black retracts ...c7–c6. The Rb6 can then be unpromoted at e1 without leaving the White king in the lurch. The rest is easy.

229 **(Fasher)** It is tempting to introduce a new White queen by retracting ...KxQa6. However, taking back ...Kb6xQa6 doesn't lead to a helpmate in one, while taking back ...Kb5xQa6 is illegal, since White has no previous move. To arrange a helpmate in one, it seems likely that a new White piece will have to be introduced, so retracting ...d7xc6 looks promising. Too promising, in fact, since there are apparently three solutions:

1) retract ...d7xQc6 and play 1 b6 Qc8.

2) retract ...d7xBc6 and play 1 Ba2 Bb5.

3) retract ...d7xNc6 and play 1 Ba2 Nb4/b8.

The only way to decide between these is to conduct some retro-analysis.

First the BBb1 must be a promoted pawn. The four Black pawns in the diagram are Black's a, b, c and d-pawns, so the pawn which promoted at b1 must have been the e-pawn originally, reaching b1 via captures at d6, c5, b4, a3 and b1. The remaining Black pawn captures occurred at b6 and a5, making seven in all. Taking into account the newly resurrected piece at c6 and the fact that the c1 bishop died on its original square, this accounts for all the missing White men. Notice that White's f1 bishop cannot have reached b1 and all the remaining captures took place on black squares. It follows that this bishop must be the piece to be uncaptured at c6, since all the others were taken earlier. So only solution (2) is valid.

230 (Haas) Just as in Kofman's problem (Diagram 222), White already has a mate by 1 Kxg7 and 2 Rf8, if it were possible to prove that Black can't castle. The solution is for White to retract Rb3xBb1. Consider the kingside pawn structure. The e1 bishop must have entered before White played g3, so the sequence of moves must have been f2xe3, WB plays to e1 and WN plays to f1 and only then g3. It follows that WBf1 must have been captured on its home square, so that the Ba4 is a promoted pawn. Apart from the WBf1, there is just one remaining White piece available for Black captures, namely the queen, which was taken at g5 or g6.

Black's last move could not have been ...b2–b1=B or ...c2xb1=B, as both these require another Black pawn capture. Therefore Black's last move must have been ...Rf5–b5+ and, by the same logic, this move wasn't a capture. Thanks to the choice of b3 for White's rook in the retraction, his previous move has to be b5xa6+. The pawn at b5 must have made a capture earlier to arrive at its present position behind the b4 pawn (remember Black isn't allowed another capture). So White has made two captures with the pawn currently at a6 and three with the pawns on the e-file. The BBf8 was never available for a pawn capture, so a quick count proves that the pawn which promoted to become the bishop at a4 made at most one capture. This pawn must have been either the a-pawn or the b-pawn, so the only possible promotion squares are a8 and c8. If c8, it must have been the b-pawn, but it takes too many captures to get round Black's b-pawn. Thus the a4 bishop was born by a promotion at a8, and Black can't castle because his a8 rook must have moved. Normally 'can't castle' problems rely on proving that the king has moved, but this one is a rare exception.

231 (Plaksin) Retro-analytical studies are rare beasts, but this one is well worth a close examination. A book shouldn't end without leaving something for the reader to do, so I will give the results of the retro-analysis without going through the detailed arguments required to establish each point. After having persevered through the rest of this chapter, you shouldn't have too much trouble filling in the details.

It is possible to prove that no captures or pawn moves took place during the previous fifty Black moves and forty-nine White moves. Hence

White has only to play a non-capturing non-pawn move to claim a draw under the fifty-move rule. If he doesn't do this he will lose, for Black has a decisive material advantage in the diagram. There is precisely one such move available, so White plays 1 Ne6 and claims his draw. Of course, it may be that more than fifty consecutive moves have already taken place without a pawn move or a capture, because one can never prove that pointless oscillations have **not** occurred. But the study is still sound, because 1 Ne6 is the only move which **guarantees** the draw based only on the information present in the diagram.

It is impossible to specify precisely what the position was 49.5 moves ago, but it must have been similar to this.

Even though some pieces might have been on different squares, the pawn structure **must** have been like this. White plays (these are ordinary forward moves): **1 exd4 2 Re4 3 Rh4 4 Rh7 5 Rg7 Bh7 6 Rg8 7 Kg7 8 Rb8 9 Rb7 10 Bb8 11 Ra7 12 Ra5** (Black plays waiting moves the whole time) **13 Re4 14 Rh4 Bg8 15 Rh7 16 Kh6 17 Rg7 Bh7 18 Rg8 19 Ba7 20 Rb8 21 Rb7 22 Bb8 23 Ra7 24 R7a6 Kb7 25 Rb5 Kc8 26 Rb4 Kd8 27 Ra5 Ke8 28 Rab5 Ra7 29 pass** (e.g. Rc4) **Rb7 30 Ba7 Rb8 31 pass Rd8 32 Bb8 Ra7 33 Ra4 Rb7 34 Ba7 Rbb8 35 Rba5 Rbc8 36 Bb8 Kf8 37 Ra7 Re8 38 Rb7 Rcd8 39 Ba7 40 Rb8** (Black waits with his queen) **41 Rc8 42 Bb8 43 Ra7 44 Rb7 45 Ba7 46 Rcb8 Rc8 47 Nf4 Red8 48 Ne6+ Ke8 49 Nf8 pass 50 Kg7 Qh4**, and we have Diagram 231.

Bibliography

1   Albert, *Ideal-mate Chess Problems,* California, 1966.
2   Bán, *The Tactics of End-games,* Corvina Press, Budapest, 1963.
3   Barnes, *Comins Mansfield: Chess Problems of a Grandmaster,* British Chess Problem Society, 1976.
4   Barnes, *Pick of the Best Chess Problems,* 2nd edn, Elliot Right Way Books, 1983.
5   Chéron, *Le Jouer D'Échecs au Pays des Merveilles,* Lausanne, 1982 (in French).
6   Kasparian, *Zauber des Endspieles,* Walter Rau Verlag, 1974 (in German).
7   Kasparian, *555 Miniature Studies,* Erevan, 1975 (in Russian).
8   Kasparian, *Domination in 2545 Endgame Studies,* Progress Publishers, Moscow, 1980.
9   Kasparian, *Remarkable Studies,* Erevan, 1982 (in Russian).
10 Kazantsev and others, *The Soviet Chess Study,* Moscow, 1955 (in Russian).
11 Kofman, *Selected Studies of Kaminer and Liburkin,* Moscow, 1981 (in Russian).
12 Kraemer and Zepler, *Im Banne des Schach-Problems,* Walter de Gruyter, 1971 (in German).
13 Kubbel, *Selected Problems of L. I. Kubbel,* Moscow, 1958 (in Russian).
14 Lipton, Matthews and Rice, *Chess Problems: Introduction to an Art,* Faber & Faber, 1963.
15 Lommer and Sutherland, *1234 Modern End-game Studies,* Dover, 1968.
16 Lommer, *1357 End-game Studies,* Pitman, 1975.
17 Mansfield, *Adventures in Composition,* Liverpool, 1948.
18 Nunn, *Tactical Chess Endings,* George Allen & Unwin, 1981.
19 Petrović and others, *FIDE Problem Albums,* Zagreb, 1961.
20 Rice, *An ABC of Chess Problems,* Faber & Faber, 1976.
21 Rice and Dickins, *The Serieshelpmate,* 2nd edn., Q Press, 1978.
22 Vladimirov, Kofman and Umnov, *Grandmaster of Chess Composition,* Moscow 1980 (in Russian).
23 Vukcevich, *Chess by Milan,* Ohio, 1981.
24 Whitworth, *Leonid Kubbel's Chess Endgame Studies,* Cambridge, 1984.

This list is intended as a guide to those who wish to read further about chess problems. More than a thousand books have been published on the subject of chess composition, so it is very much a personal selection.

Many chess problem books are hard to obtain, especially those originating in Eastern Europe. Fortunately the British Chess Problem Society runs an efficient book procurement service, in addition to producing its own bi-monthly magazine, *The Problemist*. Both the magazine and the book service are highly recommended (Secretary: C. A. H. Russ, Darwin College, University, Canterbury, Kent CT2 7NZ, Great Britain).

I have not dealt with the more specialised aspects of problems in this book. [14] and [20] provide clear definitions of the many technical terms used in problem literature, although they deal almost exclusively with direct-mate problems. Most problem books are compilations of one composer's work, or a selection of 'best' problems. In the first category, [3], [12] and [22] are outstanding. [22] is the collected problems of Lev Loshinsky (1913–76), probably the greatest ever composer of three-movers. The best of the second category is [19], a series of books covering the period from 1914 to the present day and aiming to give the very best of twentieth-century composition. Like many books in the list, these are quite a daunting prospect for the beginner, since the problems and solutions are given without any commentary. After having read *Solving in Style* the reader should be sufficiently familiar with problem conventions to tackle them.

If you are not so interested in direct-mate problems, but fancy a diet of helpmates or selfmates, then in general you will be out of luck, since for some reason problem books have tended to steer clear of anything not completely orthodox. However, [1] has a high proportion of helpmates, while [21] covers the serieshelpmate field thoroughly. Finally, [5] is a remarkable study of extreme effects in problems; the analysis is exceptionally detailed.

Perhaps your ambition is to compose yourself. In this case you won't find much guidance in problem books. Luckily the one book dealing with composition, [17], is excellent.

The remaining books in the list are for study enthusiasts. [15] and [16] are the standard study compilations in English, although again the lack of commentary gives a very dry impression. [2] is highly recommended for over-the-board players who want to read about studies, since each position is introduced in entertaining style. The Soviet composer Kasparian has produced a number of excellent study compilations. One of them, [8], has been translated into rather peculiar English, but after all it's the chess that counts. [11] and [24] are amongst the best collections of the work of individual composers; both books contain accurate and careful analysis.

Finally, many books dealing with over-the-board endings have studies scattered through them. I will pick just one, [18].

Index of composers

Numbers refer to diagrams

Further Gambit Chess Books

www.gambitbooks.com

Chess Training for Budding Champions
Jesper Hall
"Hall offers very useful synopses at the end of each chapter highlighting the key points covered. He also offers the student exercises and, perhaps most importantly, suggestions for further reading. This book is highly recommended to aspiring students (1600-2400), as well as chess trainers" – *John Donaldson, Inside Chess Online*

Understanding Chess Move by Move
John Nunn
"A wonderful book about 30 wonderful games. The analysis is first rate, the commentary cogent, and the production excellent. What is there not to like? In the end, I couldn't find anything to fault, and that is why it earns the highest rating. Buy this book, you will not be sorry" – *Randy Bauer, Randy's Revealing Reviews*

101 Attacking Ideas in Chess
Joe Gallagher
"The latest in an excellent series...Gallagher discloses various attacking stratagems which should benefit all aspiring students of the game" – *J.J. Walsh, Irish Times*

Fundamental Chess Endings
Karsten Müller & Frank Lamprecht
FCE is the first truly modern one-volume endgame encyclopaedia: a masterful work that analyses and assesses all major endgames. Key principles are explained, and the authors also emphasize the practical side of endgame play, giving rules of thumb, principles and thinking methods.
"A book has emerged that looks to be the new standard for endgame evaluations... I recommend this book highly" – *Cecil Rosner, Winnipeg Free Press*

The Taimanov Sicilian
Graham Burgess
This popular opening (1 e4 c5 2 ♘f3 e6 3 d4 cxd4 4 ♘xd4 ♘c6) is one of Black's most flexible choices in the Sicilian Defence.
"Burgess has done an impressive job compiling up-to-date information" – *Einar Gausel, Dagbladet*

Test Your Chess
Steffen Pedersen

"The examples are well chosen and challenging. *Test Your Chess* is a useful training book for players from 2000 to 2400 that are serious about improving their chess. This book will improve the conscientious reader's analytical skills and increase his understanding of the game." – *John Donaldson, Inside Chess*

Understanding Pawn Play in Chess
Dražen Marović

Chess owes its extraordinary strategic depth to pawns. They can be blockers, battering-rams, self-sacrificing heroes, or if mishandled they can be weak and provide targets.

"Contains over 100 complete games, each demonstrating a particular pawn strategy...an excellent book" – *Alan Borwell, Scottish Correspondence Chess*

World Champion at the Third Attempt
Grigory Sanakoev

It is rare that a Correspondence World Champion annotates a collection of the finest games from his career with such detailed notes. Sanakoev's dazzling sacrificial attacks are especially instructive as they have had to withstand the most scrupulous analysis.

"A remarkable book of commentary and games" – *Bob Long, The Chess Gazette*

How to Be Lucky in Chess
David LeMoir

Some players have an inexhaustible supply of chessboard luck. No matter what trouble they find themselves in, they somehow manage to escape. Here LeMoir aims to help ordinary players, who may have little time for studying chess, to make the most of their abilities.

"LeMoir here adopts a no-nonsense uncomplicated way to show club-standard players just how best to lure opponents into making errors" – *J.J.Walsh, Irish Times*

Storming the Barricades
Larry Christiansen

"A true feast of initiative-based, dynamic, hard-hitting chess. It is also good to see a sparkling, modern selection rather than the same old classics that lovers of chess literature are so used to. The examples for *Storming the Barricades* are almost entirely drawn from the last three decades and even include games from 1999. It makes a fine textbook for attacking play for the new Millennium, especially for club-players and above" – *Jonathan Levitt, Club Kasparov*

The Slav
Graham Burgess
"Burgess has done a very conscientious job. He gives you a very good survey of what has happened up to now and in openings where he has personal involvement, like the 5 e4 Gambit, he offers a great deal of personal insight... a first-rate opening book" – *John Donaldson, Inside Chess Online*

The System
A World Champion's Approach to Chess
Hans Berliner
One of the most successful correspondence players of all time explains his own controversial set of chess principles.
"The strength of the book is the insight it gives of how a World Champion Correspondence player approaches chess and selects his moves. There are many issues that Berliner covers that will make you think even if you do not agree with them" – *Australian Chess Forum*

The Gambit Guide to the Benko Gambit
Steffen Pedersen
"We are quite comfortable labelling The Gambit Guide to the Benko Gambit as the best work to date on this opening... it should quickly become the book of choice on the Benko Gambit" – *Glenn Budzinski, Chess Cafe Web Site*

The Road to Chess Improvement
Alex Yermolinsky
Winner of the United States Chess Federation award for Best Chess Book
A United States Champion offers solutions to the real-life problem of improving one's chess. With refreshing candour Yermolinsky passes on insights he has gained over years of playing and teaching.
"...a magnificent achievement, by far the finest book I've ever seen on the subject of practical play" – *Matthew Sadler, New In Chess*

The Gambit Guide to the English Opening: 1...e5
Carsten Hansen
"Hansen is very honest in his summaries. The reader really can trust his recommendations ... [he] has found a number of mistakes in GM analysis ... a must buy" – *Richard Palliser, Hull Chess Club Magazine*

The Symmetrical English
Carsten Hansen
"If you play these systems for either side, this is now the new 'bible', more original and user-friendly than Bagirov and more up-to-date than Watson" – *Phil Adams, Checkpoint*

Dynamic Pawn Play in Chess
Dražen Marović

How should pawns be used in the fight for the centre? How does the central pawn-formation affect planning for both sides? These questions are central to understanding chess, and are answered by this wonderfully instructive book.

"A fabulous feast of energetic examples illustrating the irresistible power of pawns" – *Paul Motwani, The Scotsman*

The Gambit Guide to the Modern Benoni
John Watson

The Modern Benoni, which arises after 1 d4 ♘f6 2 c4 c5 3 d5 e6, is one of Black's most swashbuckling openings.

"Watson gives a lot of new ideas and tries to improve on existing theory. Most of the time he is successful ... a fine book" – *Søren Søgaard, Seagaard Reviews*

Chess Champion from China
Xie Jun

The remarkable story of how a young Chinese girl rose to become Women's World Champion.

"Jun comes across as a character of warmth and humility as she charts her first steps as an innocent in the Western world. Highly recommended." – *John Walker, Oxford Times*

The Dynamic English
Tony Kosten

This is the aggressive player's guide to a traditional opening, 1 c4. Includes recommendations against every black defence.

"... you couldn't wish for a better book" – *Schach Markt*

How to Beat Your Dad at Chess
Murray Chandler

"My husband and I coach a scholastic chess team and we really like your book *How to Beat your Dad at Chess*. We recommend it to kids all the time. We have a son who is 12 who is being coached by a Master named Andrew Whatley and he has recently discovered your book and is recommending it to all his students as well" – *Sharon Mayes, Chess Nuts Chess Supplies*

Vishy Anand: My Best Games of Chess
Vishy Anand

British Chess Federation Book of the Year

A splendid collection of 57 of Anand's best games, featuring detailed and entertaining commentary.

"A cracker ... you are bound to enjoy every page" – *CHESS Magazine*

Play the Open Games as Black
John Emms
A detailed guide, from Black's viewpoint, to facing such openings as the King's Gambit, Vienna, Scotch, Four Knights, Italian Game, Bishop's Opening and the variety of oddball gambits White can try after 1 e4 e5.
"Fills an important niche in the market" – *John Pugh, Chess Post*

101 Chess Opening Traps
Steve Giddins
This compilation of common opening traps is essential reading, as it focuses on traps that club players are most likely to fall for.
"To my delight and amazement [my opponent] fell straight into the trap." – *Alec Toll, Open File*

The Gambit Guide to the Bogo-indian
Steffen Pedersen
After 1 d4 ♘f6 2 c4 e6 3 ♘f3 the underrated move 3...♗b4+ enables Black to dictate the opening battle from move three.
"Pick out the bits headed *Quick Summary* and gain some valuable insights into this ambitious opening for Black." – *Bernard Hanison, Chess Post*

Understanding the Grünfeld
Jonathan Rowson
"The most satisfying aspect of Rowson's book is the depth of explanation he provides. He does not talk down to his readers. On the contrary, he assumes you are his equal and a willing companion in a fascinating search for truth in the Grünfeld" – *Craig Pritchett, The Herald*

John Nunn's Chess Puzzle Book
John Nunn
This innovative chess puzzle book will stretch you to the absolute limit. The reader is put in the real-game situation of having to find the best move, not knowing what the theme or goal is.
"An excellent tactical battle manual built around 250 test positions with clear solutions given in impressive detail" – *Douglas Bryson, Scotland On Sunday*

The Seven Deadly Chess Sins
Jonathan Rowson
The author delves into chess psychology to investigate the main reasons why chess-players blunder.
"Rowson has broken ranks by writing about playing chess as it actually is rather than as it ought to be and should be greatly commended for this. This is a book which, in contrast to the vast majority of its brethren, I will continue to visit and revisit" – *Jon Speelman, The Independent*

Learn Chess
John Nunn

"*Learn Chess* by Grandmaster Dr John Nunn is ideal for anyone who's just starting out now, with keenness to develop into a successful player" – *Paul Motwani, The Scotsman*

101 Chess Opening Surprises
Graham Burgess

This book contains an amazing array of opening thunderbolts, each assessed both in terms of soundness and its ability to surprise and shock.
"A collection of tricky little-known lines of play which can catch out even well prepared opponents" – *Leonard Barden, Evening Standard*

The Main Line French: 3 ♘c3
Steffen Pedersen

The French Defence is one of the most popular chess openings – and with 3 ♘c3 White confronts it head-on. The result is often a ferocious battle. Black tries to destroy or damage White's central pawn phalanx, and some of the variations (such as the Winawer Poisoned Pawn) are amongst the sharpest in opening theory.

Secrets of Practical Chess
John Nunn

This acclaimed book is packed full of useful advice on how to make the most of your existing talent, be it defending difficult positions, studying openings or avoiding common mistakes.
"I have about 15 of Nunn's books and none have ever disappointed me. I thoroughly recommend this book, especially to any player who ... wants to know how to set about improving" – *Luke McShane, Sunday Express*

S.T.A.R. Chess
Paul Motwani

Grandmaster Motwani goes into Warp Drive to explain Strategy, Tactics, Attack and Reaction, in a book chock full of good advice, puzzles and anecdotes.
"The most refreshingly different book for a very long time" – *Ken Bloodworth, Western Morning News*

The Ultimate Chess Puzzle Book
John Emms

1001 puzzle positions – grouped by an interesting variety of classifications – to help you improve your tactical skills.
"... exceptional ... the perfect resource for improving your game by studying tactics and it's accessible to players of all strengths" – *Mark Donlan, Chess Horizons*

The Gambit Guide to the Torre Attack
Graham Burgess

1 d4 ♘f6 2 ♘f3 e6 3 ♗g5 is a very attractive system for White as it enables him to set the agenda from the outset.

"This excellent book should be in the hands of all students ... very well produced" – *George Koltanowski, San Francisco Chronicle*

Secrets of Rook Endings
John Nunn

"In 50 years' time *Secrets of Rook Endings* will be regarded as one of the truly great classics of the twentieth century ... it is as close as any book can ever realistically come to perfection on its subject" – *Julian Hodgson, British Chess Magazine*

Chess Highlights of the 20th Century
Graham Burgess

"Even in writing an eminently accessible, popular book, Burgess has still bothered to put a great deal of effort into details which correct the historical record.

"Burgess's selection of games and key positions is just superb, and can hardly fail to delight even jaded fans. The goal of the book is to delight the reader with a journey through our chess past and with a host of fun and intriguing games ... 'Chess Highlights of the 20th Century' succeeds in that regard" – *John Watson, The Week In Chess*

Secrets of Modern Chess Strategy
John Watson

British Chess Federation Book of the Year
United States Chess Federation Book of the Year

From the moment of appearance, John Watson's masterpiece was hailed as a modern classic. Taking up where Nimzowitsch left off 70 years ago, Watson shows how the way chess positions are handled has changed greatly in modern times.

"No matter what your level of play, you will marvel at the insights ... Watson teaches you the classical rules of chess, and then illustrates how those rules often must be broken" – *Cecil Rosner, Winnipeg Free Press*

The Petroff
Lasha Janjgava

This defence has soared in popularity over the past few years, as with 1 e4 e5 2 ♘f3 ♘f6 Black avoids all perils of the openings like the Scotch Game or Ruy Lopez.

"... a very comprehensive and thorough guide to the Petroff ... equally valuable to players of both the Black and the White pieces" – *Alan Sutton, En Passant.*

101 Winning Chess Strategies
Angus Dunnington

Without strategy, a chess game is just a series of tactical tricks. A good strategy binds together the tactics, and enables a player to make methodical progress towards victory.

"With ample diagrams to illustrate the ideas, this is the perfect travelling companion on planes, trains and automobiles" – *Gary Lane, Chess Moves*

Secrets of Pawnless Endings
John Nunn

This book unites grandmaster and machine in the search for ultimate answers. Following on from his successful book *Secrets of Rook Endings*, John Nunn turns his attention towards endgames without pawns. Using computer databases which can state with certainly the correct result of the positions considered in the book, John Nunn has extracted the most important information and presented it in the form of guidelines and key positions. Since the first edition of this book was published, the databases for many six-man endings have been created, resulting in some surprising and paradoxical discoveries. The coverage has therefore been expanded to include the most interesting features of these endings.

The Most Amazing Chess Moves of All Time
John Emms

From thousands of candidate games, John Emms has selected the 200 most stunning, dazzling, incredible chess moves ever played – moves which can be impossible to find, even when you know they are there!

"Mini introductions or hints accompany each position, and the solutions almost all contain the complete gamescore, which I believe is a considerable bonus in this kind of book" – *James Vigus, Dragon*

The Botvinnik Semi-Slav
Steffen Pedersen

Most of today's top grandmasters have relied on the razor-sharp Botvinnik System (1 d4 d5 2 c4 c6 3 ♘f3 ♘f6 4 ♘c3 e6 5 ♗g5 dxc4) – especially in make-or-break situations.

"This system ... is certainly not for the faint-hearted. What I particularly like about the Gambit books are the introductory chapters, which in a few pages explain the typical strategic and tactical ideas" – *Alan Sutton, En Passant*

The Queen's Gambit & Catalan for Black
Lasha Janjgava

This useful repertoire book shows how Black can counter 1 d4 with the solid, classical reply 1...d5. Once White's starting advantage is countered, Black is ready to break out and seize the initiative.

"... a very thorough job" – *Chris Rice, Weekend Chess Magazine*

Secrets of Chess Intuition
Alexander Beliavsky & Adrian Mikhalchishin

Intuition is a key element of success in chess, but many people believe that it cannot be trained. Beliavsky and Mikhalchishin show otherwise. By treating various aspects of intuition in turn, the authors aim to develop it in the same way as other chess skills. Examples of intuition in action back up the general concepts, and a set of exercises tests the reader's grasp of the principles underlying chess intuition.

An Explosive Chess Opening Repertoire for Black
Jouni Yrjölä & Jussi Tella

A complete opening system for Black based on the move 1...d6! against any first move by White.

"Overall Yrjölä and Tella's coverage of 1 d4 d6 2 c4 e5 and 2 ♘f3 ♗g4 (138 pages in total out of 272 overall) is excellent and fills a significant void in chess literature" – *Richard Palliser, Chess Moves*

Instructive Modern Chess Masterpieces
Igor Stohl

50 outstanding modern games analysed in extraordinary detail. Grandmaster Stohl presents his findings in a manner that is both instructive and entertaining.

"... hugely impressive. The opening stage is replete with references to other relevant games, and the middle-games and endgames are well explained, in words as well as variations" – *Phil Adams, The Manchester Chess Scene*

The Sicilian Sozin
Mikhail Golubev

"The heart of the book is the coverage of ♗c4 versus the Najdorf (dubbed the Fischer Attack where Golubev likes 5...a6 6 ♗c4 e6 7 ♗b3 ♘bd7!) and the Sozin and Velimirović Attacks. These chapters take up almost 200 pages and are filled with detailed coverage including a lot of original analysis. The Sicilian Sozin is must reading for those who play either side of this fascinating opening" – *John Donaldson, Blitz Chess*

Chess Recipes from the Grandmaster's Kitchen
Valeri Beim

The various 'recipes' explain key principles of chess strategy and thinking methods in chess. Topics covered include tactical ideas in the middlegame, liquidation to the endgame, the technique of analysing variations and inverted thinking in chess. Throughout, you will be presented with new ways of looking at chessboard issues that will help you develop a deeper understanding of the game. Every chapter contains stunning examples of the themes, together with challenging exercises where you can put your new insights to the test.

101 Brilliant Chess Miniatures
John Nunn

An entertaining collection of sensation games of 25 moves or fewer, with the accent on instruction. The innovative format of three diagrams per page enables the book to be read without a chess set.

"Short victories between Grandmasters do not occur every day. Highly recommended" – *Lubosh Kavalek, Washington Post*

64 Things You Need to Know in Chess
John Walker

An experienced chess teacher provides the essential knowledge that will both help readers to start winning games immediately and lay the foundation for a deeper understanding of chess tactics and strategy. Each 'thing' is explained in an easy-to-follow lesson, which is followed by exercises that enable the reader to check that he or she has fully understood the concept.

The Meran System
Steffen Pedersen

This system, which arises after 1 d4 d5 2 c4 c6 3 ♘f3 ♘f6 4 ♘c3 e6 5 e3, is one of the main parts of the Semi-Slav, the most combative line of the Queen's Gambit.

"... a five star rating...Steffen continues to produce excellent material for Gambit" – *Michael Blake, IEGC Newsletter*